BEARING THE BRUISE

A Life Graced by Haiti

ETHAN CASEY

www.ethancasey.com

BLUE EAR BOOKS

First published in 2012 by
Blue Ear Books
P.O. Box 85315
Seattle, WA 98145-1315
USA

© Ethan Casey, Blue Ear Books
www.ethancasey.com
info@ethancaseymedia.com

ISBN: 978-0-9844063-2-6

Credits:

Cover Design:
  Jason Kopec, tagcreativestudio.com

Page Layout and Design:
  Jennifer Haywood, Blue Ear Books, Seattle, WA

Printer:
  Scott Morris, Morris Printing Services, Arkansas City, KS
  www.morrisprint.com

Project Manager and Copy Editor:
  Sharon Green, Panache Editorial, Inc., Colorado Springs, CO
  panache2004@comcast.net

Photos:

p. 5: Fr. Ed Morgan, Fr. Octave Lafontant, and Fr. Dayle Casey in Haiti, circa 1990.
p. 75: National Highway 1 between Hinche and Cap Haïtien. Photo by Pete Sabo.
p. 175: Clockwise from left: Marseille, Édrice, Yovens, Fritz, and Ti Gerald at Saut d'Eau, September 2011. Photo by Jennifer Haywood.

CONTENTS

Choosing Haiti 1

PART ONE 5

    Chapter 1: "Sure!" 6

    Chapter 2: Averting Our Eyes 22

    Chapter 3: A Ghastly Feeling of Impotence 50

PART TWO 75

    Chapter 4: Suspended Revolution 76

    Chapter 5: *Mais tu es en Afrique!* 89

    Chapter 6: Eating Misery 103

    Chapter 7: Meeting Mr. Clean 119

    Chapter 8: On the Streets 134

    Chapter 9: "Isn't the World Just Going Nuts?" 158

PART THREE 175

    Prologue: Paying Attention and Taking Notes 176

    Chapter 10: "I'm Goin', Man" 180

    Chapter 11: In the Ruins 199

    Chapter 12: Man of the South 221

    Chapter 13: Making Things Work 252

    Chapter 14: To Be Continued 281

Acknowledgements and Further Reading 307

Bay kou blie, pote mak sonje.

He who gives the blow forgets;
he who bears the bruise remembers.

— Haitian proverb

CHOOSING HAITI

"Wee-eek up!" I heard from below my window. "Wee-ee-eek up!"

"*Ki moun ou cheche?*" I called. Who are you looking for?

"*Ou menm*! Paul Farmer wants to see you."

It was only nine in the evening, but it had been a long day of hard travel. I forced myself to sit up and dress.

It seemed I came to Haiti anymore only when something bad had happened. This time, the occasion was the second abrupt and forcible ouster of President Jean-Bertrand Aristide, who had been such a divisive central figure in Haiti's drama since the late 1980s. On February 29, 2004, Aristide had boarded a U.S. plane at the airport in Port-au-Prince and somehow ended up in the Central African Republic. Farmer, the co-founder of Partners in Health, subject of Tracy Kidder's bestselling book *Mountains Beyond Mountains*, and author of *The Uses of Haiti*, was not alone in calling it a coup. Others were pretending not to hear the hard questions Farmer and many Haitians were asking about the incident's circumstances. Most Americans failed even to notice that it had happened. One American who had noticed was Dick Cheney, whose comment was characteristic: "We're glad to see him go."

Earlier that year, when the cable news channels had been carrying disturbing accounts of "rebels" mobilizing against Aristide in provincial Haiti, I had been in Pakistan. The semester I had signed up to spend teaching at a university in Lahore ended in early February, and I returned to my home in a London suburb. Matters were coming to a head there as well after my long absence but, when I had a choice to make, I chose Haiti. I always chose Haiti. I quickly wrote and submitted the book I was writing on Pakistan, explained myself as best I

1

could, then fled the suburbs again. I couldn't not go to Haiti at such a time, or so I told myself; and if I had wanted to stay in the suburbs, I would have stayed in the suburbs in the first place.

So, at what turned out to be decisive cost to my personal situation, I chose Haiti yet again.

I was still groggy as the burly Haitian and I walked out of the compound and across the road. "You're a writer?" he asked in Creole as we picked our way up a dirt path toward a small house hidden away on a wooded hilltop. His name was Ti Jean.

"Yes," I said. "I'm not as well known as Tracy Kidder ..."

"*Se zanmi mwen*," said Ti Jean. He's my friend. I felt one-upped.

A tall man wearing little John Lennon spectacles stood at the entrance to the yard in front of the house. "I'm Paul Farmer," he said, offering his hand.

It felt like meeting Kurtz at the end of the long journey upriver, but the air of mystery dissolved quickly. In the light Farmer was a bland-looking white guy in early middle age, younger than I had imagined. He wore a light-blue Haitian shirt with stitched palm trees and stylized peasant figures on it. In his small front room he had set out glasses and bottles of rum and Prestige beer on a low table.

They were wary at first, and I blundered by describing the events surrounding Aristide's departure as "complex."

"Haitian professionals don't really buy that peasants and slum dwellers ought to vote," asserted Farmer. "People who can express themselves in international languages are not on the side of a popular vote. They're just not, sociologically. The poor happen to be ninety percent of the population here. Reporters, even of goodwill, don't talk to the poor. That was the purpose of *The Uses of Haiti*: to say, 'Look, these people are human.'"

Ti Jean claimed attention and deferred to no one, and he felt insults keenly. If you could communicate with him in Creole, you quickly recognized a shrewd and alert intelligence. "In the U.S.," he said, "I've never seen a Haitian go into a store or a restaurant with visible firearms. But in Haiti, Americans go into stores openly armed all the time. When I see you writing, it doesn't make me hate you. When I see Paul with a stethoscope, it doesn't make me feel bad. But when I see an American soldier in Haiti, it makes me want to kill myself."

"This must be a lot like what you got in the Islamic world," remarked Farmer. "These are the people I work with, and this is how they talk to me. But Haiti is America's oldest neighbor. You can only have one oldest neighbor, and for the U.S. this country is it. It's not Iraq or any other country."

Farmer later told me how Ti Jean had gone from being a manual laborer to being his right-hand man.

"Everybody has to have a hobby, right?" he said. "Well, mine is planting trees, more than anything else. Trees. But once a place is reforested, then you have to plant other things. So I started with trees, and I'm still into trees, but I also plant other things: perennials, small plants, house plants, whatever, but outside. Water plants, bog plants. And when I would go back to Boston to be on service at the hospital there, I'd be gone for a month solid. And so I'd ask my neighbors, 'Would you mind watering my plants?' And they'd always say, 'Oh please, Doctor Paul, we'd be so happy to water your plants for you. You're such a fantastic guy, great doctor, we'd be thrilled.' And I'd come back, and everything would be dead.

"I tried various neighbors. And you get kind of sheepish thinking, well, you know, it's not like there's a lot of water around, it's not like things to eat are coming out of these plants and trees. They're ornamentals. And so I never really could feel too put out. I always felt kind of sheepish. And Ti Jean was at the time, as he would say, lifting sacks. He would wash the cars, the vehicles, the ambulances, and on Fridays go to a local market and carry back these huge bags of things. And I would just see him in the courtyard. His brother was a patient of mine; he was one of eighteen kids. I knew lots of people in his family. Whenever they were sick, you know. He's obviously a pretty sharp character, and I asked him would he mind watering my plants. And I came back from being in Boston for a month, and everything was *lush* and *verdant*." He emphasized the adjectives with relish. "I had been expecting the worst. And I said, 'Wow, Ti Jean, man, thank you so much for doing this. I owe you big-time. I'd like to do something for you.'

"And he said, 'I'd like a computer.'"

"And I was completely floored by that, and I said, 'What do you want a computer for?'"

"And he said, 'Oh, did someone ask you that when you asked for your first computer?' And I said, 'Ouch.' And it just so happened I had just been given a new computer, so I had two. And I did give him a computer. And now his chief complaint these days is likely to be, 'I told you I'm sick of Windows 98. I want Windows XP 2000.'"

"The masses have no one sticking up for them anymore," Ti Jean insisted. "Even now, with Aristide in exile and all the repression, he would be elected again for seventeen years. You can call this a government. We call it a *tchoul*, a lackey. It's not elected. They're *jobbeurs*, Bush's hired hands. Haiti is a small country. But it's the first independent black country. That's why Aristide was overthrown. Aristide is a black man who wants to stay black. Rich Americans and rich Haitians conspire to make sure Haiti will always be a *tchoul* state. On February 29, 2004, they restored slavery to Haiti. All Haitian people elected a president. As soon as all Haitians elected him, they blocked international aid. And then when they kidnap him, they restore aid. It's like *The Lord of the Rings*."

I asked Ti Jean whether he believed Aristide had been kidnapped.

"They kidnapped him from his house and took him in handcuffs to the Palace," he said. "Paul Farmer doesn't know this. I know this. I have a good source."

Ti Jean walked me back across the road and left me with a lot to think about.

"*Merci*, Ti Jean," I said at the door to the guesthouse.

"*Ou merite-l*," he said. You're welcome.

The literal meaning of the Creole clause *Ou merite-l* is *You deserve it*. But was it true? And I couldn't know whether Ti Jean had meant it literally. I guessed maybe not.

Farmer told me later that, after that first meeting, he had said, "Ethan's progressive," and Ti Jean had replied, "It seems that way, but wait until we read his book."

4

PART ONE

CHAPTER 1

"Sure!"

If, at age sixteen, you go from an all-white town in Wisconsin to Haiti and back, you never go all the way back. I never really did go back to Oconomowoc, but I always went back to Haiti. Other interests, adventures, worries, disasters, and crossroads came and went, but Haiti always returned to insist on my attention.

I find it easier to narrate how I became involved with Haiti than to analyze why. My father is an Episcopal priest. In 1994, when events compelled me to begin revisiting my experience, I asked him how it had all begun. Another priest in Wisconsin had led a group of medical and church people to Haiti in 1979, as "a substitute for a planned trip to Nicaragua, which got short-circuited because of the revolution there," he told me. A couple in our parish went in 1980 and got my father involved in 1981. The group worked with Father Fritz Lafontant, a Haitian priest in Mirebalais on the Central Plateau. Every group included physicians, veterinarians, usually a dentist and a pharmacist, nurses, and hangers-on like me. Married couples often went together. The idea was to go to Haiti, repeatedly and predictably to the same place, for ten days or two weeks, two or three times a year, to bring basic medical attention to whoever showed up.

"You became involved with Haiti 'accidentally' at first," my father reminded me. In 1982, when I was a junior in high school, he had planned to take my older brother with him, but "his schedule wouldn't permit him to go, so I came home one day and asked if you'd like to go in his place, and you said, without hesitation, 'Sure!'"

I heard this as an echo. My father's high school baseball coach in

Dallas in the 1950s had warned that "the nigras" were about to take over the big leagues. "I thought that was fine if they were good," said my dad. "I imagine he might have thought it was the end of civilization. Playing with blacks, though, was rare for us in Texas. I recall playing one afternoon in a game somewhere in Dallas when there were only two, maybe three of us who were white. I don't know how it happened; I think I was just asked if I'd like to, and I said, 'Sure!' I recall thinking it was a mildly radical thing to do, something most of my friends wouldn't have been caught dead doing."

I once put to him a notion I had cultivated: that his flight from Dallas at twenty-one had set a pattern I felt compelled to follow. For me this was a usable conceit. He had never been given to either loquacity or second-guessing of choices made long ago, but he considered it politely.

"I didn't go as far afield as you guys did," he allowed. "But I did feel a need to"—he paused and chuckled—"get out of town."

On my way to Haiti for the first time at sixteen, I had no clue what I was letting myself in for. But what most of my friends wouldn't have been caught dead doing was to me an opportunity and an adventure.

✳

In Port-au-Prince we stayed at a small hotel owned by a Dominican named Ernie, on Delmas 29 near the airport. A short walk away was a Kentucky Fried Chicken, and across Delmas was a local chain called Chez Tony. The drive to Mirebalais took most of a day, on a winding uphill road. If two vehicles met on the mountain road, one had to edge dangerously close to the cliff to let the other creep past.

"One of my memories of that first trip is of your talking into the evening at Ernie's with the kids," my father reminded me years later, "and of your sitting in the back of a pickup at Fr. Lafontant's house with a kid saying, 'No, no, no, no' over some homework you were helping him with." The children were everywhere in their checked school uniforms: chanting their lessons in neat, obedient rows, studying beneath dim street lamps at night, boisterous and laughing. People in our groups brought bags of balloons for the children, and we took turns blowing them up. *Ba-m blad!* cried the boys—Give me a balloon!—and the girls stood timidly aside. "It was either that year or the next that the veterinarians had you giving shots at one of the crowded clinics," my father wrote, "and even at 16 (17?) the Haitians all thought you were a doctor because you gave shots and were a 'blanc.'" On the way back to Port-au-Prince, we stopped in a village called Trianon to give inoculations. One of our doctors had arranged it with the village "president," and the old man had told his people, and they had come. The president's wife brought out china cups and saucers and served us strong Haitian coffee, and the president sent a man up a tree with a machete between his teeth to cut down a coconut. And he had a brown bitch that was all skin and bones and low-swinging dugs, and her puppies all wore red ribbons. "They won't be alive next year," said one of the vets. But the next year when we returned, the pups were fully grown and the mother had recovered.

Early 1983 was a time when everything was going very well indeed. The Brewers had just gone to the World Series, Robin Yount was Most Valuable Player in the American League, and I was about to graduate high school. Three groups went from Milwaukee to Haiti that spring, and my father arranged for me to miss part of my last semester of high school so I could stay there for six weeks. "I left you in the care of Sister Joan Margaret at St Vincent's," he reminded me a decade later, "and you stayed with Dr. Albright, traveling around. I recall Sr. Joan's telling you, as I left you with her, that the meal times at St. V's were such and such sharp—and that if you missed them, well, then, there was 'Chez Tony's down the street.'" Sister Joan had been in Haiti for forty years, running St. Vincent's School for the Handicapped. She got around slowly with a walker but ran the place with an iron hand. Steve Albright was a groovy young dentist who had quit his practice in Milwaukee to drive around America. He went around with a toothbrush stuck behind his ear. He had left his car in Seattle and flown to Miami to join us in Haiti, bringing with him the famous final episode of *M*A*S*H* on videotape and a copy of a brand-new national newspaper called *USA Today*. I helped Steve pull teeth at St. Vincent's and together we drove up the coast, snorkeled in the bay at Club Med, and visited the Albert Schweitzer Hospital in Deschapelles, where I shivered on my cot with pus-filled sunburn blisters. Steve paid for my room at the Club Med. "It's all right," he said. "Some other time you'll pay for somebody else."

At the end, in the Miami airport, the mood was always melancholy. But something about Haiti had gotten under my skin. I studied *Let's Learn Creole* and the book of Haitian proverbs that I had bought at the Baptist mission up the mountain from Port-au-Prince, at Kenscoff. *Ampil ti patat fe chay.* Many little sweet potatoes make a load. *Moun ki ede ou achte choual gro vant pa ede ou ba-l manje nan sezon sek.* He who helps you buy a horse with a big stomach during the rainy season won't help you feed it during the dry season. *Moun grangou pa ka tande.* The hungry person can't hear you. *Byen mal pa lanmo.* Almost dead is not dead. *Ti neg fe sa-l kapab; gro neg fe sa-l vle.* The little guy does what he can; the big guy does what he wants.

I read Graham Greene's novel *The Comedians* and a startling new book about how zombies are created called *The Serpent and the Rainbow*, by a young Harvard ethnobotanist named Wade Davis. At a library sale for fifty cents I bought a travel book called *Black Haiti: A Biography of Africa's Eldest Daughter*. "The workers sing in the fields, and against the black tide of their recurrent lives the spectacular crises stand out," author Blair Niles had written in 1926. "Peasants have sung and toiled in Haiti, danced and sung and drummed, sorrowed and wailed, while the great figures have moved passionately through their parts." Of one Haitian, Niles wrote: "His candidate for the Presidency had lost. And then he'd had, of course, to take to the 'bush.' In order to save his life he'd gone up into the hills. It was always wise to give a new President time to settle down into office and to forget just who had taken up arms to elect his rival."

After my parents moved to Colorado Springs in the mid-1980s, my father continued going to Haiti. One day at the Episcopal cathedral in Port-au-Prince, he and another priest named Ed Morgan met Father Octave Lafontant, Fritz Lafontant's brother.

"We sat at the table outside the gift shop and I asked him if it was possible to begin some programs with him that would maintain the church connection as well as the medical," my father remembered, "and he said, 'Sure.' I'll never forget our first trip from Jeannette one day to 'scout' out Petit Trou"—Petit Trou de Nippes, a town on the north coast of Haiti's long southern peninsula. "All day—seven of us in a four- or five-person, *small* jeep, over all the rivers and through all the mud holes, with our medical gear sliding off the top of the jeep and sliding all the way down the mountain ... and our retrieving it ... and when we got back to Jeannette that night, I talked the day over with Ed."

"We just can't do it," the Americans told the Haitian. "It's too far and too difficult. We'd never get our people and stuff there."

"If Jesus wants us to go, we'll go," replied Octave. "And besides, I've already bought the land [for the church]."

That conversation led to the founding of the Colorado Haiti Project, which still works in Petit Trou. My father pursued his work from year to year with a doggedness that I now know comes only from a staunch and hard-won serenity. But what good did any of it really do? The liberal impulse requires rectification. Not a damn bit of good, I think my father would rejoin. And more good than you can possibly imagine.

✳

By February 1986, when a popular uprising forced President Jean-Claude "Baby Doc" Duvalier to flee Haiti, I was finishing my junior year in Madison and preoccupied with my own worries. After an ominous two-week silence, I got a shocking letter from my first serious girlfriend. An older female friend read it, took my hand, and said: "As you journey through your twenties, you'll realize that life really is just one damn thing after another." I walked past a bulletin board, saw a flyer for the University of Wisconsin College Year in Nepal Program, and thought, "Why not?" By August I was in Kathmandu.

Three years later I washed up in Berkeley, where I commuted to a tie-wearing office job in San Francisco. My brother rescued me from that by inviting me to spend the summer traveling with him around central Europe. I said, "Sure!"

It's hard to know, anymore, where one's own naivete ended and a collective wishfulness began. On a wall in Berkeley, I read:

Phony Communism is Dead!
Long Live Real Communism!
Mao More than Ever!

I read a lot, that spring of 1990. I read *This Way for the Gas, Ladies and Gentlemen*, Tadeusz Borowski's chilling book of stories set in a death camp: "'Gentlemen,' said the officer with a friendly smile. ... 'I know, of course, that after what you have gone through and after what you have seen, you must feel a deep hate for your tormenters. But we, the soldiers of America, and you, the people of Europe, have fought so that law should prevail over lawlessness. We must show our respect for the law. I assure you that the guilty will be punished.'" Milan Kundera taught me to phrase my response in the form of a question. "The dictatorship of the proletariat or democracy?" he asks in *The Unbearable Lightness of Being*. "Rejection of the consumer society or demands for increased productivity? The guillotine or an end to the death penalty? It is all beside the point. What makes a leftist a leftist is not this or that theory but his ability to integrate any theory into the kitsch called the Grand March." And at Cody's bookstore in Berkeley, I bought what would become a landmark book. *The Rainy Season: Haiti since Duvalier* by Amy Wilentz would prove as prescient about the rise and significance of Aristide, though tainted by a disingenuous leftist wishfulness. Wilentz wanted Haiti to lead the way in the Grand March.

✳

In Europe, my brother Aaron and I and our West German friend Ralph paid five Deutschmarks each to a dour woman behind a window at Friedrichstrasse, the only U-bahn crossing point into East Berlin. We rode to Lichtenberg station to catch the 8.48 train to Prague. Ralph had a way of speaking in full paragraphs.

"There were so many coincidences that led to this revolution," he said on the train, "that it could have happened before it did, or it could have happened ten years from now. East Germany wasn't always a corrupt state. When it was founded, and for many years afterward, people believed in the ideal of a socialist utopia. Still now, especially for people of his generation"—he meant the man sitting next to him— "some people believe in this ideal. For a while, after the revolution but before the election, there was a discussion about a *dritte Weg*, a third way between socialism and capitalism. But now, since Kohl's policy of just swallowing East Germany into the Federal Republic, that discussion is over. It will not happen."

The man next to Ralph was on his way to Dresden for an acquaintance's fiftieth birthday party. He was fifty himself and was a librarian, and had lived in East Berlin all his life. His hair was unkempt in a genial, bookish way, and his thick glasses gave him a mildly startled look.

"A year ago," he told me in German, "no one would have believed that the whole system would fall apart like a house of cards."

I asked if he was glad the revolution had happened.

"Yes, of course. But our country will have to adjust to a whole new frame, a whole new way of life. It will be difficult."

"Now we can travel," said the wife of the other couple.

"Would you like to visit other countries in Europe?" asked Aaron.

"Oh, yes. Of course, it is expensive." She smiled. "Maybe we can't travel as much as we would like, but just knowing that we are free to buy a train ticket makes us happy."

At a party in Budapest we met Christi and Vlad, Romanian brothers whose jazz band held a collective visa for Austria. The brothers had missed their train to Vienna.

"Our band is very angry," said Christi. "They don't know where we are. They know we are in Budapest. But where are we in Budapest?"

To Vlad I said: "I remember seeing on television in December …"

"The revolution," he answered. "I might be dead. I am dead two times almost. I am speaking, 'Ceaucescu bad, Ceaucescu bad.' One time I go around a corner. And pow! One meter behind me. You understand? One meter. Another time, I sit down. If I don't sit down, maybe I'm dead."

I told him I had been moved by pictures of Romanians waving their country's flag with a hole where the Communist emblem had been.

"That is problem," said Vlad. "If we don't have that in the middle, our flag is same as Chad. So without Communist, people see our flag and think it is Chad."

I asked about Ion Iliescu, the new president.

"He is a fucking liar, man. He is friends with Ceaucescu. He speak to the—in French the word is *paysans*."

"Peasants."

"He speak to the *paysans*—the farmers—he speak, 'I give you—' What is this? *La terre*."

"Land."

"Yes! He speak, 'I give you land.' But is it Iliescu's land? He is a liar."

On the train to Debrecen in eastern Hungary, the woman across the aisle asked where I was from. She wore grey denim trousers, a knit vest, and a t-shirt. Her hair was dyed blonde. I lowered the *International Herald Tribune* I was reading. "America," I said. "Where are you from?"

"Romania," she said. "I am Hungarian."

Her name was Eniko, from Valea lui Mihai, across the border from Debrecen. She had gone to university in Cluj, the capital of Transylvania, the Hungarian-majority province of Romania. She had just finished an academic year teaching math and physics in Budapest; until the previous September, she had never been outside Romania. She hoped to return to Budapest but didn't know if she would be granted another visa. "Do you read a lot about oofoes in America?" she asked.

"Excuse me?"

"Do you read about oofoes?"

"Oofoes?"

"Yes," she said impatiently. "U-F-O—oofoes."

"Um, yes …"

"People from other planets come on oofoes."

"Yes."

"There are two kinds of people from other planets: little green ones, and tall ones."

"Yes."

"Do you read a lot in the newspapers about them in the United States?" I could tell she wanted me to say yes.

"Yes." I changed the subject. "I remember seeing on television in December …"

"Ceaucescu."

"Yes."

"Some people think now that perhaps he is not dead," said Eniko. "That pictures we saw were of a double or a dummy."

"Some people in America think that Elvis is not dead," I remarked. She laughed. "Yes. There's something I don't understand. He had so much money, but he was so unhappy. He drank too much, and he took drugs. I hear a lot of Americans take drugs. Why? Marilyn Monroe was unhappy too. She took drugs too."

"When Americans hear the word Transylvania," I said, "we think of Count Dracula."

"Yes. He was a—what is the word? Like Ceaucescu."

"A lord?"

"Yes. A lord. He was a lord, and he killed many people, thousands of people. Then people began telling stories about him."

"Move a bit to one side, dear," said an Englishman at the Berlin Wall to his wife who posed, in a blue dress, gamely wielding a hammer. "Excuse, please," said an Italian woman to someone standing between her and the camera. "We are taking a photograph." She and her husband leaned through a gap and smiled, each holding a fist-sized chunk of concrete. A man in shorts took a picture of a girl taking a picture. An Asian man caught it on video. At Checkpoint Charlie, which had been ceremonially demolished about ten days earlier, I overheard a teenage American girl say proudly: "I took this piece off the Wall myself." There was no need to pay workers to dismantle it: just give each tourist a commemorative hammer.

"The trains are crowded," said the man next to me on the train to Dresden, the same 8.48 from Berlin that we had ridden to Prague five weeks earlier. "Now is beginning the vacation time." He was thin and grey-haired, with a Roman nose and a sad face like a beagle's. He was silent most of the way, but as we approached Dresden he suddenly became talkative. He pointed out the window. "Those are wine-yards," he said. "This is one of the beautiful parts of our country."

"Yes," I said. "I've heard Dresden is nice." I couldn't resist adding, "I hear it was even more beautiful before the war."

He laughed. "Yes. But—but that is the result of a war."

"Yes."

"We started the war," he said. "We started the war …" He shrugged. "We've had a bad half-century."

"I think the next half-century will be good for Germany," I said. "Germany will be very big and strong."

"Yes," he agreed. "The border nations are not happy."

"Like Poland and France?"

"Yes." He smiled wryly.

Did he think the revolution had been a good thing?

"Oh, yes," he said tiredly. "It was the only possible solution. The economy has become so bad."

Had people disliked communism per se, or were they fed up with the bad economy?

"That is a very difficult question. Where are you from? Sweden?"

"No," I said, surprised. "America." We were speaking in English.

"Oh! You speak well. Not like other Americans."

The train neared the platform. "Five years ago I bought a house," he said. "Very near the Wall. It was so cheap then: 130,000 marks. Now, suddenly, it is already worth two million marks."

"Deutschmarks?"

"Yes. I am a rich man," he said sadly. "So now I can take some of my Deutschmarks and make a vacation in Prague."

He had been six years old in 1938: too young to have fought in the war, but he remembered seeing synagogues burn. He had lived in East Berlin most of his life. "This last year has been the most interesting time for me in the last thirty years," he said, a gleam in his eye. "But it was nervous too. 'What will happen next?' we asked."

✻

In Haiti, the fall of Baby Doc in 1986 had been followed by an unstable period of elections and coups d'état that Haitians call a *parenthèse*. During that time, a young Roman Catholic priest named Jean-Bertrand

Aristide began making his mark as a leader of the urban poor. Amy Wilentz's book *The Rainy Season* is an unavoidably important document of that time. "Talking to him once in his office," she writes,

> I noticed a newspaper with the front page headline "QUI ETES-VOUS, PERE ARISTIDE?" Who Are You, Father Aristide? I pointed to it and said, "So? Who are you, anyway?" This time he did laugh, and he said, "You'll see, you'll see. Over the years, that's the only way to prove my sincerity. That's the only way in Haiti." It became a running joke whenever we talked. "Who are you, Father Aristide?" I would ask. He always said the same thing: "You'll see." Eventually I did see, but it took a long time. As the years wore on, his courage and integrity were challenged again and again, by the regime, by the hierarchy and by the political situation. He was attacked with guns and machetes and sticks and rocks. Sometimes, I didn't know whether he was dead or alive. And then he would re-emerge, sometimes in a state of nervous prostration—thin, frail and wavering—and sometimes strengthened by the trauma, but always with his faith in himself and in his cause unshaken. In those days, he seemed unconquerable, but in the end he too would be brought down by the hard facts of Haiti.

The fall of the Berlin Wall caused a massive geopolitical earthquake that was felt as far from its epicenter as Nepal and South Africa and Kashmir. The aftershocks are still being felt everywhere. As Jalil Andrabi, a Kashmiri lawyer who documented human rights abuses by the Indian military, told me in 1994, "We thought that if people of Romania can go out on the streets and get rid of a dictator, why can't we go out on the streets in Kashmir?" Many Haitians had similar thoughts, and the vehicle they found for expressing them in words and actions – or that found them – was Aristide. As they had done two centuries earlier, in 1990 Haitians posed starkly the most awkward of universal questions: Do we really believe in government of, by, and for the people?

The autumn after the fall of the Berlin Wall, my dad invited me to join a Colorado Haiti Project trip. Ernie's had closed, so in Port-au-Prince we stayed at Wall House, a guest house off Delmas run by Canadian missionaries. The road to Petit Trou was washed out so we went to Jeannette, a lovely assemblage of huts stretching over many hills, named during the colonial period for the mistress of a French planter.

The routine was familiar: mornings and afternoons in a makeshift clinic, weighing babies, horsing around with young boys, teasing shy girls in ribbons, giving out vitamins and pills and worm medicine. Lunches of cheese-and-tomato sandwiches and dinners of rice and beans and fried bananas, idyllic evenings playing bridge and smoking cigars. Thanksgiving fell during our stay, and one day my father returned from Port-au-Prince driving a Land Rover with two live turkeys in the back, tied together at the feet. We—the visiting *blancs*, Père and Madame Lafontant, and their retainers and servants—had a memorable service and dinner. The boys who hung around in the yard were not invited to join us.

"They have to know that this is *my* house," said Père Lafontant. "It is not *their* house."

Haiti had become a place I wanted always to return to. But much had changed. One of the nurses had brought a container of handwipes that she used between patients, advertised on the label as effective in killing HIV. And the country's political future was uncertain.

A Haitian doctor joined our group, a plump young man with an easy laugh and a big heart, hopeful and eloquent in French, with a deep and melodious voice. He and I worked near each other in the clinic during the day and had long, earnest conversations in the evenings. He praised my command of French and said he wanted to improve his English. He was interested in the Kennedy assassination and asked my opinion; he felt sure Johnson must have had something to do with it. I asked him about AIDS. Did he know that Haiti was infamous in the outside world as a place of origin for the epidemic? Yes, he knew. Had he known many people with AIDS? Oh, yes; *une vingtaine* of his own friends had died, and in his work he had encountered *des centaines*, hundreds of cases.

He was a sentimental linguistic democrat, and a hopeful patriot. "*Autrefois on ne pouvait pas parler Creole dans les bureaux,*" he told me. "*Mais maintenant si on parle Creole, c'est tout à fait normal. A un certain epoch, si vous parliez Creole dans un bureau, on pouvait vous dire, 'Expwimez-vous en fwancais, monsieur.' Mais maintenant, on ne fait pas.*

Les gens acceptent si vous parlez Creole n'import-e ou."

"We love Creole very much, and we cannot abandon it," he said. "We must not abandon it, because it is *une partie de l'âme haïtienne"*— a part of the Haitian soul. "We love French very much also. *C'est une langue importante, c'est une langue internationale, qui nous permettra d'avoir des relations avec l'exterieure."*

The doctor said many proud and happy and hopeful things in the same vein. At our last dinner together, he offered a toast. He was very happy to know that there were Americans like us, he said, who loved his country and came to help; he would never forget us.

At the end of the trip we rode over the spine of the southern peninsula, on roads not repaired since they had been built by forced labor during the 1915–34 occupation of Haiti by the U.S. Marines. On the far side of a valley we rode through, a massive pile of earth had fallen in a heap: an entire mountainside brought down by the erosion caused by deforestation. In Jacmel my father and I stayed two nights at Le Jacmelien, a beachside hotel where surf played in your ears as you slept. A ways down the beach, a freighter lay washed up and abandoned.

I had ridden down the mountain from Jeannette to a hospital in the coastal town of Léogâne with Stewart Abbott, a big, bearded young obstetrician from Greeley, Colorado, and a Haitian woman who had just given birth. We had sought out the pharmacy, bought I.V. equipment and solution, and appropriated a room so Stew could examine the woman, who had a vaginal tear and a uterine infection that would have been fatal if she hadn't come to our clinic. To get there, she had walked several hours. Afterward, riding over the mountains to Jacmel, I taped Stewart's thoughts on a microcassette player. "I think the frustrating thing about that whole episode was orchestrating the trip," he said, his mouth touching the recorder's microphone as the bus's gears ground relentlessly in the background. "The jeep was available. But because the woman had to take her family to take care of her, and had a newborn that she had to nurse—they had to run home and get the baby—that probably took about an hour that we were sittin' around while this poor woman was just feeling miserable. That was the real frustrating thing. I felt so helpless there."

He was diffidently beginning to form professional opinions. "The impression of the hospital, I'm still processing," he said. "There were lots of doors that were closed: the laboratory, and radiology, and pharmacy—it looked like there were departments there, but it sure looked like they weren't working. I don't know what the availability of services was. At least the public areas seemed clean."

Family members had to buy supplies and medicines, as we had done for Simone. "That's sure my impression," said Stew. "And not only that. They need to provide the services, I believe, like bathing and meal preparation for the patient. That's why someone from the family needed to come with Simone. It seemed an eternity watching the nurse make a bed for her. A frustrating thing was the whole lack of regard for time or suffering. They knew that she had a problem, and I believe they accepted that she had a problem, but it sure didn't seem that there was a lot of motivation to do anything about it."

He had seen a woman with an enlarged goiter, possibly cancerous; a man with a leg swollen from elephantiasis; another man with a badly abscessed tooth from too much sugarcane ("I understand that that may be the only source of nutrition for some of these people for a period of time. Again, it was a helpless feeling to know that I am not trained to do any dental extractions or dental work"); a teenage boy with an enlarged spleen; a woman with a tumor in her breast about eight centimeters across. "I'm not sure surgery would really alter the course of her disease," he said. "She was complaining of some backache, and may well have had some spread to the bones."

But most of Stewart's patients had suffered only from the usual run-of-the-mill ailments. "Mostly, I think we provided an opportunity for the local people to see a physician," he said. "They all seemed to have chronic complaints revolving around their stomach or intestinal systems, and also generalized symptoms such as fevers and weakness. Those symptoms most likely correlated with malaria. And since we didn't have any laboratory facilities, not even a microscope, to help diagnose some of that or to rule it out, we elected to treat most everyone with sweats and fevers and weakness as if they had malaria. Most everyone else had stomach symptoms that we elected to treat as being worms. We've been told there are worms in the public water supply."

I was curious to know, since he was an obstetrician, whether back home he ever performed abortions, or was asked to.

"It says right in my Yellow Pages ad, 'No Terminations,'" he said. "So don't even ask. That's my policy."

I asked how he and his wife had decided to come to Haiti.

"We were at the annual Christian Renewal Conference this summer, and one of the afternoon workshops was a presentation about the project," he said. "We had been thinking for some time that we wanted to do some type of Third World work or experience, because we know that we've been blessed with so much in our home, and my practice has grown dramatically, and we felt that it was important for us to share that somehow. But rather than signing up for two years with the Peace Corps right away, we thought that maybe a short trip was less threatening, and that we could certainly do that, and maybe that would help us know if there was more of this kind of work in our future."

In the courtyard of the cathedral I spoke with Pat Hudson, a member of my father's parish, who also was in Haiti for the first time. "I've had two thoughts going through my mind since I've been here," she told me. "One is trying to imagine what life would be like without any occurrences, without events, other than the ordinary, everyday family events, so that when the truck goes by with white people in it and they throw balloons out of the truck, it's a really big thing—not for the adults, but at least for the children. Then you have to wonder too: Has the church really made a real difference in their lives? And it may not be that we've saved so many lives; it may just be that we bring the outside world in, and they're exposed. But is that a good thing or a bad thing? I don't know yet. I think Haiti is a country for big questions.

"When you see a country in such bad shape as Haiti is, you're tempted to think, How could we move in, in a very big way? Let's lay something on this country. It's a temptation to think, What would you do if your means were unlimited? The big temptation would be to, I think, clean it up, lay some kind of program on it. Of course this is what we tried in the past too—very often with very disastrous results. But I can see how people were tempted to do that. If nothing else, I think I understand how big, mistaken programs come to be."

I observed that the Colorado Haiti Project was a small program.

"Of course you always hope that a little bit is going to do something," said Pat. "We all know it's pretty much just putting a Band-Aid on a gaping wound. But, we try! And I think probably the point of this whole mission is not really so much what we can do for 'these people,' but it's just awakening ourselves to the terrible tragedies in the world."

I asked why she had come.

"I got involved for a couple of reasons," Pat said. "One, being on the vestry, I feel people on the vestry have a responsibility to support programs. Number two, I hadn't seen any other women my age who had come down here and done this. I think that was kind of an important thing: to show other women my age that they could do something quite adventuresome. Number three, curiosity. Number four the challenge, and maybe a little bit the scare of coming to a country like Haiti, about which we haven't heard anything good. And, to see for myself."

✳

But the conversation from that trip that has haunted me was one with Père Lafontant, one quiet evening in Jeannette. Haiti's first-ever genuinely democratic election was due in less than three weeks, and I asked him who he thought would win.

"Aristide will win," he responded. Then he lifted a finger: "—if he lives."

Did former World Bank official Marc Bazin, whom the United States supported, stand a chance?

"Between you and me, no. Aristide is too popular."

Which candidate did he support?

"I support the candidate who will be the best for the country."

Which one was that?

"God will choose the right one."

I didn't buy this. Had God chosen, say, Hitler?

"*Oui. Bon-Dieu a choisi Hitler, mais Hitler a trompé Bon-Dieu.*" he said. God chose Hitler, but Hitler deceived God.

CHAPTER 2

Averting Our Eyes

On September 30, 1991, the first democratically elected president in Haiti's long history was ousted by the army. I heard about the coup from my father. Haiti had had many coups. But this one was different, because Aristide was different. Wasn't he?

"The President and his staff have been arrested and taken to the army headquarters," foreign minister Jean-Robert Sabalat was quoted as saying on the front page of *The Globe and Mail* of October 1—I was living in Detroit, where the Canadian paper was available in sidewalk boxes. Another minister said: "We're in serious trouble." Among the "charges" against Aristide was that he had been "meddling in internal army affairs." Twenty-six people were reported dead, including a small child at an orphanage founded by Aristide and the preacher and dissident politician Sylvio Claude. The next day's news was that Aristide somehow had sent a statement to the Haitian embassy in Washington. "They have a very long list of people they plan to kill still," he said. "They will kill them like flies. Do everything possible to stop people from dying. It's General Raoul Cedras who mounted this coup d'etat. He started killing everyone. They're going to kill everyone still."

In his *New York Times* column of October 3, Thomas Friedman wrote: "Bush Administration officials said they were determined to reverse the coup in Haiti, having spent a great deal of time and energy over the years trying to produce a democratic government in Port-au-Prince, but President Bush said he was not inclined to use American military force." Quickly the administration backed away from even this equivocal commitment. "After Father Aristide was ousted in a coup last Monday," reported the *Times* on October 6, "President Bush and Secretary of State James A. Baker 3d both demanded his reinstatement with no conditions. But today, officials said they concluded that Father Aristide must publicly disavow mob violence and work toward sharing power with the Parliament."

In *The New Republic*, Amy Wilentz wrote:

> Part of Aristide's problem as president has been that he had continued to behave as though he were just a liberation priest. "I see myself as a president in opposition," he said during the last weeks of his administration (nothing could be truer now). … After a 200-year wait, surely the Haitians have earned the right to be governed by the man they elected. It is unlikely that in any future election they would come out to vote for anyone else.

A landslide was about to sweep away many people and things and assumptions. But one thing that didn't change much was my father's work. "Dear Participants of the January 31–February 12 Haiti mission," he wrote on October 5. "As all of you know, things are happening in Haiti right now! I've been trying to call Father Lafontant to get some firsthand reports, but it's not possible to get through by phone. I have written him to assure him of our prayers.

"As some of you know, things like this have happened in the past several months before our missions, and then by the time we're ready to go things are stable again. Always, we have experienced only minor problems when the time comes for us to go. It's impossible, of course, to know at this point how this particular coup will end, but I am hopeful that by January and February we'll be able to proceed with our missions. … Meanwhile, remember the Haitian proverb, which is designed to get Haitians (and us) through events such as those taking place in Haiti right now: 'If you're flexible, you're too rigid. You've got to be fluid.'" But on November 21 he wrote:

Dear friends in Christ:

> Father Lafontant called me this morning with the sad news that it is his judgment that it would be best for us to cancel our January and February missions to Haiti. Father Lafontant said that things continue to go from bad to worse, that fuel is almost gone, that

electricity and water are in increasingly short supply, and that the consulate [sic] had yesterday urged the few remaining Americans in Haiti to leave. Further, a meeting planned for today in Colombia between Aristide and those currently in power inside Haiti has apparently fallen through, making the news on the streets in Port-au-Prince very discouraging. Given all this, it just does not look to him as if things would be sufficiently stable in January and February to be safe even if some agreement were arrived at soon—and even that does not look likely.

"This is, in many ways, a pivotal Sunday of the year," my father told his parishioners the following Sunday in his sermon, based on the Gospel reading John 18:33–38a. "It's the celebration of Christ the King. ... As Jesus stands before Pilate, who is about to turn him over to the executioners, Pilate asks Jesus if it's true that Jesus is a king, as the Jews were claiming. 'Are you here to challenge my authority, my power? Are you here to challenge the authority and power of Rome? Are you a king?' asks Pilate. 'If so, I'll have to dispose of you.'

"'Well,' says Jesus, 'You are the one who says I am a king. But this is why I was born—to bear witness to the truth.'

"'Truth?' says Pilate. 'What is truth?' And Pilate turned Jesus over to be executed.

"Last Thursday night, the book discussion group discussed a small book entitled *In the Parish of the Poor*. It was written by Jean-Bertrand Aristide, a priest who is now the exiled President of Haiti. The book was published in 1990, the year Father Aristide was elected President. And in the Foreword to the book, Amy Wilentz asks how one can account for Father Aristide's extraordinary following among the masses of the Haitian people, among those desperately poor who have no power in Haiti and who have no claim even to any of the substance and life of their own country. And Wilentz concludes that it is because Aristide speaks the truth to those who are in power, even putting his own life in jeopardy to do it. The masses of the poor are committed to Aristide, she says, because Aristide speaks the truth when he tells the world that the poor in Haiti are exploited by the wealthy and the army in Haiti as well as by the cold country to the north.

"That's what Father Aristide has to say in his book and in his sermons and speeches since the mid-1980s. Then Father Aristide was elected President of his nation. He himself was placed in authority, and he exercised that authority for a few months in 1991. And then, on September 30, just two months ago, those with the firepower—the army and the wealthy, those who stand to lose if the poor actually rise up with Aristide and claim their share of the resources of Haiti—removed Aristide from power and sent him into exile.

"Why? The reasons are complex, and I'm not going to try to analyze them all this morning. But the *basic* reason is that truth and power in this world do not mix well. A year ago, as a priest who was responding to his vocation as prophet, as one who seeks to speak God's Word to his people, Father Aristide could substantially speak the truth, because that was his purpose, his aim, the reason for his life. But once *inside* the government, once he was President with at least some of the world's authority at his disposal, once he became responsible not only to God and to the poor in Haiti but to *all* elements of Haitian society, Aristide has found that the truth can bite you if it's spoken too boldly—or acted upon. He has found that in the world, including that part of the world of which he is president, those who have more concern for their power or their self-interest will often sacrifice truth to power and self-interest. So now Father Aristide in Caracas and the army in Port-au-Prince are negotiating. They are trying to determine whether power and truth can share the same office, or what mix of truth and power might be acceptable to all concerned.

"Jesus, standing before Pilate two thousand years ago, witnessed to the truth. And part of the truth is that in the struggle between truth and power and self-interest in this world, truth is often sacrificed to power, because of sin. So Pilate handed Jesus over to be crucified, because Pilate did not know what truth was, and did not care. Or rather, better, because in Jesus, Pilate looked Truth in the eye, just as the Jews had, and he recognized there the threat of truth to his authority and his power and his own self-interest. And, fearing the truth, he had Truth put away."

✳

I had arrived in Detroit that summer to help a local reporter named Michael Betzold research a book on Tiger Stadium, the city's historic baseball park, and the controversy over whether it should be replaced. The larger issue was whether a city with a Third World infant mortality rate, or a state that included such a city, or any entity in a world that included such a city, had any good reason to subsidize a for-profit business by spending hundreds of millions of dollars of public money to build a demonstrably unprofitable new physical plant. During the frenzied four months Mike and I spent producing *Queen of Diamonds: The Tiger Stadium Story*, I began to see that the question is not always who is right and who is wrong, but who holds power and who defines the terms. And I began to extrapolate: If They aren't telling me the truth about Tiger Stadium—as I now knew They weren't, because I was doing the work of learning about it for myself —what else might They not be telling me the truth about?

"We shouldn't have to be writing this book," I complained.

"I know you think you're a literary genius and all," said Mike. "But I think you have the makings of a journalist."

One day, Detroit mayor Coleman Young and the similarly jowly billionaire strip-mall developer Al Taubman faced the cameras, looking like two of the pigs in *Animal Farm*, to announce that they had reached an agreement about a new stadium. Such deals usually turned out to be smoke and mirrors, but invariably local media billed them as tremendously newsworthy events. The TV reporter was gushing about how much "power" had just emerged from behind closed doors.

"'You are powerless. You have no power.' That's what they're saying," said Mike in disgust. Mike's friend Frank Rashid showed me the new car plant built on land donated by the city in the face of threats from Chrysler Corporation to leave town. He showed me Belle Isle, the once beautiful island park in the Detroit River, now run down. He took me to a concert at the lovely Orchestra Hall that his sister Kathy, an artist, had helped restore. He drove me along the river, where what would have been a nice view across to Canada had been obliterated by a concrete wall. He pointed out the surreal change that came over Jefferson Avenue as it crossed from Detroit into the affluent suburb of Grosse

Pointe. He introduced me to local people who were investing their own money and effort in the painstaking work of rebuilding Corktown, the neighborhood around Tiger Stadium. Through this guided tour of the big defeats, so readily visible to anyone who remembered the things that had been lost, and the modest successes, all human in scale and fragile, I began to sense what was at stake.

And I began seeing history in a new way. Never for a moment had Detroit stood still. Its industrial boom in the middle of the twentieth century had drawn migrants by the million: "ethnics" from eastern and southern Europe, blacks and whites from the South. Detroit was the most American of cities: the corner of Michigan and Woodward was the site of the world's first traffic light. The Davison was the world's first freeway. Westland, just north of Eight Mile Road in Southfield, was the world's first suburban shopping mall. Hudson's had been the world's biggest department store. General Motors was the world's largest corporation. More potato chips were consumed per capita in Detroit than anywhere else on the planet. Labor was plentiful, so wages could be kept low enough to suit the car companies. Housing was chronically scarce, and the city became a tinderbox of racial, ethnic, and class animosities. The lid blew in 1943 and again in 1967.

By the time I moved there in 1991, the physical city was a burned-out shell of its former self. Detroit had been a city of neighborhoods, blocks of single-family houses sprawling over many square miles. Now, you could walk the length of a city block with nothing on it but weeds and rubble. In Corktown, history could be read like tea leaves: a brick or wooden house built around the turn of the century, maintained just to the point of being habitable; across the street, what in the 1860s had been a German immigrant's house on a ribbon farm running all the way to the river, now restored and gentrified by a gay couple; down the block, a crack house. On the next block, the charred wreck of a house burned by its owner for insurance. Across the street from that, an empty lot. This was the street I lived on.

The devastation had been swift and all too recent. If you didn't know what had been lost you wouldn't miss it, but people still in their thirties carried memories of buildings, neighborhoods, whole swathes of the city that simply no longer existed. My friend "Baseball John" Miramonti remembered the Olympia Arena, lovingly decorated with bas-relief murals, where the Beatles had played, and where from the upper deck you could look straight down on Gordie Howe skating past; the Red Wings now played in Joe Louis Arena, a featureless building like a warehouse that blocked a view of the river and was named after Coleman Young's personal hero. People remembered Poletown, the Polish neighborhood where hundreds of homes and dozens of churches had been razed to build a new General Motors plant, on the false promise of a net gain in jobs. Where the cultural heart of Detroit's black community had been now ran Interstate 75. One day Baseball John and I snuck over a wall into the old train station, built in the 1920s with copper roofing and fourteen floors never fully occupied before the building closed in the early 1980s. We walked all the way to the roof and enjoyed the view: Canada to the south, the GM Building to the north in the distance.

Detroit's downtown had been impressive, and at night the city of yesteryear could still be seen, in a ghostly way, because so little had been built more recently. Who was to blame was a rhetorical question that hovered over the skyline and seeped unspoken into conversations. The battle lines were black and white, and it was difficult and trying for even well-meaning and intelligent people to cross the line starkly marked by Eight Mile Road, the frontier between the city and what Coleman Young called "the hostile white suburbs."

Detroit's revolution had come in 1973 when it elected Young, its first black mayor. The groundwork had been laid by white flight of a speed and scale not seen in other cities and beginning as long ago as the 1950s, when the *yang* of industrial triumph had already carried within it the *yin* of its own demise, and accelerating after the 1967 riot. In 1973 Detroit's blacks, feeling it now was their city, elected a man willing to consolidate and perpetuate his own power by using race as a trump card, while cultivating mutually useful understandings with the very white business people he excoriated. Many whites despised Young and equated him with blacks, and blacks with Detroit, and averted their eyes. For their part many blacks, even long after the promise Young had seemed to embody had become a bitter memory, defiantly kept I SUPPORT MAYOR YOUNG stickers on their car bumpers. Part of the trouble was that everyone on both sides was in the right. The younger Young had been a courageous dissident and principled advocate for workers, especially but not only blacks. Once in power he did what he had to do to stay there, for twenty long years.

Frank Rashid showed me his old neighborhood. His Lebanese family had come to Detroit from Illinois, and his father had opened a grocery store. The store was still standing, but it was now the only building on its block, and it had been closed ever since the 1967 riot. On the day of the riot Frank and his father had cowered on the floor among scattered canned goods, until some of their black customers led them to safety. Frank, who taught English at a local college, called Detroit's racial syndrome "Faulknerian."

"People will use blacks as scapegoats for other problems," he said. "I had an uncle who resented my father and used our living in the city with blacks as a way of getting at him." In Faulkner, "you see it over and over again in the call back to the land, what the land was before 'we' whites ruined it with the cotton crop and by cutting down all the forests. Because the vehicle that allowed us to do that was the slaves, we hate and resent and blame the vehicle." During the boom in Detroit, he said, "the blacks came into our neighborhoods. The fight over housing was very, very serious. It was brought on completely by the auto industry, which drew up whole bunches of people for which the city was not prepared. We ended up with the 1943 race riot as a result. The car companies made this town what it is. They brought my family here too. Not to work in the plants, but to sell groceries to the workers in the plants. To me, Faulkner wasn't writing about the South. He was writing about Detroit. Detroit needs its own Faulkner."

Detroit fascinated me from my first day there. By the same token it bruised me, and making sense of it became more difficult as one became a part of the city's daily life oneself and came to feel the oppressive weight of collective but very personal guilt and shame, just like every other Detroiter. When, abruptly and painfully eighteen months later, I decided that I had to leave, the streets and buildings around me became insubstantial, as though fading from view. I had felt oppressed by the claustrophobic, incestuous, cannibalistic social and political atmosphere, horrified that I might become habituated to it. Now, relieved and reprieved, I wanted only to avert my eyes.

✳

Just before I left Detroit, in December 1992, the exiled Aristide came to the Hyatt Regency hotel in Dearborn to give the annual Cranbrook Peace Lecture. In person, the first thing that struck me about him was a childlike demeanor, an odd shyness or diffidence. His command of English was imperfect, and many of his phrases and images were hackneyed and forced. He leaned heavily on a metaphor of the crane, symbol of the sponsoring Cranbrook Peace Foundation. He played to what he knew was a sympathetic crowd, and they cheered on cue.

"The spirit of the crane was with us once again in December 1990," he said. "As you know, we won the first democratic elections. … As you know, the flight to democracy was not peaceful." He recalled the infamous September 1988 attack on his parish, St-Jean Bosco. "We met those same weapons on February 5, 1991. Those weapons can burn our people, our houses, our churches. They cannot burn our love." He paused for applause, then added: "We still love those who commit crimes against humanity." On the night of the coup, he had prayed that the soldiers would be divided over whether to kill him. "May God help them to get divide," he said he had prayed. "And because they divide, I am still alive. I did not want to have power, but spreading love. … I prefer that way." He outlined his political plans. "We will remove from the army General Raoul Cedras and the thugs who led the coup with him," he said. "The only way to restore democracy in Haiti is to restore our constitutional government. When our refugees leave Haiti to come to the United States, there is a jobs problem. When President Clinton helps to restore democracy back, the Haitian will stay in Haiti. You can be sure about that."

The awkward crane image recurred. "The same spirit of unity that helps the crane to soar" should guide all Haitians. "The action of the few cannot impede the flow of history. Like the crane, all of Haiti must

30

move in the vee formation and take flight." The army, he said, "uses weapons for drugs trafficking, to protect a structure of corruption," but it was "possible to stop those military in a nonviolent way." It was "not fair" that forty percent of the national budget went to the military. "Because our constitution says we have to have an army, I respect the constitution. But not that kind of army." He spoke of "professionaliza-tion" of the army, of separating the military from the police.

"The only thing we need is the support of the international com-munity passing from statements to action," he asserted. Then, we would see "the fruits of love, the fruits of peace." Of President-elect Clinton he said: "The way he talks about refugees tell us the world can have a man who will pass from statements to action." Haitians had been watching the U.S. election avidly. "They thought if President Clinton is elected, then democracy will happen. If you mention the name of President Clinton in Haiti, you might be arrested and beaten and put in prison."

He spoke of Haiti's poverty. "In Haiti, for each ten thousand Hai-tians, we don't have two doctors, just one point eight. You cannot be-lieve that, but it's a fact. Our politics want to be different. Serving people, instead of using people to make us richer. For us, a man or woman is God. We cannot talk about peace without sharing love, be-cause no love, no peace, no peace, no love."

A panel was on hand to ask questions. Someone asked about the army.

"Unfortunately," said Aristide, "they use their money from drugs trafficking, corruption, to lie to the world. … They present a face of Haiti to you, and they hide the real Haiti." After the coup, the military "realized there is something irreversible: the will of the Haitian people to live in democracy." And he asked: "If you want to help us, don't help the people who are killing us."

Dr. Jean Elsie, president of a group called Espoir, asked Aristide why he should go back to Haiti.

"First, because I love my country," he said. "Secondly, because of the mandate coming from the elections. The elections were free, and it's a mandate for five years, and it's not already five years."

"If you go back to Haiti," asked someone else, "what should the people here tonight expect to happen?"

"You can expect a commitment to live in democracy," said Aristide. "François Duvalier chose the weapons—it's a bad way to be president. When I will be back, you can expect from me someone who will realize he cannot go as fast as he could go."

Someone from the audience asked about *père lebrun* or necklacing, the mob practice of assassinating someone by throwing a burning tire around his neck.

"During our seven months," replied Aristide, "we never had any case of victims from necklacing or *père lebrun*. The first case happened precisely the day of the coup, September 30, 1991. The country is a broken glass. The pieces are down. We have to pick them up. How do we do that?"

He ended by acknowledging a group of Haitians who had come from Lansing, directing to them the trademark slogan of his movement: "*Ou sèl ou feb. Ensem nou fort. Ensem ensem nou se lavalas.* Alone you are weak. Together we are strong. All together we are like a flood. Indeed we are *lavalas*. Thank you."

✳

"I should have known Detroit couldn't hold you," said Frank Rashid sadly. Another friend challenged me: "Leave if you have to," she said, "but at some point you're going to have to turn back and face Detroit again." At this point, I didn't know when that point might be. Feeling beat up and defeated, I headed west to Colorado. During the long days driving alone past snowbound cornfields, I wondered why places like Haiti and Detroit made such claims on me. When I had returned in 1991 to the Upper Midwest, it had been to settle in a badly decayed neighborhood deep within America's all-purpose pariah city. Haiti's name likewise had long been a byword for bad and scary things. The litany of its afflictions was long and familiar: the slave revolution of 1791–1804 that had achieved its hard-won and bitter freedom, not acknowledged by the United States until 1862. The infamous tradition of corruption and political instability. Voodoo. The Duvaliers, Papa

Doc and Baby Doc. African swine fever and AIDS. Now, since the coup, tens of thousands of unwelcome "boat people" were washing up on beaches in Florida. What made the scorn easier to excuse was that so much of what we wanted to believe was in fact true. Haiti really was unstable, dangerous, impoverished. Also like Detroit, Haiti was haunted by the ghost of a ruined landscape. Perhaps this vestigial memory of past beauty and dignity was what was so painful. Loving Haiti as I did was an exercise in frustration, emotionally draining, complicated. I thought of it as loving a dying friend. But why the scorn? From what, precisely, are we so quick to avert our eyes?

My engine blew up outside Kansas City, and I stumbled across the Great Plains in a one-way rental. My father was taking a group to Haiti in the second half of January and had invited me along. I said sure. In the days before we left there was a flurry of news and rumors, a sense that something was about to break. Haitians were feverishly building boats, hopefully awaiting the inauguration of the American candidate who had pledged: "If I were President, I would—in the absence of clear and compelling evidence that they weren't political refugees—give them temporary asylum until we restored the elected government of Haiti." The *New York Times* reported that Clinton was holed up with his advisers in Little Rock, pondering his promises. The night before we flew to Miami, we learned that Clinton had reneged on his pledge to change Bush's policy of forcible repatriation. He had suddenly discovered "a clear and legitimate distinction between political and economic refugees."

"*Your* president," said my father to me.

That evening I spoke on the phone with Father Ed Morgan, who had preceded us to Haiti by a week. The conversation was staccato because of a delay and static on the line.

"Have you heard the latest?" I asked him.

"I don't know," he said. "What's the latest?"

"I've just heard Clinton is reneging on his promise."

"Well, we're hearing here that Aristide is coming back."

"Wow! What's your source?"

"My source is the *New York Post*," he said, a little offended.

"The *New York Post*?"

"I mean the *Washington Post*."

About fifteen of us gathered at four the next morning in the Denver airport. We stayed overnight in Miami. "No halt to repatriations" read the *Miami Herald* headline, above the fold and over a large color photo. Again we heard the rumor that Aristide had returned.

The next morning's banner headline was U.S. BARRICADING HAITI. A flotilla of Coast Guard vessels had been sent, presumably at Clinton's behest, although he hadn't yet been inaugurated. Front-page color illustrations showed the various kinds of planes and ships that constituted an "arsenal of air and sea power." THWARTING AN EXODUS, read the caption.

The black American driver and a grey-haired man from Surinam loaded our many duffel bags into the van. The driver was not at a loss for words.

"Clinton got a lot to deal with right now, man," he told me. "Somalia. Eye-rack. And Haiti. So he's got to deal with those other places in the Middle East first. He can't even deal with the economy. He's got to put off Haiti for now."

"But he's got to deal with Haiti pretty soon, I think," I suggested.

"Oh, yeah. I think Bush is testing his foreign-policy expertise, if you ask me."

I asked him about Haitian refugees.

"There's just too many of 'em here now, Haitians and Cubans too," he said.

"What would you do if you were a Cuban?"

"I don't know. I spent fifteen months in Vietnam fighting what they got—oppression. But if I was in their shoes? I don't know. Me bein' an American, I can't see going to another country except my own. I can't see going to another country just to go to jail. Because that's what it is where they keep 'em—barbed wire, and head counts, and all. Some of 'em been there a year, year and a half. And it's no good saying you'll send 'em to other parts of the country. They all just come back here. They got the tropical weather here, they got the same foods they're used to, and they're closer to home. As soon as Castro's gone, we'll have another influx of Cubans. And we can't take any more. Miami gonna sink. Maybe we should just say no more refugees from anywhere for ten years or something, 'til this country's back on its feet."

*

To see the world from above is a great privilege. In Haiti the mountains rise almost directly from the sea; what they must have looked like when there were still trees on them, one can only imagine. From above, Haiti looks like a life-size topographical map of itself; every feature and coastline is naked to the gaze. "I was returning without much hope to a country of fear and frustration," writes Greene in *The Comedians*, "and yet every familiar feature as the *Medea* drew in gave me a kind of happiness." *There*, as our plane drew in, was the Isle de la Tortue; *there* was the main island's north coast. *There* were the undulant hills and river valleys of the Artibonite; *there* was where the northern peninsula curved to join the narrow mainland north of the capital. *There* was Highway One. Port-au-Prince in the bright sunlight, curving and spreading around the bay and up the slopes of the hills in all directions. La Gonâve: the long, empty island in the bay. And the bright blue bay itself, dotted with fishing boats, more detail visible as the plane descended, every feature familiar and strangely comforting.

Knowing the Coast Guard blockade was there, one had the sensation of flying across a dimensional barrier or permeating a membrane. I felt as if a friend of mine – a dying friend, a friend with AIDS—were being summarily rejected by a rich neighbor. Were we then Samaritans? But my reasons for returning to Haiti were essentially selfish. As we stood waiting in the aisle of the plane, I saw that the woman in front of me, one of our group, was browsing in a catalogue, reading an ad for a garlic shredder.

Stepping onto the tarmac this time was not oppressive but pleasant; in Colorado it was deep winter. As usual, I had brought just enough clothes and too many books. NE PAS MONTER DESSUS, said the sign above the baggage carousel, in French and English. DO NOT STEP THEREON. The customs check was perfunctory; soon we were outside among the crowd milling by the buses and tap-taps and taxis, and instantly I recognized the human odors that tell me I am in Haiti.

Down Boulevard Harry Truman and through Carrefour there was almost no traffic. Gasoline was cheaper than it had been, about $3.75 per gallon, but engine oil was up to six or seven dollars a quart. No one went out, Ed Morgan told us; people stayed inside and listened to their radios. The military government had scheduled elections to the Senate for January 18, but most Haitians saw these as only lending the junta a spurious legitimacy.

DIEU SEUL MAITRE, read the tap-taps, the colorful, playfully decorated pickup trucks used as public transportation. PARTY COOL MAN. VOICI DAD. I LOVE YOU BABY. A TOI SEIGNEUR. And, quintessentially: PATIENCE: TOUT EST MYSTERE. *Aba Aristid*, I read on a concrete wall in Léogâne. *Vende peyi pou pouvwa.* Down with Aristide, who has sold the country for power. And on a billboard: *SIDA: Nou tout ka pran.* AIDS: We all can get it. We rode past the abandoned Reynolds bauxite plant, then two and a half hours to go the bone-jarring last twenty-seven miles.

✳

And at last we were in Petit Trou de Nippes. Two young men greeted us. One played a guitar, and together they sang:

> *Jesus, je t'aim-e,*
> *Parce que tu m'as sauvé …*

I love you, Jesus, because you have saved me. Too soon that first evening, I said to Father Lafontant: "*Je veux discuter avec vous la situation politique.*"

He shrugged.

He proudly showed me the new cistern and outhouses he had had built.

"*Eske Titid ap vini anko?*" I asked. Will Aristide come back?

He shrugged again.

Father Lafontant was in his way aristocratic, dignified, driven, dedicated to his own local work. He had little patience for the convulsive and violent vicissitudes of politics. I had learned this about him in 1990, and now it began to sink in.

The next day was Sunday, and the Episcopal bishop came in his purple shirt to perform his yearly round of baptisms. The locals gathered in the corrugated-iron shed that was the church: the foundation of a new church building had been laid nearby. Mothers and fathers, wizened elders, impeccably dressed and well-behaved little girls, stiff little boys gathered. The bishop spoke of *la dignité de chaque être humain* and baptized *au nom Papa, Piti e Saint-Esprit*. To us *blancs* he said in English: "We thank you for your sacrifice. We know that each of you have two or three cars in your garage. We know sometime that God will take care of the road, the way he take care of everything." And he spoke of the coming "*grand, grand, grand, grand fête dimanche prochaine*," the big party next Sunday.

We had the afternoon free. I strolled down the road. A red Land Rover approached from behind. I waved it down and asked for a lift.

"*Pa gen pwoblem*," said the man driving. No problem. He was a local official of the party of Sylvio Claude, the Protestant minister who had been a popular favorite in the 1990 election until Aristide entered the race, and who had been assassinated during the coup. Three others were in the Land Rover. I got in.

The driver's name was Williams. "Williams Régala?" I asked, naming a well-known *méchant* Duvalierist. There was a pause, then everyone laughed.

We talked politics. "Under Jean-Claude it was stable," said Williams. "There were no *zinglindos*. But now …" Zinglindos were gangs of armed thugs who ruled the streets at night. The men dropped me in the town. One of them stayed with me. He was probably in his late teens, and his name was Ismael.

"*M-renmen peyi blanc*," Ismael told me. "*Peyi blanc rich ampil*." I like white countries. White countries are very rich.

He had been to Guantanamo Bay, where he had been questioned by U.S. authorities, rejected for asylum in the United States, and returned to Haiti. He led me past the town's square, past plastered houses and wooden huts, and out of town to the cockpit: dirt squares surrounded by palm logs and railings, roofed with banana leaves. Many pairs of eyes watched me. I was asked for "one dollar," given to understand that this was the price of admission.

"*Pa genyen,*" I said, which was true. I had no money in my pockets. There was general laughter: mocking but, so I hoped, also welcoming.

A long time passed. There was much discussion and milling around. Young men held and stroked their cocks, some of which had their heads covered with socks. Every once in a while two cocks would be set down in the pit and tested against each other. The cocks would fan their neck feathers like cobras, looking fierce and jumping toward each other while their owners held them on strings. The problem was to find two cocks that were "equal," Ismael explained. Women squatted nearby over stoves, selling fried foods. Older men played dominos.

"*Gen de pou batay,*" said Ismael finally. Two well-matched cocks had been found. The crowd crushed in several layers against the pit; the owners squatted inside, whittling on the spikes on the back of their cocks' legs to sharpen them.

But it was a false start. The scene was repeated—discussions, comparisons, sharpening of spikes —in the other pit. While we waited, a young man named Jean-Pierre told me in good English about life at Guantanamo Bay.

"It was nice, man," he said. "Them feed us good. I translate for migration people."

"INS?" I asked. The U.S. Immigration and Naturalization Service.

"Yes. INS. Here is my idea." He showed me a laminated card with his photograph on one side.

"Your ID?"

He grinned. "Yes. My ID."

Jean-Pierre had been interned in Camp 2 at Guantanamo but, because of his language skills, he had been free to show his ID to visit other camps. "Look around, see what's going on," he said.

A man was walking around inside the pit blowing a whistle, pushing people behind the palm logs. Suddenly, without ceremony, two men dropped two cocks on the ground. Amid much cheering and exhortation the cocks squared off, then went after each other with their spikes.

For a long time one chased the other in circles, first clockwise, then counterclockwise, lunging every so often for its neck. I was jostled and found myself unable to see. I elbowed my way back to a view of the action. At long last one of the cocks sat panting in the dirt, its foe stood over it in triumph, the referee blew a long note on his whistle. The cocks' owners rushed to pick them up and take them a few yards away to suck the blood from their heads and legs. Winning bettors jumped inside the pit, cheering and yelling.

✱

Walking back, Ismael told me about his own trip to Guantanamo. In May 1992, he had paid $100 to go there in a boat with eighty-seven people. The boat had taken on water and had to return to Haiti's southern peninsula.

I asked why he had gone.

There was much gang violence now in Port-au-Prince, he said. *Zinglindos* terrorized, robbed, even entered houses to murder people. In the countryside there was less violence, though many *chefs de section* were *méchants*. Zinglindos would knock on people's doors claiming to have news of Aristide. When the people opened their door, the zinglindos would enter the house, steal, kill, and *viole se*.

I didn't understand the phrase.

"Cut," he said. "Cut your sister."

On the road we met two other young men, the brothers who had been singing about Jesus when we arrived. I was to spend much time with them over the coming days, asking and answering questions, walking with them along this road. From them I learned a little of what it was like to pin one's hopes on a packed, rickety boat crossing six hundred miles of open sea.

Didn't they know attempting a sea journey was dangerous?

"*C'est la vie*," said one of them. He planned to try again in February.

Why had he left the first time?

Zinglindos had broken into his house in Port-au-Prince, he said, and he had escaped to a friend's house in the mountains. He had paid $180 for passage to Guantanamo—more than Ismael, because his boat had a motor. He had stayed in Guantanamo two months, until his petition for political asylum in the United States was rejected and he was returned to Port-au-Prince.

Did he know about the announcement Clinton had just made, that he would continue the Bush policy of forcible repatriation? Would it change his mind?

No, he would try again regardless. So would Ismael.

But why?

Although they could die in boats, both of them said, they could just as easily die on the streets of Port-au-Prince.

Would they change their plans if Aristide returned?

"Can Titid stop the terror?" asked Ismael. "Can he control the army?"

That evening I chatted with the two young Haitian doctors attached to our group.

"*Et qu'est-ce que tu fais comme métier?*" asked the woman.

"*Je suis journaliste.*"

"*Et allez-vous écrire au sujet d'Haïti?*" asked the man.

"*Oui.*" I would write a few articles after I returned to the States, I told them. I had planned to send a story to a paper from here, but I didn't think I should.

"*Absoluement que non,*" said the woman, shocked at the very idea. "If the army found out a journalist was in the group, there could be big trouble for everybody." The army was paranoid, she said. Checkpoints like the one we had endured on our way to the village—the one that had seemed so comical when the soldier came out of the guard hut zipping his trousers and tucking in his shirt—the checkpoints and passport checks were dead serious, not at all like the lethargic exercises I had known on previous visits. The army was in control, not at all happy with Americans in general, and extremely skittish with Clinton about to take office.

We talked about the 1990 election. She disdained Bazin, the former World Bank man. "His campaign was like an American campaign. He made all these ads for TV. Beautiful ads. But who in Haiti owns a TV?" Aristide's campaign had been entirely different. But he should not have run. "He is a leader. He is not a president. You understand the difference?"

She explained to me the rules bourgeois Haitians follow about when to speak Creole and when to speak French. One spoke French with one's parents and one's spouse, she said. Her husband had courted her in French, and it would have seemed odd to revert to Creole after they married. One spoke Creole with servants and when gossiping. She could not imagine gossiping in French. "That's why I don't gossip with my mother!"

"But surely the French gossip in French," I offered. We all laughed.

We discussed the future of Haiti and of the world in general. I suggested that perhaps the idea of sovereign countries was dying. Perhaps Haiti and a few other countries were fated to be rescued by, or subjected to, a new kind of overt colonialism.

"*La Bosnie*," she agreed. "*La Somalie*."

*

One of my young friends told me he had escaped being killed three times. It didn't matter if you were political or not, he said. If you were educated, they didn't like you.

His brother told me his Guantanamo story. At two o'clock in the morning on April 11, 1992, he had left from a small island off the southern peninsula, in a wooden boat with a motor. He was at sea three days. At first it was fun, but then came the high wind and the rain. The boat left the Windward Passage near Cuba and began to take on water. A U.S. Coast Guard boat spotted them and pulled alongside. The Coast Guard took the Haitians into their boat, children first, then searched the area and found two more boats. Two days later they reached Guantanamo, where they were made to take showers, then given rice, meat, apples, apple juice, and sweets, and cots with clean sheets. After two days, he was moved from Camp 2 to Camp 5. He was given a card with his photograph and a number; this was for his interview. He was given an ID bracelet bearing the same number.

On April 22 he was taken to Camp 2B, where he was interviewed on April 24. "Why did you leave your country?" they asked him.

"Because of the political problems," he replied.

"What sort of political problems?"

"I was a supporter of Aristide."

"Where did you leave from?"

"A small island near Petit Trou de Nippes."

On April 25 he was moved to Camp 2A. One evening in church, he lost his ID card. He was taken to have another card made, then made to sit through another interview, in which he was asked the same questions and gave the same answers. After the second interview, he was moved back to Camp 2B. He was asked to provide addresses of friends in the United States. "Return to your tent," they said. "We are going to call your friends in the U.S." A French "policeman," a naturalized American, took him and several others to a camp for rejected applicants, to be returned to Haiti. In this camp he stayed two days. He was put in a boat and returned to Haiti, to Port-au-Prince. Because of the violence in the city, he returned immediately to his town. If someone said Aristide was coming back, the police got angry and the person had to hide. It was better to stay in the countryside. In the army, there were good men and bad men. The bad ones killed people, then drove them up the coast to a place called Ti Tanyin, where they dumped them by the truckful in mass graves. Everyone knew about this place.

"I would rather die in a boat than get shot," he said.

Was there any hope?

"If Aristide returns, there is hope."

And if not?

"*Si Aristid pa tounen*," he said, "*pa gen espwa*." If Aristide does not return, there is no hope.

✳

My father suggested some questions he thought I should ask the two brothers. Were many people still planning to get in boats on Wednesday, the day of Clinton's inauguration? If the two brothers went again, would they go alone, or would they take their families? Did they not know that Clinton had arranged the Coast Guard blockade with Bush?

Father Lafontant said something I still didn't understand: Aristide, he said, could not be both prophet and president. But now Haiti and the international community were stuck: he was the legitimately elected president.

Ed Morgan had been thinking about the embargo and felt he had discovered two important points. The United States defined Haitians as economic, not political, refugees, he said; yet it used an economic means that affected the poor—the embargo—as a political tool. Second, Haiti had always been poor. If Haitians were economic rather than political refugees, then why were so many suddenly fleeing now?

The group's work was no different than on previous trips. I spent my days with Susan Hatch, a plump, maternal nurse-practitioner from Denver, examining children and pregnant women, translating questions and instructions, telling mothers when and how to give our medicine to their children. On the day Bill Clinton became President of the United States, Susan Hatch and I examined a four-month-old male baby. He weighed two and a half kilograms. His tiny feet were grossly swollen, and his skin was translucent and unnaturally tight. His body was covered in scabies. He lay motionless on the table, sporadically emitting feeble cries.

Another nurse, Marti O'Dell, told me of the woman she had seen that day. The upper half of her right breast was completely eaten away by cancer—"blown away," Marti said. On the breast was a lesion at least four inches in diameter, its lip an inch thick, "rock solid," with rough edges. The woman had had a biopsy in a nearby town, but for lack of a hundred dollars could not afford a mastectomy.

At four in the afternoon on the twenty-first, I saw a three-year-old girl with kwashiorkor, her belly vastly swollen. Kwashiorkor happens when blood goes from the blood vessels where it belongs into the interstitial spaces in the abdominal cavity. This happens because of a lack of protein. It's common in Haiti.

The Haitian woman doctor saw a woman who almost certainly had HIV. She had tuberculosis, fever, and diarrhea, and her hair was beginning to straighten. The day before, the doctor had seen the woman's husband. Thirty-five percent of the population of Port-au-Prince now was infected with HIV, she told me. But the good news was that AIDS was much less prevalent in the countryside.

I asked: With so many people, especially men, fleeing violence in Port-au-Prince …

Yes, she said. They will spread HIV in the countryside.

She worried about the result if she herself were to be tested. She had delivered two babies without gloves.

"Why?" asked someone, incredulous.

"The woman was about to have it right on the front porch," said the doctor. "There was nothing I could do. I had to deliver it."

On our last night in Petit Trou we ate by lantern—the generator had been down since the night before—then sat in reflective postures in cane chairs and on the ground. The male doctor was dark and thin, mustached, less confident than the woman. He came from Jérémie at the remote tip of the southern peninsula, site of the infamous Vespers, when Papa Doc Duvalier had massacred the town's mulatto elite. The doctor's own family was black, not mulatto; he had done well in school and had finished second in his medical school class. His parents had been college-educated, but he knew little about his grandparents, or at least he volunteered little. He believed one of his great-great-grandfathers might have been white.

I told him I was sad and didn't want to leave.

"Separation syndrome?" he said, and smiled.

"The little boy who was having the seizures," Marti asked him. "The parents took him away because they said it was spirits. What will happen to him?"

"They will take him to a *houngan*"—a voodoo priest—"and of course he will die. If he doesn't get better in a day or two, they will say there is nothing they can do."

"So basically, they will let him die."

"Yes, of course," he said, tired, a little irritable. "He will die."

I had grown fond of the two brothers. "Marti says that you are indispensable," I told the older one.

"Yes, yes," he agreed. "I am indispensable." He paused. "I spend many days now with you," he said. "And Ted, and Marti. When you go, I will feel—a gweat sadness."

"I too will feel a great sadness."

There was another pause.

"But we can write letters to each other," I said.

"If I don't go to Santo Domingo, we can wite."

"If you go to Santo Domingo, tell Father Lafontant your address."

He shook his head vigorously. "I can't tell Father Lafontant if I go to Santo Domingo." He and his brother were only provisionally in the priest's favor, because they were politically active, supporters of Aristide. The younger brother had worked for an *atelier* in Port-au-Prince and now was trying to sell coffins that he made himself. He showed me two he had made, stacked on his front porch. His asking price for one was $150; he hadn't yet sold any. Regardless of whether business improved, he planned to go to Cuba again in two weeks.

Just before Mass that last evening, miniature farewells anticipated our departure the next morning. "When you think you will come back here, to Haiti?" asked the older brother.

"I don't know. Maybe next year," I said, implausibly.

"In ninety—ninety-four."

"Maybe."

I imagined the prospect with pleasure, but with a greater sadness that acknowledged the unlikelihood. A year from now I would be in Thailand, and he planned to be in Santo Domingo.

"Ethan."

"*Oui.*"

"When you wite the informations, please don't wite the name of me, and my bwudder. You understand? Because the Haitian police is very week-ed. Yes?"

"Yes. Of course." But I felt sad: I wanted to name my new friends. Three children were holding my hands. One of them was the brothers' adorable youngest nephew and my father's godson.

"*Mwen renmen ti moun yo ampil,*" I said.

"And they love you too," said the older brother. "Jesus say, 'Let the little kids to come to me.'"

*

The Land Rover broke down several times on the tortuous first leg of the long drive back to Port-au-Prince. The problem was dirt in the gas lines; the only way to repair it was to blow through a hose and hope for the best. Hours later in Carrefour we saw a car burning in the middle of the street, ignored by the many bystanders and by the policeman in khaki and dark glasses lounging in front of the station, his rifle between his legs in an insolent pose. It was Sunday but, even so, the emptiness of the downtown streets was eerie. Some members of our group had been here in January 1991, just before Aristide's inauguration. Now, as we rode past the picked-over carcass of a Volkswagen, they spoke quietly of the pervasive euphoria of that time and of *pere lebrun* or necklacing. In my mind there were two Haitis: the remote, peaceful, rural place I knew, and the violent and desperate slum portrayed in newspapers and shown on TV. Now the two were overlapping and merging in disturbing ways.

VIVE TITIDE said a graffito we drove past. Long live Aristide. Along Boulevard Harry Truman I looked out the window and thought: Of the few people I see on this street, one in three has the AIDS virus.

We had heard on the radio the day before that Jesse Jackson was in Port-au-Prince, and that there had been a small, apparently unsuccessful uprising in the military. Now, back at Wall House, we learned that a general strike was planned for tomorrow. You could tell how serious a general strike was by whether the tap-taps, playfully painted passenger pick-up trucks, were running. On the balcony we sipped Prestige beer and watched a large cloud of black smoke rise from somewhere very near the airport, at the base of the hills. Something seemed about to happen. But it was impossible to tell truth from rumor unless you were out in the streets, seeing it for yourself, and not really even then. Word of mouth was the only news we had. The issue of *Newsweek* on the coffee table was from the previous November.

The Walls had lived several stints in Haiti over more than two decades, and Mrs. Wall spoke to me for a long time that evening. The embargo had created thirty-two millionaires, she said. The other Caribbean islands were treating it very loosely indeed, and an African country was selling cheap oil to the junta. The only sanctions that would work would be if the regime's U.S. bank accounts were frozen and effective measures were taken to keep oil from getting in. Prices kept rising, and it went without saying that there were no tourists.

"The people who have money get their things in," said Mrs. Wall. "And the poor have no food, and no money to buy it with." In November when Clinton had won, there had been much excitement and building of boats. The boats were a profiteer's dream: a few people got rich building them and collecting fares. "People can change in a minute here," she said. "They can be a saint one minute, then the Devil the next. They'll do whatever is for their benefit—or their safety." Just down the street, police had found a man holding a photograph of Aristide and had killed him. The police were known to burglarize houses. In the aftermath of the coup the violence had been terrible. "You couldn't mention the name Aristide. If you mentioned Aristide, you got killed. But seven months earlier, if you didn't mention Aristide, you got killed. The people who don't talk, they're the ones who are doing good for the poor, but don't have the guts to let on." In December 1991, Aristide had announced from exile that he would be returning in three weeks. "Lo and behold, so many people were killed here just after that. He really should have been smart enough to know he shouldn't say things like that." Violence then had been arbitrary. Her own husband, a white foreigner, had been stopped by police and threatened with being sent to the notorious prison Fort Dimanche.

"And another thing is voodoo! They put hexes on each other and everything." She told me of a man in the countryside who didn't like his daughter's boyfriend, so he had made her stand out in a field. "Just like you read about in the Bible, you know? But they will never put a hex on a real believing Christian. Not even the voodoo doctors will put a hex on a Christian." There had been a real, live Tonton Macoute—Duvalierist vigilante—right next door. He seemed like a decent and devout man, held prayer meetings and everything. "Knew his Bible inside and out." And he had turned out to be a Macoute. She told me of the night when Baby Doc had fallen, in February 1986. A mob had attacked Papa Doc's "eternal flame" outside the parliament building, dousing it with bare hands and spit. Many had believed and hoped that the reign of terror had ended that day.

Mrs. Wall said good night—"Goodness, I really should be careful what I tell you!"—and suddenly I felt very tired.

The next day we drove around the city and did some shopping. Graffiti were everywhere. PE LEBRUN SE SEL REMED MAKOUT, read one. *Père lebrun,* necklacing with burning tires, is the only remedy for Macoutes. VIV TITID, read another. NOU SE LAVALAS. We are *lavalas,* the flood. Waiting at one shop, I asked our driver his thoughts.

"I am not a specialist in politics," he answered with a laugh, arms folded, leaning against the van, eyes darting.

The flag at the U.S. embassy was at half mast. Whenever I went to the Haitian countryside, invariably something newsworthy happened in the outside world. One year I got all the way back to Miami before learning that John Belushi had died. Another time it was at the Hotel Montana above Port-au-Prince that I heard about the fall of Margaret Thatcher. This time I scribbled in my notebook: "Clinton shot? Reagan dead? Nixon dead?" Like the cloud of smoke rising from near the airport, the flag at half mast seemed an untoward omen, and I felt disconcerted by my ignorance. But things were not as they seemed. The smoke came from a post-harvest burning of fields. The lowered flag was for the death of Thurgood Marshall.

While others looked at paintings at an art gallery, my father and Marti O'Dell and I walked to St. Vincent's School for the Handicapped. In recent years, the legendary Sister Joan Margaret had made many trips to Florida for medical treatment, and she had abandoned her walker for a wheelchair. She was not expecting us, but when we arrived she happened to be in.

"Sister, I'm Father Dayle Casey," said my father. "This is my son Ethan. Ethan stayed here at St. Vincent's for some time in 1983."

"Yes," said Sister Joan and bestowed a smile on us both. "Yes. It's good to see you, Father."

"And this is Marti O'Dell. Marti is a nurse."

"Hello, Sister," said Marti.

"Hello."

Sister Joan told us that after forty-nine years at St. Vincent's, she would return this year to her order's headquarters in Massachusetts. If we had come just a few months later, we would not have found her there. She wasn't retiring, mind you. She was moving on to new things, new work. She was turning the running of St. Vincent's over to a middle-aged priest. She laughed and smiled a smile of deep satisfaction.

"When you get to be eighty-eight," she said and chuckled, "I think it's time for someone younger to take over."

✳

That night was our last night in Haiti. I met a young man that evening, a technician gracious and articulate in the way of so many bourgeois Haitians, eager to talk politics. Aristide genuinely wanted the good of the poor, he told me, but until his ouster he had been naïve as well as arrogant and unduly provocative. "*Depuis le coup, je pense qu'il assiste a l'école politique*," he said. Since the coup, I think he's attending political school. He was proud to be Haitian and would not consider leaving. "I have a good life here." But sometimes, he said, he felt ashamed of his country. If he were Clinton, he too would set up a blockade against boat people.

"If I were a starving peasant," I responded, "I too would flee to Miami in a boat."

"Yes," he agreed. "I would too."

I felt a fondness for this serious, poised young man. "We can't expect others to solve our problems," he said. "It is up to Haitians to solve Haiti's problems."

✳

To my father that evening I said: "I don't want to leave."

"Well," he said, "it's time to move on to the next thing."

CHAPTER 3

A GHASTLY FEELING OF IMPOTENCE

The next thing for me was Southeast Asia. My friend had warned that I would have to face Detroit again, but at this moment I wanted only to be as far away as possible. Just as years earlier I had fled Madison for Kathmandu, so now, to put distance between myself and Detroit, I felt it necessary to go to Bangkok. But it wasn't only Detroit I was running from; it was the entire United States of America and everything it represented to me.

I was still too inexperienced to understand or even fully identify my own urges, and what I also failed to understand was that there's nowhere to run away to. And anyway, on this planet at least, you can't get away from America. But in fleeing America I was encountering Asia, and from Asia it turned out there was a lot for me to learn.

One thing I learned in Asia was the need for humility and patience when faced with complexity and ambiguity, whether factual, moral, or both. Asia taught me that to understand the world is a more urgent priority than to judge or change it, and that an action or stance can be at once morally wrong and politically right, or vice versa. And, reporting from Asia for newspapers with limited space and attention spans and with priorities and perspectives different from my own, I both learned the discipline and felt the frustration of explaining something irreducibly complex—Thai politics, say, or the situation in Cambodia—to uninformed readers far away, in eight hundred words or less.

And I never really left Haiti. It was with the eyes of one who had seen Haiti that I saw chronically desperate Cambodia, and tortured Burma, and deforested Thailand. In my bones I knew that these places were not behind the times, but ahead of the curve. The appalling immediacy of life and death, the perpetual urgency of politics in Haiti had changed me; having set foot there meant that to remain innocent would have required greater exertion than to acknowledge the world's seamlessness and the implications of my own involvement.

✳

It was the last historical moment before the Internet kicked in and media became truly global and intrusively ubiquitous, and working at the *Bangkok Post* newspaper I had the benefit of access to the wire services' full feeds. But, in fact, resorting to this soon became unnecessary. Events in Haiti were accelerating, to the point that soon the *Bangkok Post* was running stories on its crisis weekly and then daily on its world news page and, eventually, on the front page.

Closer to home Aung San Suu Kyi, daughter of Burmese independence hero General Aung San and standard-bearer of the movement for democracy that had erupted in Burma in 1988, was approaching the end of her fourth year under house arrest. Like Aristide, Suu Kyi had been alert and brave enough to ride an extraordinary historical moment and to articulate and channel into a popular movement the frustrations, resentments, and hopes of the large majority of her country's people. Suu Kyi and her movement, like Aristide's *lavalas*, attacked the Achilles' heel of entrenched brute power: its conscience.

Burma was an instructive topic to follow with a view to gauging just how free the press was in ostensibly democratic Thailand. The Outlook section of the *Post* had a stable of haughty young women reporters who specialized in long, self-righteous articles about environmental destruction, women's issues, and human rights. These would decry one or another outrage to do with Burma from time to time. One of the editors of the *Sunday Post* was half Burmese, and he saw to it that there were always plenty of articles and editorials in the Perspective section. And leader editorials, some of which I wrote, could bash the Burmese junta, known by the acronym SLORC, and even Thai government policy toward Burma with few holds barred. In news coverage, on the other hand, any awareness that people were routinely being murdered and enslaved next door was smothered beneath layers of euphemism, elision, and deference. Too, of course, the *Bangkok Post* was published in English.

The attitude of the Thai government, hence of the Association of Southeast Asian Nations or ASEAN, was articulated by foreign minister Prasong Soonsiri at a press conference I attended in September 1993. Citing "many complex issues [that] remain" in Burma, Prasong excused the SLORC for emphasizing "stability and security" and suggested that "democracy will perhaps follow." He insisted that outsiders should not interfere with "the means by which a government solves its own domestic problems" and claimed Japanese foreign minister Tsutomo Hata, on a recent visit, had "expressed agreement with Thailand's policy of constructive engagement and believed it was constructive."

"Constructive engagement" was the preferred official response to the regime in Burma. Activists pressed for a trade embargo. U Khin Nyo, editor of the U.S.-based newsletter *Burma Review*, had told me that the U.S. government "not only does not impose economic sanctions" on Burma, "but it does not discourage companies from investing." The U.S., he said, would not be hurt economically by leading a strict embargo against Burma. The U.S. should start an embargo with other Western countries, then "pressure ASEAN and China. If the U.S. pressures China, it will drop Burma like a hot potato. Economic sanctions are not like a battle. You have to be patient. If the U.S. had started sanctions in 1990, the regime would be doing different things now."

I asked Khin Nyo if he saw parallels with Haiti.

"The Haitian government is negotiating with the U.S.," he said. "How can you say the embargo is not effective? The Nobel laureates visited Thailand. If their visit was not effective, why is the SLORC angry with them? If the Haitian government transfers power, they will be killed. But Aristide offers them amnesty, so now they are ready to negotiate with him. The SLORC will negotiate or surrender only if that is their only option. Aung San Suu Kyi was arrested because she attacked Ne Win, for the first time in thirty years. They asked her if she would amnesty them. She said the people will judge whether they should go to trial. Then she was arrested."

Aristide's power, such as it was, seemed analogous to Suu Kyi's: it was moral power, or rather moral authority. This kind of power didn't compute in the calculations of military rulers. Or rather they did understand it, and it terrified them. Terror was what such regimes inflicted on the people they ruled, but the rulers too were terrorized; they knew they were guilty and that those who resisted them were justified. This was why such rulers were called "paranoid" and "cowardly," why the Cedras junta would not yield to Aristide, why the SLORC would not release Suu Kyi. But as long as Suu Kyi remained under house arrest and Aristide remained in uncompromising exile, the people Aristide called "evildoers" felt rebuked. "The evildoers run and hide, they hide in the shadows," Aristide had written in *In the Parish of the Poor*,

> hoping darkness will protect them and allow them to continue committing their crimes, their massacres, to continue to enforce their repression. ... Beware the person who feels angry upon hearing the words of truth. Hiding the truth is like trying to bury water. It seeps out everywhere.

✳

To read about Haiti in assembly-line news reports was disorienting and demoralizing. The country I was reading about was a cartoon of the country I knew. The language in which the stories were written resembled English but consisted of ready-made phrases—*restoring democracy*; *the Americas' poorest nation*—and low-rent metaphoric imagery: the Security Council was going to "clamp" an embargo on Haiti; unhappy Haitian legislators wanted aid to start "flowing" again. All this from writers and editors who would swear that what they were giving us was just the facts, ma'am. All language is mediation, all communication is alchemy: I experience something directly, I put it into words, I transmit the words to you in the blind faith that you will understand them to carry the same meaning, or even merely to represent the same facts. Because we crave sharing meanings in common, we tacitly find a lowest common denominator and communicate in fictions, conventions, and abstractions, in a shared evasion of responsibility. The medium through which knowledge and understanding can jump the gap between us is a blend of moral qualities: honesty, empathy, respect. You have to trust that I know what I'm talking about, and that I mean what I say. This is what makes real reporting not a commercial or even professional undertaking, but a vocation. But prefab industrial journalism, the dialect of the powers that be, was now my main source of current information on Haiti. None of it meant much to me. But the equally political language of dissidence left me cold too. "In politics," warns C.L.R. James in *The Black Jacobins*, his great history of the Haitian Revolution, "all abstract terms conceal treachery."

"I guess all you can really do is be a witness," a friend at the *Bangkok Post* said to me around this time. This is what Edith Mirante, an American who had spent years in the 1980s sneaking into obscure areas of Burma, had done in *Burmese Looking Glass*. What struck me about her book was its very personal tone. Mirante wasn't writing polemic or preaching; she was telling her own story and trying to understand. Later she became an activist, but that's a different story. First things first. And she knew that simple explanations don't suffice. "The longer I spent around the Burma war zone," she wrote,

> the more interested I became in World War II's China-Burma-India theater of operations. "The war in Burma *is* World War II," I often told people who required a simple explanation of what it was all about. "The Karens and other tribes backed the British and Americans against the Japanese invaders. The Burmese had helped the Japanese, thinking it would be a good way to get rid of the British colonists. The war supposedly ended. The Japanese left, the Americans left, even the British left – but the Burmese and the ethnic minorities kept right on fighting." Burma had always had ethnic rivalries, but outright warfare had stopped until World War II brought it all boiling to the surface again.

With the discipline of a genuine writer who knows what is and what is not a part of the task at hand, Mirante did not even mention Suu Kyi until page 327. She was narrating not Burma's recent history per se, or the case against the SLORC, or even the complexities of the unending multi-ethnic civil war, but her own deepening involvement with and painful, obsessive love for a country where she had lived some important episodes in her own life, and for the people she had known there. As the reader from one page to the next became vicariously more involved, the author's personal story and the story of Burma became inexorably enmeshed. I reached the end winded, but wishing for more.

Around this time, mid-1993, the Governors Island agreement was supposedly being attempted, with U.S. and UN negotiators trying to strong-arm Aristide into granting amnesty to the junta, in exchange for his planned return in October. The agreement was agreed to, sort of, by all parties, then reneged on by the junta. Then came the humiliation of the USS *Harlan County*, which approached Haiti on October 11 but turned around within sight of Port-au-Prince the next day, because of a small number of armed protesters at the port.

In journalistic terms, the aborted invasion was an occasion for me to write about Haiti. But I wasn't ready; I preferred to avert my eyes; I was on the other side of the planet. And I flinched.

And other writers gave me little comfort or cover. Haiti was an ideo-logical Rorschach test, in which each writer saw only what he or she wanted to see. In his book *Year 501*, Noam Chomsky quoted anthro-pologist Ira Lowenthal: "Haiti was more than the New World's second oldest republic, more than even the first black republic of the modern world. Haiti was the first *free* nation of *free* men to arise within, and in resistance to, the emerging constellation of Western European em-pire." In an article in *The Atlantic Monthly* titled "Voodoo Politics," on the other hand, former USAID official Lawrence E. Harrison rejected Latin American "dependency theory," which "argues that the advanced countries got rich by exploiting the poor countries." Harrison asked: "If Haiti is not a victim of imperialism, how can its tragic history be ex-plained?" His answer was that it was cultural: "The imprint of African culture, particularly Vodun, and slavery on Haiti, sustained by long years of isolation from progressive ideas, open political systems, and economic dynamism, is, I believe, the only possible explanation for the continuing Haitian tragedy." As Upton Sinclair said, it's difficult to get a man to understand something when his salary depends on his not understanding it.

I didn't want to be a political writer. What I wanted to say was only that I loved Haiti. But I couldn't write about the country without addressing its situation. I struggled to find expression for what I was feeling as well as for what I now believed: that the United States government was deliberately, if only semi-consciously, draining the marrow from Aristide's ability to deliver on his promise of genuine societal change in Haiti. It would not return him to office unless it first stripped him of any real power. That was the purpose of his exile. In my article published in the *Bangkok Post* of October 17, 1993, I quoted what Aristide had said about Haiti's election of 1987:

> Haiti had to prove it was "moving toward democracy." Only if we elected a government would the cold country to our north, and its allies—other former colonizers—send us more money and food. Of course, that money and that food corrupt our society: the money helps to maintain an armed force against the people; the food helps to ruin our national economy; and both money and food keep Haiti in a situation of dependence on the former colonizers.

"These are words to ponder," I ventured, "when we read pernicious bromides about 'abuses on both sides' and 'restoring democracy.' Aristide has been arrogant, naïve and incendiary; but he is Haiti's freely elected president (the only such in the country's long history) and should not have been squandered." I wanted also to convey just why it was that I loved Haiti. I recalled the passage in Graham Greene's novel *The Quiet American* in which Pyle goes to Fowler, the English narrator, for "background" on Vietnam. Through Fowler, Greene comments movingly that Pyle "would have to learn for himself the real background that held you as a smell does," then recites an eloquent litany. The best I could do was to recite a litany of my love for Haiti. I listed the spontaneously friendly peasants and their utterly charming children; the intense restfulness of evenings in the countryside; the ubiquitous morning roosters, and the haunting late-night voodoo drums; cockfights; the mountains that rise almost directly from the sea; the sight of La Gonâve island in the distance from the coast of the southern peninsula; the freighter beached at Jacmel. "I love that when my father and I go to Haiti together he is happy," I wrote. I remembered an excruciating passage in *The Black Jacobins*:

Thousands of small, scrupulously tidy coffee-trees rose on the slopes of the hills, and the abrupt and precipitous mountain-sides were covered to the summits with the luxuriant tropical undergrowth and precious hardwood forests of San Domingo. The traveller from Europe was enchanted at his first glimpse of this paradise, in which the ordered beauty of agriculture and the prodigality of Nature competed equally for his surprise and admiration.

"How very long ago that was," I wrote. "Haiti's virgin mahogany forests are long gone (whole sides of mountains can be seen where they have fallen in giant heaps), and there certainly remains no 'ordered beauty' anywhere. And for the people, there may no longer be any hope."

✳

"You have many books, sir," said the slender young man behind the money-exchange window at the airport in Kathmandu. I had brought four books with me on the plane. As I reached for my wallet, I set them on the counter.

"Yes. I have many books."

His smile widened and he did the South Asian head-wobble. "You are a *wo*-racious reader."

It was good to be back.

In 1990, the year that began in the wake of the European upheavals and ended with Aristide's election in Haiti, Nepal had had its own revolution, overthrowing the absolute monarchy and ushering in a tinpot semblance of democracy. The official opposition in Nepal's new multiparty parliament was the Communist Party of Nepal (United Marxist and Leninist). In 1994, having left my desk job at the *Bangkok Post*, I wanted to see for myself how things had changed.

Kathmandu was not quite the place I remembered, and yet every familiar feature gave me a kind of happiness. The city still had its distinctive smell: equal parts dust, rotting garbage, incense, and apple pie. In the morning you still heard roosters and saw dogs and cows foraging daintily in the garbage heaps. There still were bicycle bells, handsome Tibetan women with smiling eyes and striped aprons, monks in burgundy robes, cheeky children ("Hello! One rupee!"), gentle police officers stylishly directing traffic at roundabouts, young men strolling hand in hand.

With democracy had come a flood of goods from India and a relaxation of restrictions on importing automobiles. There now were traffic jams, and privately owned storefronts where you could call or fax overseas, and motorists and pedestrians wore the ghostly white face masks I had grown accustomed to seeing in Bangkok. The Pepsi logo had become ubiquitous. On Mondays you could tour the Royal Palace. A casino had opened. In Thamel, the tourist quarter, one now saw as many Kashmiris as Tibetans. And electricity was routinely rationed, according to a varying regime: sometimes there was electricity in the morning and evening, sometimes there was a blackout every other day. Nepal sold sixty percent of its hydroelectric power to its huge neighbor. The Hotel Buddha kept candles on hand; the Potala Guest House had its own generator.

I asked a young man named Rana about the trade embargo India had imposed on Nepal in 1989.

"Nepal send water India," he explained. "'I don't give water,' say Nepal. Also India say, 'I don't send everything.' That time India not send kerosene petrol to Nepal. That time peoples angry. India say, 'You make gummint democracy-tic, I send kerosene petrol.' Not have Nepal more money. People all angry, right? Everything no has, Nepal. Everything send outside. Everything buying Nepal. Everything increase. Sell electricity to India, but no for Nepal. Money is put in the pocket and not make, not develop."

The Nepali Congress party had 113 seats in the new parliament; the CPN (UML) had 69. "Congress party give the jobs. Gummint have police army. Communist Party no have police army. Only people. Public has only i-stone and i-stick. Gummint have gun and also police army. Public died twenty people."

I asked which party he supported.

"I don't like party. Because any party same. Communist Party make gummint also same, I think."

Rana introduced me to a travel agent nicknamed Om, a husky, enterprising man in his early thirties with a stylish mustache.

"No matter who comes in power in India, they won't change their foreign policy," Om said. "India is enemies with Pakistan, they're enemies with Bangladesh, they're enemies with Nepal, they're enemies with Sri Lanka."

There had been riots in Kathmandu the previous June and July. A new dam was being built in western Nepal, on which Nepal and India had drafted an agreement. But the agreement favored India; hence the riots. "The rich people are, well, they're rich," he said. "The Communists will look after the poor. The people who are not doing so all right are the middle class."

"Like yourself, for instance," I suggested.

He laughed. "Yes, that's right."

A university lecturer named K.B. Maharjan had launched a new mimeographed periodical called *The Trend*. He was not a member of any party, he stressed. "I don't go chasing after power. *So* many Panchayat [royalist] people joined the Nepali Congress after 1990. Some joined the Communists, but many more joined the Nepali Congress. My Congress friends all think I am Communist, my Communist friends all think I am Congress." He spread his hands and smiled. "What to do?"

Nepal's post-revolutionary democracy faced its first serious test during my stay, with the "troika" of Nepali Congress leaders feuding among themselves and Prime Minister Girija Prasad Koirala surviving a no-confidence vote brought by the Communists. I met CPN (UML) chairman Man Mohan Adhikari in the front room of his modest house, with kitschy tourist posters from London and Paris on the walls. Adhikari was a grizzled, affable man of seventy-four with bad teeth, an ill-trimmed grey beard, and a topi. He had spent fifteen years in prison in Nepal and India. A young relative served us tea.

Did Adhikari regret that the no-confidence vote had failed?

He did not. The motion had been pro forma; the situation had demanded it. "I wish that this parliament should live its full term," he said. "Because of this political crisis, investors are getting scared. I don't see any party that has more support in the international field than the Congress. Nepal's stability depends on their stability. Even if we are left, we have to accept the realities of the modern world. It was easy for us to bring democracy, but it has become harder and harder to consolidate it. Now, the ball is in the Congress court."

He noted the difficulty of holding new elections. They could not be held during the summer; that was the rainy season and the time of the budget session. "Even if there are mid-terms, they could only be held after one year. From our side they won't have any problem. We will shout in the parliament, we will shout in the streets. If they fall because of their internal difficulties, that will set a bad precedent."

Would the Communists be prepared to form a new government?

It would depend on the King and on Nepal's international friends. "We were in the interim government. We were in the height of the movement. We have accepted the monarchy. We have accepted pluralism. Unless we can prove that we are the legal government, we don't have the right." A full term for the Koirala government—the first elected since the revolution—would be best for all concerned. Ordinary people wanted simple, ordinary things, Adhikari told me: "simple education for their children, simple two square meals. I am very proud of them. But because of the squabble in the parliament, because of the struggle with the leaders, they have become apathetic. Our country had always been autocratic country. Democracy for them means real freedom. They gave such tremendous sacrifices." Democracy in practical terms should mean that "support and aid"—from the West and from international agencies such as the World Bank, of which Nepal was one of the world's largest per capita recipients—"can be utilized properly under a democratic system."

I asked how relations between the parties had reached such a pass.

"The prime minister is a very hard-headed man. He is a very hard-line anti-Communist. Our relations are not cordial, not warm. But even then both parties should play the game according to the rules of the game. Sometimes you have to carry your bitterness in your heart. I do not think that power will fall in my lap. I have to win it. How? Through the democratic process. Rome was not built in one day. It was easy for us to bring democracy, but it has become harder and harder to consolidate it."

As I was leaving, I remarked that ordinary people in my country were fed up with politicians. Adhikari chuckled and told me a story. Once, in the United States, he had ridden a train. "There was a lady, quite elderly lady, who was very kind to me. And then she saw my lapel—I was with the UN delegation. She asked if I was in politics. When I said yes, she was aghast! I explained that we struggled for democracy in Nepal. She understood, but she was aghast about politics in the U.S. Only about forty percent of people vote!"

✳

On March 20, 1994, I flew from Kathmandu to Delhi. On the plane I was given a complimentary copy of *The Rising Nepal*. At the bottom of the briefs column on page 5 were two short paragraphs from the official news agency of the People's Republic of China:

Haiti violence Intensifies

Mexico City (Xinhua):

Violence has intensified in the Haitian capital of Port-Au-Prince and its surrounding areas since January 31.

This was revealed by the Organization of American Sates [sic]-United Nations (OAS-UNO) civilian mission in its report published here Friday.

Throughout four months traveling around the subcontinent, I followed the long-looming U.S. invasion of Haiti in the *International Herald Tribune*, *USA Today*, and the Indian papers and magazines. Each Haiti headline gave me a sinking feeling, what George Orwell called a ghastly feeling of impotence, that quickly became familiar. It remained within my power only to read and think about Haiti, and to write about it. Inexorably it dawned on me that Haiti was becoming a daily news story worldwide. The impotent feeling was especially ghastly when I saw front-page headlines in *USA Today* and thought: I have to pay fifty rupees for this rag. By the time I returned to Kathmandu in late June the papers were having a near-daily Haiti-fest of stories, photos, and commentary, cresting with a spasm of front-page coverage in the second week of July, when an invasion seemed imminent.

An issue of the *New York Times* that I happened to see in India included an op-ed by Thomas Carothers, senior associate at the Carnegie Endowment for International Peace:

> The political problem in Haiti is not simply that the military refuses to allow [Aristide] to return. It is that Haitian society is profoundly polarized between an entrenched business and military elite, some of whom are violently anti-democratic and some of whom are not, and the great mass of ordinary Haitians, who deeply hate the elite and in 1990 chose a leader who promised a fundamental redistribution of power.

This was inarguable, but Carothers went from there to suggesting that the Clinton administration must "consider alternatives that don't depend on the immediate return of President Aristide. The paradox of Haiti policy is that the longer we hold out for the best of all possible worlds, the more likely we are to end up with the worst." And he asked: "Do we want to send a signal to Russia ... that it is acceptable for dominant regional powers to use force to solve their neighbors' internal political problems?"

I was out of touch with the American mood, but I sensed that the place name "Haiti," like "Vietnam" before it, was taking on new shades of meaning, and that it had become a stick with which new lines were being drawn, and old ones redrawn, among Americans. I read that Randall Robinson, executive director of the TransAfrica Forum, was courting death on a hunger strike against the policy of forcibly repatriating Haitian refugees, and that six members of the U.S. Congress had held a sit-in in front of the White House. Jesse Jackson had urged Clinton to support Aristide and to oppose "fascist forces in Haiti" just as he "reinforced" Boris Yeltsin in Russia.

On June 30, back in Kathmandu, the *Herald Tribune*'s front page featured a photo of rubber-gloved U.S. Coast Guard workers rescuing a Haitian baby "while aiding another boatload of Haitian refugees." The page 3 story from the *Washington Post* was about the administration's decision to reopen the U.S. base at Guantanamo Bay in Cuba because of an increase in boat people: 1,486 Haitians intercepted at sea on Monday and more than 700 over the weekend. "This is the surge that we had to worry about, the influx that swamps the system," said a Clinton official. Aristide had refused administration requests that he urge Haitians to stay home. And a new poll showed that "support for the idea" of an invasion "may be growing," although "a large majority of Americans question whether U.S. vital interests are at stake in the island nation." The previous four days, according to AP, had been "the busiest period in Coast Guard history."

An invasion seemed days away at most. Whatever its intentions, surely no competent White House would let matters reach such a crescendo without acting. Being able to follow Haiti's tragedy only at several removes was excruciating, but I told myself I didn't want to be one more piranha in a hot-news feeding frenzy. And it was comforting to be away from it all; Nepal for me was what Nottingham had been for Greene: "a focal point of failure, a place undisturbed by ambition, a place to be resigned to, a home from home."

But suddenly this was so no longer. One morning, I caught sight of the *Kathmandu Post* headline: "Koirala resigns as PM, proposes mid-term polls." With the annual budget session imminent, the "Group of 36" dissident members of parliament from the ruling Nepali Congress party had abstained from a vote, engineering a defeat for the prime minister by 86 votes to 74.

It was Nepal's first constitutional crisis since the 1990 revolution, and no one knew where it might lead. K.B. Maharjan was at once apprehensive and exhilarated. "Whatever happens, it will happen for the first time in Nepal," he told me. "This is a true example of experimentation with democracy!"

Might the palace re-assert power, maybe even throw out the constitution?

"If the King was very assertive, you can be sure that something like that would happen. But he is not that smart, and he is not assertive. He is a happy-go-lucky type." On the other hand, there were "lots of palace supporters who would like to repeat the history. It is the embassies that the palace is afraid of."

What about India?

"India is not very interested in our democracy. It is interested in its business."

The King accepted Koirala's resignation, dissolved the House of Representatives, and scheduled mid-term elections for November 13. The move's constitutionality was highly disputable, but this was the first opportunity to test certain clauses of the new constitution. No one was sure how much power the palace retained. The date set for the mid-terms was awkward: too close to winter and to the Hindu festivals Dasain and Tihar.

"People in Nepal, they think the festivals are more important than the elections," said Om, the trekking agent, shaking his head. "People thought we would have something new. And now we have the democracy and nothing is new. It is a new system, but the same methods."

I went again to see Adhikari. The two international factors that chronically affect Nepal were in play now, he said. "What India wants is to restore power to the King."

The King could then be prevailed on to dissolve the clause in the bilateral trade and transit agreement that limited India's access to Nepal's natural resources. The Western powers, for their part, had been convinced that the King was ineffective and should be limited to a constitutional role. Now they might have changed their minds, and might agitate for him to be granted emergency powers. "The King dissolved parliament on the advice of an unpopular and discredited prime minister with one purpose: to discredit both Koirala and the parliamentary process," said Adhikari. His disgust and disappointment were palpable. Given the chance, he would have tried to form a caretaker government in cooperation with the "Group of 36" Congress dissidents, then called elections. Denied that chance, the Communists now opted to lead street protests and strikes. The party had to protect its own interests. "Everybody has a compulsion," he said. "We also are trying to survive."

Making ready to leave, I told Adhikari that I hoped he would consider me something more and other than a journalist. "I was here as a student seven years ago," I explained. "I speak Nepali rather well. I'm not just a news reporter."

He brightened. "You are a friend of Nepal!"

"That's right."

"Whenever I meet foreign friends of Nepal," he said happily, "I always find them very friendly. They all say (except the Indians, of course) that they want to see political stability in Nepal, so the country can develop."

K.B. Maharjan arranged for me to interview Ganesh Man Singh, the 79-year-old "supremo" of the Nepali Congress, who was ill in the hospital. "I too am excited that you will interview Ganesh Man-ji," K.B. said to me, over his shoulder as we rode on his motorbike. "I was not certain he would agree to an interview. He is a *very* important man. He is Gandhi of Nepal!"

In a small, bare room at Bir Hospital, I pressed my hands together in the traditional *namaste* greeting and bowed. Prone and immobilized, a metal contraption riveted to his head, Ganesh Man Singh smiled in reply. I was made to sit on a stool beside his bed; I had to lean near and strain to catch his words. His frailty limited my time. After a few tries, I gave up asking questions and simply took down his words.

"The fledgling democracy is in great danger," he whispered. "I cannot say that the democracy can be saved. The moment democracy finishes, nationalism also finishes. We have not lost our courage. Ones who are in favor of democracy all are fighting hard. As the fishes cannot be without water, so we cannot be without democracy. This time not only democracy is in danger, nationalism is in danger."

Adhikari had visited him three days earlier. The Congress supremo had urged the Communist leader to reach an understanding with the Congress dissidents. I asked what they had talked about.

"You have already decided to launch the movement," Singh told me he had told Adhikari. "Therefore you must try your utmost to involve all the forces of democracy."

"They are trying their utmost to save democracy," he said. "How far they will be successful is another question. If the democrats boycott the mid-term poll, the people also will be with the democrats. Now, *seemingly*, it is only the leftists boycotting. Democratic Nepalis are waiting, what the democratic leaders will decide. As compared to the coming movement, the 1990 movement is very small. The shadow of the coming events is already cast. They have already launch-ed processions, launch-ed public meetings. These are all the signs of the coming events."

Nepal always had struck me as a surpassingly gentle society, its politics so stable as to seem nonexistent. I knew it had an army—in 1986, as a student, I had sprained my ankle playing basketball with soldiers—but it had never occurred to me to wonder what purposes it served. Nepal was where you went to get away from it all, like Bob Seger. But times had changed; there was no getting away from it all anymore. Now, soldiers exercised in ranks every morning in the Tundikhel, the giant park in the center of Kathmandu. They did push-ups and ran in place; they were taller and bigger than other Nepalis.

"That is an expression by the King that 'I am still there,'" Adhikari told me.

The Communists had hired three-wheeled taxis to drive around flying the red hammer-and-sickle flag and blaring anti-Koirala slogans through loudspeakers. Thousands were gathering to hear speakers in the park. Today, on my way to the hospital, I had stepped aside on a winding back street to let pass two dozen soldiers. They wore blue uniforms and helmets and wooden batons on their belts and were marching as casually as a group of soldiers in formation can march, seemingly headed nowhere in particular, being what's known as a uniformed presence.

"Still, our police force and army are very much loyal to the King," said K.B. Maharjan. "This is very important."

I asked Ganesh Man Singh how the military might figure in the coming events.

"What gummint can do without making the police walk?" he replied. "It affects the people how much? That is the question. The police and army will make the people scared. If the gummint is successful, they will keep the people scared. But I don't think we will be scared."

The world is of a piece, I came to realize; and all writing is occasional prose.

✳

I returned to Bangkok. My father had telephoned several times over the previous week. I called him back.

"I tell you, Clinton just seems to be *reeling* about Haiti," he said.

"Clinton seems to be reeling about a lot of things," I observed.

My dad had just visited Israel and Jordan for the first time. Arab areas, he said, were "just like Haiti." I laughed.

"I mean that seriously," he said. "Little kids and chickens running around, some guy walking his donkey down the street, old men sitting on a porch playing checkers." Israel was entirely different. He had been in a store, not sure if the prices marked were in dollars or shekels. "I asked the woman, who was obviously from Ohio or somewhere like that, 'Excuse me, are the prices in shekels or dollars?' She said, 'Think for a minute. Are we in the United States?' I said, 'Some of the shops list prices in dollars.' She said, 'Only the Arab shops.' What I should have said," he added, "but I wasn't quick enough, was, 'Then I'll go to the Arab shops.'"

I caught up with my Australian drinking buddy Micool. The fifth anniversary of Aung San Suu Kyi's house arrest was two days away.

"She's meant to be released," said Micool.

"What? Have you heard something?"

"No: She's *meant* to be released, by law. They can only hold you in house arrest for five years. But they've already said they're not going to release her."

"The one general said he was willing to meet with her."

"Sure. He'll go to her house and have tea with her. He's not going to talk politics."

Micool was writing a book about the Death Railway built between Thailand and Burma during World War II, by Japanese-held prisoners of war. He had a contact inside Burma, a European contracted with the SLORC to do engineering work. "He rang me up and told me he's having this seminar summarizing all his research. He said he'd like me to come, he'd try to get me a visa. He came through for me, but the SLORC let me down. They said, 'No fucking way is some *farang* journalist coming to that seminar.'"

"So that was it for you and the SLORC."

"That was like the last straw." Then Micool surprised me by saying, "Until you came back, I was thinking about writing an editorial on Haiti. *Newsweek* had a really interesting article on 'Invading Haiti: The Debate.'"

"Yeah, I saw that. What are you going to write?"

"Well, now that you're back, I'd better let you write it."

I asked what he would have written.

"No way was America going to invade Haiti during the World Cup," he said. "No host country has ever invaded another country during the World Cup."

"The O.J. Simpson thing was bad enough," I agreed.

"Yeah. Now, if the World Cup had been in *another* country, America *would* have invaded. It would have been the perfect time."

"You think that's why ...?"

"It's totally obvious."

"Has anybody published this?"

"It has *not* been published."

"Well, go ahead and write it."

"No, no. Now that *you're* back ..."

"I guess it is about time for another Haiti editorial," I said, my heart sinking. "If they run the Burma one on Tuesday, maybe Peter'll give me Thursday for a Haiti one. I bet they'll invade in the next couple of months."

"Mate, I think it's gonna be sooner. In the next two weeks."

Bob Halliday, a burly and hyper-literate New Yorker who wrote the *Bangkok Post*'s popular restaurant reviews under a pseudonym that was Thai for "Sea Frog," urged me to read Kafka. "He was one of those prophetic writers," said Bob. "He saw it all coming long before it came. It's all there in *The Trial*."

We talked about the running sore that was Burma.

"My friend Wendy says none of it is ever going to be redressed, because there's no morality in politics anymore," Bob said. "In the old days there used to be morality in politics."

"Surely they were pretending back then too," I objected. "Some countries pretend their actions are based on morality, and others don't. That's where the confusion comes in."

"Well, yes, I suppose so. I read all your editorials," he said, meaning the ones I had sent to the *Post* from India. "I can always tell which ones are yours. For one thing, the word 'Haiti' is a tip-off. I liked the one about how the whole world is a mess. That was yours, wasn't it?"

In India I had read volumes two through four of George Orwell's *Collected Essays, Journalism and Letters*. I reminded Bob of something he had said just before my trip: that Orwell's terminal commitedness could get to be a bit much.

"I read those four volumes like eating a box of candy," he said now. "But he's just so *fucking* committed. Sometimes you just want to say, 'Back off!' I mean, the rest of us aren't *that* stupid." He chuckled. "But I guess you had to be committed in those days, in the thirties and forties."

On July 31 the UN adopted Resolution 940, authorizing the United States to form a multinational force to use "all necessary means to facilitate the departure from Haiti of the military leadership." Around the same time, Boris Yeltsin seemed to deserve credit for something he had *not* done: he had not invaded a tiny entity in the Caucasus called Chechnya, which was trying to secede from Russia. "Intervening in Chechnya's affairs with force is out of the question," Yeltsin had said. "This would be so messy and bloody that no one would forgive us." I wondered what might have been saved—in human lives, in hope, in tree cover on Haitian hillsides, in his own credibility—if Clinton had stood by his campaign promise to support Haiti's democratically elected government and to give temporary refuge to "boat people." Or if he had invaded Haiti in October 1993, when the USS *Harlan County* had turned around and General Cedras had declined to "step aside" as scripted. Or even if the January 15, 1994 deadline had not been toothless. Yeltsin seemed to be showing that sometimes politics is only the melancholy art of forestalling the unthinkable.

Recent events in two small countries I knew personally had led me to posit that human affairs operate along three axes. First is the left/right axis. In Nepal, the Communist Party of Nepal (United Marxist and Leninist) was "on the left." Aristide had won a landslide election victory in Haiti in 1990 by saying forthrightly and often that the rich are rich because the poor are poor. This was "leftist"; it also happened to be true. Second is the right/wrong axis: every political action or event has moral implications. The bombing of Hiroshima, for example, might have been self-evidently wrong, yet Truman responded to political compulsions, or perhaps even believed he was creating a *political* situation *morally* better than if he hadn't ordered the bombing. People can act politically with the intention of doing moral good, yet be mistaken and do wrong, unintentionally. Meanwhile, everyone involved must consider his own interests. As Man Mohan Adhikari had told me in Kathmandu: "Everybody has a compulsion. We also are trying to survive." The third axis represents geography and power. "The little guy does what he can," goes the Haitian proverb; "the big guy does what he wants."

I said these things in a think piece published in the *Bangkok Post*. Then, suddenly, it was Cuba and Cubans we were compelled to watch and read about. Although a riot in Havana on August 5 seemed the immediate spur, it was hard to avoid the impression that Castro's choice of moment to encourage his people to take to homemade rafts was connected to Clinton's helpless foundering on Haiti. In an abrupt reversal of longstanding U.S. policy, all Cubans picked up at sea after August 20 were sent to Guantanamo Bay or to Panama. "They will still have a big problem," said one of the 14,616 Haitian boat people already at Guantanamo. "All of the problems the U.S. has created will not fit on Guantanamo Bay."

The term "boat people" was one of those neologisms, like "safe havens" or "humanitarian relief" or "fundamentalist" or, later, "homeland security," that slipped into the language quietly and consensually enough that many soon honestly forgot not only their origins but that there had been a time before they existed. With "boat people" there was something more at work: for what, after all, was its origin? To remember when we first began speaking of "boat people" was to feel the same shiver evoked by Vietnam veteran John McCain, when he asked if U.S. troops in Haiti could be kept safe from "a bomb in a café." "People remember Somalia," said McCain's fellow Republican Senator Nancy Kassebaum—a polite way of saying what it was people really remembered, but still preferred to forget. Less than two decades after its original currency, "boat people" had acquired a science-fiction ring like, say, "lizard people" or "men from Mars." Even more chilling was the constant talk of "refugee flows," as though human beings were some kind of liquid substance.

Was the situation a human tragedy, or a conundrum of imperial statecraft? Most writers weren't sure. In a "soft" feature written in a wire reporter's spare time, a few "boat people" could be given names and their stories sketched; this was "background" or "color." In an analysis like an AP piece I had read in June, the kind of writing in which governments are referred to by the names of their capital cities, "Haiti"—shorthand for Bill Clinton's dilemma—could be unblushingly called "essentially a domestic problem" for the U.S. government.

*

On September 16 there occurred a probable all-time first: a story on Haiti above the fold on the front page of the *Bangkok Post*. The full-length report on page 13 was accompanied by an illustration showing the various kinds of ships the U.S. was sending to Haiti. Immediately to its left was an item datelined Baghdad, on the effects economic sanctions were having in Iraq. "What does America think—it can change the government?" the AP quoted "a man wearing shabby trousers and torn sandals" as saying. "No way. I cannot buy shoes. I cannot buy trousers. May Allah damn Clinton and America."

Clinton was preparing to address the American people. "I know it is unpopular," he told reporters, with a sigh audible even in print. "I know the timing is unpopular. I know the whole thing is unpopular. But I believe it is the right thing."

"I would rather die" than yield power, said Cedras.

I flew that day to Hong Kong, where a Thai acquaintance who had just arrived nonstop from London said she had seen Clinton on television there. Her unclear impression was that the invasion had happened already. But as of print time for the next morning's *South China Morning Post*, it had not yet happened. Haiti filled two inside pages.

The unexorcised ghosts of Vietnam were rattling their chains. Here at the top of page 12 was a photo of protesters—captioned "students"—carrying placards outside the White House. NO BLOOD FOR VOTES, read one. The young woman holding it wore a puzzled expression, as well she might; did she suppose Clinton stood to gain politically by invading Haiti? And what was she protesting, and why? "Who would have imagined," sniffed the columnist George Will, "that when children of the 1960s Vietnam protests came to power they would seek a quagmire to get waist deep in?" David Broder of the *Washington Post* instructed us that "The lesson of Vietnam is that you don't commit troops until the country is committed to the mission."

Was that the lesson of Vietnam? I no longer knew what to think.

But certain things became clear enough to me during this climactic week: any U.S.-sponsored restoration of Aristide to office would be grudging, ostensible, and short-lived, and would have no salutary influence on Haitian politics. The Haitian elite would work to reclaim and reconsolidate its position, and Cedras and the other junta members would either remain in Haiti with impunity or retire into comfortable exile. The many self-appointed experts would grow tired of commentating about Haiti, and the American public would tire of hearing about it. Bosnia would be brought briefly back onto the front burner. Congressional pressure, or the first body bags, or "mission creep," or simply the passage of time would compel Clinton or his successor to pull "our boys" out, leaving Haitians as before at each other's mercy. Jimmy Carter, who at the last minute negotiated the immaculate invasion, would be short-listed for the Nobel Peace Prize. Life and death for most Haitians would go on much as before.

The best case from the left was made by Amy Wilentz. A few weeks earlier in *The Nation*, she had written:

Everyone wants those Haitian democrats still alive to survive this terrible period. We want the Haitian people to have some hope for the future. That is why intervention seems alluring—the U.S. Marines as a deus ex machina. But a U.S. intervention, and subsequent occupation, is dangerous for Haiti's political progress into the next three generations, whereas much sooner than that, if the embargo continues and is strengthened, this regime will inevitably be forced out for economic reasons by the strangled Haitian business class. ... Let's hope for the transformation that would come about when this regime is toppled from within, under pressure from the outside, and not for the cosmetic quick fix of intervention.

But Wilentz's conditional verb tense betrayed just how ill founded such a hope was. Why did so many writers on the left feel compelled to imagine a nonviolent state or an absence of imperialism? Was it ideological Stockholm Syndrome, a felt obligation to be constructive, to avoid being branded a nay-sayer? I'm sorry I'm a dissident; here are my helpful suggestions. Or back-seat driving: Here's what I would do if I were in charge. Either way, it was an old trap. "Too many people still believe in the State," wrote Ernest Hemingway in 1934, "and war is the health of the state. You will see that finally it will become necessary for the health of the so-called communist state in Russia."

Amy Wilentz's reputation as author of *The Rainy Season* was daunting. I wasn't eager to disagree with her. But I did. In an article for the *Bangkok Post*, I articulated my differences for the first time:

Wilentz is right to call the occupation a "quick fix." In my judgment she is willfully wishful, though, to have hoped for anything else. After three agonizing years ... I now concede that a U.S. occupation is the least bad of several awful options. This is not to say that I "support" the present occupation or any variation on it. I simply acknowledge that might and right are two very distinct things, and that it really is implausible to expect any government that wields great power to do so in the interests of the poor and helpless.

Meanwhile, people who had never been to Haiti were lining up to have their say. Hugh Sampter of Queen's Road West, Hong Kong, said this in the *South China Morning Post*: "The United States administration 'invaded' Haiti because a corrupt military dictatorship won't allow a democratically elected leader to take office. Why don't the Americans invade Burma?"

"So, America launches a military operation to protect a people's right to its own democratically elected government," said John J. Evans of Moreton-in-Marsh, England in the *International Herald Tribune*. "Salvador Allende should have lived to see this day."

"Our success in Haiti to date," said Bill Clinton in his next weekly radio address, "shows what the international community, with American leadership, can achieve in helping countries in their struggle to build democracy."

"The situation in Haiti is a suspended revolution," wrote the *Herald Tribune*'s urbane columnist William Pfaff, "waiting since 1991 to be completed."

PART TWO

CHAPTER 4

SUSPENDED REVOLUTION

Ten years later in 2004, the revolution was still suspended, but a lot of topsoil had washed away over a long decade of frustration and running crisis. A condition of Aristide's restoration was that he would have to step down at the end of his five-year term, in February 1996. He agreed to this because he had no choice, despite having spent three years of his term in exile. His successor, René Preval, was a close ally widely seen as keeping the seat warm until Aristide could run again.

This he did, and the outcome was foreordained, though the occasion failed to replicate the euphoria of 1990. I seized the excuse to visit Haiti in November 2000, just before the election. "If Aristide come in," a young man in the Cité Soleil slum told me, "I think he stay until two thousand one hundred, something like that. Because he do lots of things to make the people love him." He pointed at a water tower. "Aristide make that for Cité Soleil." A graffito nearby said, in English: WITH ARISTIDE, DON'T WORRY BE HAPPY.

"Do you think when Aristide comes back he'll be able to do things for people again?" I asked him.

"I think so. Because he say in his book."

"The Christians say only Jesus Christ can save Haiti," said someone else I met that day. "Me, I say the American people can do something to save Haiti."

A lanky teenager named James, whom I had found on the street and hired to go with me to Cité Soleil, predicted that there would be no more coups. I asked him why not.

"Because the people not sleep now," he said. "The eyes of the people open. But Haiti got big problems. Everybody just swim to get out. This country no good, no work." Many weapons from the U.S.-led occupation following Aristide's restoration had remained in the country after the soldiers left, either left behind or sold or stolen. "Now, lotta people have a gun. If lotta people have a gun, and you don't have a gun, what you gonna do? Most cops are thiefs. The cops give people weapons to kill people. If Aristide not president of Haiti, lotta people gonna die."

In April of that year a prominent journalist and sometime Aristide ally named Jean Dominique, subject of Jonathan Demme's documentary film *The Agronomist*, had been assassinated, allegedly for criticizing Aristide. It had been pretty big news and seemed like a pivotal event.

"That's all it was, was news," Betsy Wall told me. Betsy was the middle-aged daughter of the missionaries Jack and Anne Wall, of Wall House off Delmas. "But here it was just a death. He had been a Lavalas party supporter, assumed to have been killed by Lavalas party faithful." Fanmi Lavalas was Aristide's party. "It was the Haitian death of the year in North America, but here it was just another death. How stupid could you be? I don't know if martyrs are valued in Haiti."

At Wall House I asked Mark Spooner, a minister with the De Soto, Missouri-based Association of International Gospel Assemblies, where he had been at the time of the assassination.

"Where I was—oh gracious," he said. "I was above St. Marc, close to Gonaïves"—a couple of hours up the coast—"putting on a five-day seminar for pastors. It was the second day when we heard about that. They had spent two days, three days walking. There was no electricity in the area, just somebody's portable radio. There was so much fear; they wanted to go back to their congregations. So we shut the seminar down. There was nowhere for us to go but back here. And I was in the middle of it. You could see the tire burnings. We came down from the mountains and you could see it. We could see the smoke rising up. The mood of the people was one of fear. Quiet. You just could pick up that fear, once you dropped down into Port-au-Prince. The whole city was shut down. The fellow that was with me, he wanted to go home, and we couldn't even change our flights. So we ended up calling home. And one of the elders from our church, he called American Airlines.

"As we went to the airport, it was the morning of the funeral. I was told that the funeral was going to be just an hour and a half. But when the government officials went to the stadium, the people closed off the exit and wouldn't let them back out. Normally [at the airport] it's a 20- to 30-minute processing time. And we were there two hours. It was chaos, it really was. The masses of people trying to take every flight there was. The suitcases were so big, some of them took two men to pick 'em up. By the time we got to the ticket agent, the fellow who was with me—it was the first time he had been down here—he said to the lady, 'Is this normal?' She said, 'No, it's because of the assassination.'"

*

Over drinks at the Montana, the hotel of choice for well-funded ex-pats, a quiet American with one of those quasi-official institutes to do with spreading democracy and monitoring elections spoke to me on background. "You're dealing in 500 years of history," he emphasized. "Since Columbus set foot on this island in 1492, there has been only one model of government, and that is absolute dictatorship." During the 1957–71 rule of François Duvalier, for example, the country's 500-plus *chefs de section* "answered directly to Papa Doc. It always has been an all or nothing game."

I asked about the opposition parties that were threatening to boycott the presidential election.

"Look at the internal structures of these political parties," he said. "Power has been absolutely and completely centralized." It was more appropriate to speak of "opposition personalities, rather than opposition parties. Many of these parties, once the leader is out, the party dies a natural death. Any single one of these political party leaders, I can safely say, once they are in power they are going to do exactly what Fanmi Lavalas is doing: crush the opposition. The real opposition is the international community."

Aristide, he said, "talks the poor people's language. Having been a priest, psychologically he knows what makes the poor people tick. He is the only one who is really and truly represented in the hinterland of the country." He had initiated things like small loans to *ti marchands*—

market women—and literacy programs. "Those are the things that set him apart. Whatever can psychologically raise the ambition of folks, I think it's helpful. Most opposition leaders are intellectuals who've spent most of their lives outside Haiti. Aristide is in touch with the people at the grassroots level."

I asked if there was any opposition more credible than the traditional, mainstream politicians. He mentioned the Mouvement Paysans Papaye (MPP), a peasants' organization based outside Hinche on the Central Plateau. Its leader was Chavannes Jean-Baptise, who had been a strong supporter of Aristide and a strong resister against the Cedras junta. The MPP was well established and influential. "After Aristide returned, there started to be a split between MPP and Lavalas." In September, Chavannes had mobilized five thousand people for a demonstration on the central square of Hinche. "It's the first time ever that anybody's been able to do that," said the quiet American. "This is perhaps the beginning of a viable grassroots popular opposition. Nobody knows where he wants to go with this."

A European diplomat was even more blunt. "The Americans brought this man back with 20,000 troops in 1994, and now he risks being isolated," she told me. "Quite ironic, really. That's how Haiti goes. He wanted everything in the Senate. He would have had a majority [in the May 2000 legislative elections], but that wasn't enough. He wanted to make constitutional changes that would allow him to run for another term and create a new military force. He's a very intelligent person. He's a very good judge of character. He tends to discard people who might be a threat to him. Why are these people" – former allies such as Victor Benoit and Robert Malval—"now against him? You're not supposed to do that when you're a politician. You're supposed to gather your supporters around you.

"I would like to think that the people are awake enough now to say, 'We're not going to take any more dictatorship.' But I don't think that's going to happen. Everything here is a catch-22: 80 percent of education is in private schools or religious schools. There are so few doctors in this country, large areas that don't have a doctor. People here—do they really want a vote? No, they don't. They want food, they want a job." In rural areas, "people don't really know what's going on. They believe in the president as a sort of father figure. Aristide is the only person with charisma. I think they have always seen him as their only hope. But it's very difficult to want to give democracy to an illiterate people. If anything happens, it will only happen in the major towns. The rural areas will just carry on as before."

What about the rumors that Haiti had become a major transit route for drug trafficking?

"Every now and then there's a drug seizure, to keep the Americans happy. But it's very difficult to find any accurate information on the amount of drugs coming in and going out. It's in the interest of drug traffickers that this country remain in perpetual chaos. Someone told me there are so many planes coming up from South America that they're jamming the radar." Drugs were said to come into Haiti in the keels of ships, in platform shoes, in double-bottomed suitcases. The police force was inadequate in numbers, inefficient, and corrupt; the coasts were porous. The U.S. Coast Guard patrolled between Haiti and the Bahamas, looking for drugs and boat people.

The diplomat was married to a Haitian and had lived many years in Haiti. I asked her what it had been like during the international embargo of 1991–94, which had been imposed ostensibly as pressure on the military junta.

"We were paying incredibly inflated prices for black market fuel," she said. Her own family had been without electricity for three full weeks. Her husband's jobs had stopped; he had spent his time trying to buy fuel and help friends and neighbors. "They would come and sit outside my house. He felt a social and moral obligation to these people." People without money had deserted the capital, putting more pressure on limited food resources in rural areas. Between June and September 1994, the embargo had been total. "Perhaps the international community thought the people were going to revolt and throw out the coup leaders. They didn't. Haitian people have such an incredible power of resistance, I sometimes wonder what is their breaking point." The Hotel Montana had been full of journalists, its roof covered with satellite dishes.

"If anybody wanted to leave Haiti at that point, you had to go by land over the border to the Dominican Republic. You had to get permission from the army on this side, and from the Dominicans. From May onwards, we thought the Americans were going to invade. Then interest waned. The first few days after the Americans landed, they would be doing patrols around town in armored vehicles, in full combat uniforms. It became the thing to do: 'Let's go down to the airport and see what the Americans are doing.'" Clinton's restoration of Aristide, after three years of posturing and a cruel embargo, was pointless and cynical. "Haiti was used as a foreign policy 'success' to sell to the American people."

✹

An opposition politician, a Protestant pastor who asked not to be named, told me he had been cheated out of a seat in the national assembly in the disputed legislative elections in May. "There was a lot of fraud, a lot of irregularities, but all the irregularities were done by Lavalas people," he claimed. "They took lots of full vote boxes, emptied them, filled them with votes for themselves. They kept six boxes in the commissariat and filled them in favor of Lavalas. Because of that, I myself lost my election. There were many candidates who lost because of those irregularities, with the complicity of the police and the CEP"— the Provisional Electoral Council.

Was Lavalas truly popular?

"No, no, no. If there were genuine elections in Haiti, Lavalas would not win."

But wasn't Aristide still popular?

"Many people say that's true, but because they're not in Haiti. He was a priest, but he no longer has the same heart."

Why did he change?

"Because he wanted money, and he loved power too much."

I asked what was going to happen next.

"In this country, you can almost never predict what's going to happen. Aristide will win the elections, because nobody else will run."

"And after that?"

His response was a shrug.

"There hasn't been for a long time two parties both with guns," Mrs. Wall said to me. "Now there is."

"Then it was a right-wing dictatorship, a dictatorship of the rich," said her irascible husband. "Now it's a left-wing dictatorship, a dictatorship of the poor. That's the difference."

Only a couple of weeks before the presidential election, it still wasn't certain whether it would take place. In the truck on the way to Fond Baptiste, a mountain village where the Walls' nonprofit organization had a project, a Haitian who worked with them told me in Creole: "If the election doesn't happen, there will be a big crisis."

"What sort of crisis?"

"The president"—Preval—"has to depart, must depart. If the election doesn't happen, there will be no new president to take his place. The Supreme Court can name an interim president. But five of the nine seats on the Supreme Court are empty now, so the court doesn't have a quorum, so it can't name an interim president. If there is no election, I think there might be civil war. There will be a lot of violence."

"Like in '85–'86?"

"Maybe worse. Many more people are armed now. There is no army, and the police are too weak."

There were, he said, "two problems for Haiti that are actually one: an economic one and a political one. Haiti is the poorest country in the Americas. I think Haiti needs to resolve its political problems in order to be able to resolve its economic problems. If you say agriculture will save Haiti, that's not true. That's true in the long term, but in the short term you need tourism. And in order to have tourism, you need to resolve the political problems. To resolve the political problems, you need a big forum at the national level. You can't do that with violence, with an occupation by foreigners, with GIs. I believe the diaspora wants to return. But they've begun to divide among themselves. We need unity."

I asked Matthieu Lucius, who also worked with the Walls, whether Lavalas really was different from other parties.

"Yeah, I think so," he said. "They have a lot of people with them. Whatever way they do the election, they would win." In the disputed

May legislative elections, "There was some problems, absolutely. But I think that doesn't mean they should sweep away the results. If they don't have the elections, the country gonna have much bigger problems. It's absolutely necessary. It's an emergency to have the elections."

✳

On the morning of November 8, I trudged across Avenue Delmas to a cybercafe to find out the result of the U.S. presidential election, only to learn that there wasn't one. Someone brought a copy of the *New York Times* from Miami the next day, and we scoured it for clues and portents. Haitians were amused. A few days later on the seafront boulevard in Cap Haïtien on Haiti's north coast, a teenager named Edner asked me, "Which do you support, Gore or Ti Bush?"—Little Bush, or Bush Junior.

"I believe only Americans, not Haitians," insisted his friend, Donald. "If I ask a rich Haitian to help me, he will say bad things to me: 'You are a dog. You are a pig. My children can go to the United States but you cannot.' All the presidents take money for projects and put it in their pocket."

We talked about Aristide and Chavannes Jean-Baptiste, the peasant leader. Chavannes had powers that allowed him to make himself invisible and do other magical things. Aristide had tricked Chavannes by giving him a car, then sending a man to steal it back from him.

"Do you like Aristide?" I asked.

"No."

"Which one is better, Chavannes or Aristide?"

"Chavannes."

"Is Aristide good?"

"No."

"Why not?"

"If Aristide were good, he wouldn't steal Chavannes' car," said Edner. "For example, you and I are friends. If I am good and I am your friend, I will not steal your car."

"Aristide says, 'I am the friend of the poor,'" I said.

"Bluff," rejoined Edner.

✳

"We don't need coup d'état again in Haiti," a nun named Sister Carmel said to me during that November 2000 trip. "Because the political people give us the big misery." Three years later, on February 29, 2004, there was another coup. Aristide had returned in 1994 courtesy of the United States, and many were saying his departure ten years later was U.S.-orchestrated as well. In April the *London Review of Books* published an article by Paul Farmer, a Harvard Medical School professor who had founded a free public hospital in central Haiti and gained notoriety as the subject of a book, *Mountains Beyond Mountains*, published the year before by the journalist Tracy Kidder. Farmer's article was titled "Who Removed Aristide?" It asked pointed questions:

> Did the US and France have a hand in Aristide's removal? Were he and his wife being held against their will? Most of Aristide's claims, initially disputed by US officials from [Roger] Noriega to Donald Rumsfeld, are now acknowledged to be true. His enemies' claims that Aristide met with officials in Antigua—Aristide said they were not allowed to move from their seats—were undermined by reports from Antigua itself. Noriega acknowledged during a House hearing that Aristide did not know of his destination until less than an hour before landing in the Central African Republic. Even CAR officials acknowledge that no Haitian authorities were involved in the choice of destination.
>
> Many more questions remain unanswered. We know that US funds overtly financed the opposition, but did they also fund, even indirectly, the rebellion, which featured high-powered US weapons only a year after twenty thousand such weapons were promised to the Dominican Republic? Senator Christopher Dodd is urging an investigation of US training sessions for six hundred "rebels" in the Dominican Republic, and wants to find out "how the [International Republican Institute] spent $1.2 million of taxpayers' money" in Haiti. Answering these and related questions would take an intrepid investigative reporter, rather than a physician like myself, working, with some trepidation, in central Haiti. It would need a reporter willing to take on hard questions about US policies in Latin America.

I doubted I had the skills, money, or other resources to do the investigation Farmer was calling for. And you can exhaust and endanger yourself proving the truth, and They will still deny it, and the great American public will still ignore it and fail to understand. I wasn't the one to answer the questions Farmer raised but, especially at this unusually fraught moment, I had to see for myself.

*

By the time I got to Haiti, with stints en route in New York, Washington, and Miami, it was mid-July. I thought I was going there to refresh my memory and confirm things I already knew. It was only afterward that, having exhausted myself physically and emotionally, I realized how much I still had to learn.

In New York I knew a guy named Michael Smolens, an international businessman who had owned a factory in Haiti, who invited me to spend a weekend at his house in the Hamptons. Until this point I had been vague about what exactly the Hamptons were; I thought maybe they were a mountain range. One morning Michael took me to see Jason Epstein, the Random House editor and co-founder of *The New York Review of Books*, at Epstein's 1790s-vintage house in Sag Harbor. Epstein's wife, Judith Miller, was out of town, but her Mazda convertible was in the driveway. When we walked in Epstein was sitting at his kitchen table, doing the *New York Times* crossword puzzle.

"Jason, you remember my friend Ethan," said Michael.

"Sure," said Epstein, offering his hand. "Good to see you again."

"Ethan is writing a book about Haiti."

"That'll sell a lot of copies," said Epstein, with a knowing chuckle.

Back at his place, Michael insisted: "Aristide is only a blip on the radar screen." We were sitting in Adirondack chairs in his backyard, on a beautiful summer day, looking across the water at the North Fork of Long Island. "The much more interesting question is, How did a primitive African culture get implanted in the Caribbean amidst all of the other islands? Why can't Haiti get out of its own way? Why is the environment receptive and supportive of an Aristide-type figure? And why hasn't it changed?" He gave examples of what he meant. "You have your houseboy, and you have to teach him to water the lawn. But you can't tell him that when it's raining you don't water it." This was a common story. Michael buttressed it with another one, about a friend who had asked his Haitian servant to paint the lines on a tennis court. Instead, he had painted an intricate and beautiful *veve* or voodoo pattern. "A mind at that level does not have the concept of relating that design to the boundaries in a game," said Michael. "These are the things that the Aristides and the Duvaliers understand and exploit."

I asked Michael what it had been like on February 7, 1986, the day Baby Doc fled.

"That was an amazing period in Haiti, because the country had been infiltrated by socialists who were supported by people in France and Venezuela," he said. "They were empowering factory workers to rise up against their employers, to bring socialism to Haiti. After he fell, the workers started getting very belligerent. You had Haitian peasant workers quoting Karl Marx. I basically told them that this was a private business. They wanted to have elections for the workers, like a democracy. I stood up on a sewing machine and gave a speech in Creole, saying that they didn't have to work for me, but if they did it would be on my conditions. I had police and armed guards there and everything. It was an amazing time. But it was very easy to do business there. Even after Baby Doc was gone, it was still relatively easy, if you were established and had the right connections and played by the right rules."

"Even after Aristide came in, it was still like that?"

"Yeah."

"So it wasn't Aristide that affected your business?"

"No, not at all."

What had affected his business was the decision by Bush *père* to impose an economic embargo on Haiti in 1991.

"I had active intelligence sources working for me, to not be blind-sided," Michael said. "That's why the embargo came as such a shock. There was a group of us, Haiti-ophiles, who were actively involved in helping Haiti. Doing business has nothing to do with politics. Totally unrelated to politics. We were just trying to get the White House to keep things on an even keel, so we could continue to do business."

"Why do you think the White House did the embargo?" I asked.

"Just as a very strong political card. It lasted four years."

"Were you pissed off?"

"I totally lost everything. Pissed off is not the word. Furious. You wanted to kill someone. All commercial flights were cancelled, all shipping was cancelled. The workers lost their jobs. The owners of the factories couldn't collect their rent. Everyone lost. There weren't any winners." Michael himself lost "millions of dollars" because of the embargo. "Mexico was the first place I went after that. Then Romania, then Hungary, then Azerbaijan. It was a time to force me to change. Had I not changed, I would not have grown at all. I would have continued to do very well financially, but I would not have grown intellectually."

"What was Bush's motivation in imposing the embargo?" I asked again.

"It was never very clear. It was to try to strong-arm Aristide. To me it was never clear."

Also in New York I met John Altino, a.k.a. Papa Jube, music producer and close associate of the singer Wyclef Jean. "Most of the diaspora, we connected with Aristide," he told me in his office in the basement of the world music club SOBs, in lower Manhattan. "It was only because of us that he went back to Haiti. We were the ones in front of the United Nations" protesting, during Aristide's 1991–94 exile.

"Do you still believe in or support Aristide?" I asked.

"No. Because the people who put him back into power, he wasn't loyal to them. Power is the thing that can turn you into a maniac. Power can go to people's heads. He hired a bunch of idiots. To me, you're not qualified to be a leader if you don't have the wits to realize that you're only as strong as your team. He excluded the diaspora."

"If Aristide had turned out to be wiser, would you have considered going back to Haiti?"

"Absolutely. I was planning to go back. Wyclef was planning to go back."

"What happened to him?"

"That's what I'm saying. He came here for four years, he became a politician. He totally became an egomaniac, because he was going head-to-head with America at the same time that his only protection was the Navy SEALs. This guy was living in a glass house throwing stones. He didn't have no friends nowhere. He married a *bourgeoise*. Therefore he couldn't be for the people anymore, because he had betrayed them."

I asked what he thought of Aristide's leftist and black American supporters, such as Randall Robinson and Congresswoman Maxine Waters. "These guys have their own interests," he asserted.

"What are their interests?"

"Money."

I asked him what life was like for Haitians in New York.

"Haitians have a lot of sympathizers in New York," he said, "because we're hard workers, and we're known for loyalty. We're different from African-Americans. Look at the current state of black America. If they can't even fight for their own people, why should they fight for Haiti? If you look at the current state of black America, it's pitiful. Michael Moore is today's Malcolm X. That's my leader today. Michael Moore is the only one that's trying to bring light and fight the big force of the media. We're proud people. We're the first people that fought for the freedom—we didn't ask for it."

Aristide, said Papa Jube, had brought his second ouster on himself. "There's no way as a president of a country, if he had any kind of proper connection, proper advisors, proper kind of structure of a government, that they could have ousted him as they did," he said. "This happened this time, no one protested. The first time, we went into a rage. That's a clear sign."

CHAPTER 5

"MAIS TU ES EN AFRIQUE!"

The house where I stayed this time in Port-au-Prince was a hard, hot walk downhill from where the side street Delmas 75 meets the arterial avenue. You hike past squatting women offering mangos and bananas, turn left and pass the EnergiTek cybercafe, then continue down and turn left again onto gravel, stepping around the deeper potholes and over or through the smaller ones, until you get nearly to where the road ends at the edge of a ravine. This walk home from the nearest public transportation took me at least 10 minutes and was tedious at the end of a long day of sensory overload in the city. At midday, under the tropical summer sun, it was draining. The reverse hike uphill was more arduous still. Leaving the house in the morning was a decision not taken lightly; keeping an appointment felt like setting out on an expedition.

This evening, as dusk fell and the dogs began their evening conversation, I was walking only a few yards to watch the sun go down behind the ravine. This gash in the mountainside, where the sprawl of the city met the natural geography of the land, would be a stream bed when it rained. From its floor rose cinder-block houses, some of two or more stories; I looked down on their tin roofs. From the darkness on the far side came the chatter of boys playing soccer on a sloping dirt pitch. Downhill from the near end of the pitch a goat was tethered.

I sat on a rock and watched as the sun fell and dusk deepened.

"Mon blanc!" It was a woman's voice, across the road but on my side of the ravine. My white man! She added something I didn't fully catch,

to the effect that if I wanted to get to the other side I should go down here, then up over there.

"Pa gen pwoblem," I explained. *"M-abite la-ba. Mesi kanmem."* No problem. I'm staying right there. Thanks anyway.

"Oh, oui," she said. *"Ça va?"*

"Ça va bien," I replied. *"Et toi?"* I'm fine, and you?

"Ça ne va pas," she answered. *"Mwen grangou!"* I'm not fine. I'm hungry! She was stating the obvious, in a lightly mocking tone. I couldn't rejoin *"Mwen grangou tou,"* because it wasn't true. The things left unsaid between us were Haitian poetry.

"Sole bel ampil," I remarked, changing the subject. The sunset is beautiful.

"Oui," she agreed, but perfunctorily, politely, humoring me.

After a long pause she said, again, *"Mon blanc!"*

"Oui."

"Au revoir."

"Au revoir," I said.

The encounter brought *plus ça change* home to me. The relentless maelstrom of flux and loss and violence somehow added up to a wacky kind of stability, or so I sometimes allowed myself to believe. To be reminded that the big, universal questions that Haiti more than any other place brings into stark relief had not changed since I had first come here, twenty-two years earlier, was at once maddening and comforting.

✳

My host was a friend of a friend, a squat, intense Frenchman from Marseilles named Philippe Allouard. Philippe had his head shaved weekly and was a very serious Roman Catholic; he had been a novice in the Dominican order.

"Like the Franciscans, Dominicans are religious: praying together, living together," he explained. "But unlike monks, they do not work manually to earn a living. They do not stay inside the priory. They go outside to preach. In fact, the official name in the Church is not Dominican, it is Preachers." Philippe had first come to Haiti in 1999. "It was a year of decision," he told me. "I was in Haiti in order to have a different context and to decide better. And for the brothers to decide better. And at the end of the year, we just decided to stop. Obviously a vocation is not something you decide. It's something you receive. It would be really egotistic to stick to my desire and not accept their wisdom." He returned to France for six weeks in August-September 1999. "But I had already fallen in love with Haiti, so I just came back."

"What was it about Haiti that you fell in love with?"

"Light. Noises. Food. Cooking. I did enjoy it a lot from the beginning." He shared with me the diary he had written during his first year in Haiti. "From time to time I go back to it and read. I write it because I wanted to keep my first impressions fresh. Because after, you get used to everything, the bad and the good. So it's wonderful to go back to your first impressions and go, 'Wow!'"

Philippe worked in the port for a shipping company and in marketing for the Hotel Montana. He worked conscientiously at both jobs, but it was clear that the jobs served his primary purpose, which was simply to be in Haiti. "Do you ever feel any need to have a particular career?" I asked him.

"I would like to have glory, to be famous," he said. "But in the same moment, if I were to be truly successful, that would be perhaps the worst. I think it is very difficult to be truly famous and not to be full of yourself."

He came from a colonial family; his mother had been born in Gabon. "My grandfather and grandmother spent half their lives in Africa, in French Equatorial Africa. So I grew up in my grandmother's house, filled with elephant teeth and stories and everything of Africa. So my dream was to go to Africa, and I never went. And first time I came here—it was not so modern as it is now; one thing you must say improved under Aristide is the airport facilities—now there are places where people can't go, and this, but then you were first in the airport, then in a crowd. And people grabbing your luggages, and the heat. And it was just like I imagined Africa. And I was so happy. When I wrote my first letter to my grandmother with my first impressions, she wrote back and said, *'Mais tu es en Afrique!'*"

For me, just being in Port-au-Prince day after day was like an endurance trial. Taking notes on what I saw and heard around me, arranging—or trying to arrange—formal interviews with various official-type people, figuring out how to get around a rugged, hilly city with rudimentary public transportation, I began to feel how inadequate were all the earnest books by sympathetic foreigners, from the obtusely apolitical Herbert Gold to the stubbornly ideological Amy Wilentz. All the books put together could only scratch the surface, because the written word was not the right medium for such a country. "I think it's very difficult to get a holistic presentation of a country as complicated as this one," Philippe said. The prerequisite to understanding Haiti was to experience it directly with all the senses, thoroughly, without prejudice, and in three dimensions: sights, sounds, smells, a capella church songs, grinding gears, dust, roosters, dogs.

"Do you think you'll stay?" I asked.

Philippe shrugged. "I don't know. I might stay. How long, I don't know. I hope I don't refuse opportunity to know other countries. If it's a choice between France and Haiti, I choose Haiti."

"What is it about France?"

He shrugged again. "I know it pretty well already. I think it's better as a tourist."

The house Philippe rented was behind a high wall and a heavy metal gate, with an overgrown front yard in which he kept chickens. The house had no running water, and electricity was sporadic. An assortment of young Haitians came and went. A couple of them lived there; others were brothers or pals or stray chancers or girlfriends. Two of them, Josué and David, were brothers. Josué, in his early twenties, was the more mature and resourceful; David was nineteen and carefree. Philippe was generous and indulgent but could be stern. I once overheard him scolding David: *Ou pa ti moun!* You're not a child!

Another of Philippe's hangers-on was a tall, gangly kid named Junior. Junior was from near Jacmel on the south coast.

"You know, Junior hardly knows to read and write," Philippe said. "And I don't know if you've been in that room, but I have different kind of books: Latin philosophy and theology on one shelf, and French books, and a little Spanish books, and on another shelf English books.

And they get dusty, and Junior dusted the shelves. And I came back from Washington and they were all mixed up with one another, and all turned backwards! See, you've got philosophy, Thomas Aquinas, right next to Tolkien!"

"They're upside-down too," I observed.

"He has an incredibly hard head, and he can be very stubborn, Junior," Philippe said. "But in the same moment, he is excessively clever and he has a great heart. And he is very honest. I would trust him with my money."

"I think your life would be less interesting if you didn't have all these boys around you," I said.

"Yes. This is my dilemma. To have peaceful and easy life and be alone, or to have this kind of perpetual trouble. David's daughter burned herself couple of days ago. Typical accident. And the mother—okay, she is very young, but …"

"David is only nineteen, right?"

"Right."

"And how old is the girl?"

"Seventeen."

"And the baby?"

"One and half or two years. Josué! *Ki laj piti David?*"

"*Deux ans*," said Josué.

"Oh! It goes so fast," lamented Philippe.

"So you're like the granddaddy of this whole bunch of young guys?" I said.

He smiled wearily. "Yes."

My first evening there, Philippe and I got to know each other on his front porch with cigars and rum. "So – you are not perfect," he remarked. "That's a good point."

"I'm not?"

"No. You are smoking cigar. Perfect people are generally difficult to live with, and sometimes boring."

"My father also is not perfect," I said. "He smokes cigars a lot."

"That's good. It's terrible, the Protestants here—some of them. Not all of them. They preach as if it's revealed that smoking is forbidden. So in Creole if you're *levangil*, if you are converted, a real Christian, you don't drink, you don't smoke."

I thought of something a Kashmiri friend had told me about the differences between Muslims and Sikhs: "We smoke but we don't drink. They drink but they don't smoke!"

Philippe was highly literate in several languages and entertained me with the range of his allusions. He introduced me to the novelist Julien Green and to Gustave Thibon, a French author and friend of Simone Weil, who had written: "*Tout dire implique infiniement plus d'hypocrisie que tout cacher.*"

"The idea is that some things, in order to remain authentic, have to remain secret," Philippe interpreted. "In fact it's exactly the same as lying, because you just put forward everything as if it was equivalent."

Like Pascal, Thibon had a talent for aphorisms. "The details change, but the analysis is the same," said Philippe with appreciation. The book of Thibon's that I should read was called *Diagnostique*, published in 1936 and republished recently. "The good point is that it's very short."

According to Philippe, over the last century or so the world had gone to hell in a handbasket. "For centuries the Church, or the Christians, just created culture," he said, citing vernacular translations of the Bible. "In the 20th century, the Church just chase after secular culture. It's a theological problem, but it is linked to a very important cultural problem. Our trains are quicker. Our planes are quicker. But I think our minds are not quicker. It still takes a life to progress."

"Would you call yourself a conservative?" I asked.

"Yes. An important part of me is conservative. I like change, but I think I don't like revolution." Ancient scriptures and wisdom "should be irrelevant, but really it is relevant," he pointed out. "So really, a man is a man no matter when, no matter where. So that is where I think there is really a basis for being conservative."

He had been living in Paris in 1989, when the city was awash in bicentennial celebrations. "It was the end of my first year in Paris, and I was involved in some monarchist groups. So I spent a year being against the French Revolution. And by the end of one year I felt like

I was wood, a dead piece of wood. Being an activist means you are always being against something. And that is not a constructive program."

I asked Philippe to tell me about the 2000 elections in Haiti.

"Even in the mission where people were Haitian, or lived in Haiti for many years, and people were pretty cool, we were afraid," he said. "Because Jean Dominique had been killed, and it was no secret it came from his former friends, and this was a sign that Aristide was not easily able to accept any kind of dissent. Jean Dominique was more and more critic about Aristide. And he might have chosen to reveal something that he knew. It was guessed that drug trafficking, or what-what. This was rumors."

"That was the May elections?" I asked.

"And it was peaceful. No dead, except one or two in the whole country. And I think that's the reason why the first reaction of France, the U.S., the UN—what they call the international community—was to say, 'Whew! These were good elections.' So first reaction was contentment, or—*soulagement?* —relief. And it took time for the incidents of treachery and stolen ballots in the countryside to reach Port-au-Prince."

Thunder sounded in the distance.

"Ze rain is passing ze other side," said Philippe.

"You want rain here?"

"Yes! The water is running low. We missed it." He went on: "And the way Port-au-Prince dealt with this was to reinforce the power of the party. It was obvious in Ouanaminthe, for example"—in the remote northeast corner of Haiti, near the border with the Dominican Republic. "It just so happened that one guy who just came in from Port-au-Prince was elected with an important majority. So they complained, and the peace justice of the area just broke the election. And Port-au-Prince dismissed the justice or forced him to resign."

"So the presidential election was sort of under a cloud?"

"The midday Mass was cancelled. And the streets were white— *blanche*, as we say in Creole; empty – and the only people I saw were Lavalas, and they were asking people, 'Did you vote? Did you vote well?' It's menacing, because they were representing the party. It was calm, but too calm. Political courage is not very common in Haiti. People are very afraid to lose the few things that they got. And Aristide responded after to this objection, saying, '*Oui*, but Haitians are very intelligent, they go to vote one by one, so you don't see them.'"

"I don't understand," I said.

"You don't understand, because it's stupid," said Philippe. "This was the official answer from Aristide."

"I can't light my cigar."

"You have first to remove ze ashes."

I tried again.

"You can just take another one," he said.

"Thanks. I will, but I must first prove that I can—"

"—light it. This I understand."

"You always use two matches?" I asked.

"Yes. It's easier. You can light the cigar without absorbing the fumes of the matches."

I tried to light my cigar with one match. It went out.

"I'm obviously not as experienced at this as you are," I said.

"You are more perfect than I am, from a moral point of view," he said. "It's proof that techniques and morality don't always go together."

Rain began falling, lightly.

"Oh, *merci Seigneur!*" said Philippe.

"This fills the cistern," I suggested.

"Hopefully it will. If it rains a lot, it can fill up the cistern in one night. It is true that cistern are a good way to collect water. A few years ago they invited some water specialists from Israel. And their conclusion was that there is no problem of water supply in Haiti. Problem is waste. Because few people are collecting rains." Philippe had his water delivered by truck. It cost 300 Haitian dollars, or about US$40, to fill his cistern. "It depends where you are," he explained. "Higher you are, the more expensive it is. Because water comes from the plain."

He generally had to fill his cistern three times a year. "This year, at least three times. Perhaps four, I don't know. Should my cistern be bigger I would not. Because when it's raining a lot, I'm losing a lot. Water is just being spilled in the garden."

❋

One evening we had a long conversation about theology, the significance of John Paul II, whether the next Pope would be Italian (Philippe thought not), and the zone where morality overlaps with politics. "People confuse politics and morality," I asserted.

"You can be a perfect person and be a very bad politician," he said. "You can be very honest, very clever, and not be good at getting people to work together or knowing what they want. You can be a very good person but narrow-minded. You can be not perfect but be a good politician. Not only successful, but serving the community well.

"There is a link," he allowed. "Because if you do not have righteousness, you will be easily corrupted by money or by other people, and it will not be easy to resist following your interest when it is not the same as the interest of your community." He cited four ways Gustave Thibon had articulated to deal with the gap between moral ideals and reality. One was to be a saint. "… And the fourth way, if you are not a saint, is to accept that you cannot live up to your ideals, but not to give them up. Even if the standard is judging you, and judging you guilty."

Shaking hands good night I said, "Interesting evening."

"Yes, but I am not used to talking about such things in Haiti," he replied. "Politics, price of rice, whether the cistern is full or empty …"

"You have an interesting perspective on Haiti," I said, "because you're educated …"

"Well, I had good teachers."

"… and yet you live the nitty-gritty of daily life in Haiti. You take your water from a cistern, for example."

"Yes, but I have a cistern. So I am in the upper part of society."

With Philippe I experienced more directly than before the chronic low-intensity conflict that is daily life in Port-au-Prince. Coming home one evening after drinks at the Montana with his Haitian friend Pierre-Richard Sam, we stopped at a Texaco station on Delmas. "He is stealing the money," said Philippe as he climbed back in behind the wheel of his hardworking jeep. I pay two hundred dollars for the gas, and he gives me one hundred ninety-nine dollars and ninety-nine cents."

He meant 200 notional Haitian dollars. "So I ask for my change." He looked disgusted and put out, in a world-weary, French sort of way.

"Who's stealing? The kid, or the boss?"

"The boss. Because if you look at the machine, it says one hundred ninety-nine dollars and ninety-nine. So it is the boss who is stealing. And first you don't know if it is accurate anyway. *And then* it stops at hundred ninety-nine and ninety-nine."

"So you ask for your change."

"Yes."

Another time, Philippe indicated through the windshield several gas canisters, held in place by heavy nylon strips in the bed of the truck in front of us.

"See the stripe, the nylon stripe?" he said. "It's Seaboard Marine, one of the companies I work for. It's stolen from the wharf. These stripes sell on the street for less than ten dollars. Before, I made a war to try to keep the stevedores from stealing these. But then I decided it was not worth losing my life just to save some nylon stripes."

✳

I had been in Haiti not quite a week when I was robbed. It probably happened sometime between 6:30 p.m. on Friday, July 23, when I returned to the house from a long, sweaty day out in the city, and Saturday morning, when I thought to check my wallet before traveling out of Port-au-Prince. Exactly $100 was missing. It felt like a blow to the gut, and it was disorienting. The precise round figure stolen made me wonder whether I really had been robbed, or whether I had just miscounted my money.

I phoned Philippe at his office. I made a point of speaking in English.

"I left my wallet in my bag in my room," I said, "because it's a pain to keep it on me all the time, and I assumed that as long as I was here at the house, and someone was here who was responsible …" Even as I spoke, I was aware how lame it sounded.

"Yes, but that is not how it works here," said Philippe gently.

For most of the rest of that day, I wanted only to leave Haiti. I went out to the EnergiTek cybercafe up the street to send several distressed emails, then to Petionville. I walked around, with the idea of finding an Air France office so I could change my return date to Miami. I asked some people at a craft gallery for directions. Air France didn't have an office in Petionville, they said, but American Airlines was in the next street. I had nowhere else to go, so I headed there. Walking uphill, I stepped on some flimsy boards covering a big hole in the sidewalk. Even as I fell, I heard a hubbub nearby. As I broke my fall with my left hand on the edge of the hole, I looked up to see a dozen art gallery patrons rushing to my rescue. We always wish afterwards that in the moment we had found the *bon mot*. In this moment, amazingly, I found it. "*C'est ma dignité qui est blessée,*" I announced jauntily to the crowd.

They laughed appreciatively, and a mulatto matron bantered graciously back at me in elegant French, too quick for me to catch fully, something to the effect that not even my dignity was wounded, because *evidemment* I was *trop intelligent* (she pronounced the *p*), or something like that. I feigned full understanding and waved; the lady waved back; we laughed again and went our separate ways. Suddenly, I was in a better mood.

At the American Airlines office, I sat in a plastic chair with the vague and implausible intention of asking the staff there for help with my Air France ticket, drank potable water from the cooler in paper cups, and appreciated the air conditioning. The staff was extremely slow, and waiting was pointless anyway because my ticket was on Air France. I gave up on the idea of changing my flight and walked around some more. There was no haven, no escape, and even Petionville was grimy. I heard "*blanc*" from various sides, in tones that sounded mocking and rude. In Haiti how one responded, and what sort of encounter ensued, depended on one's mood or attitude. Walking back downhill from Place St. Pierre, I took a wrong turn and found myself struggling through a crowded, muddy market. But even as I wallowed in self-pity, I looked around at the women squatting in the mud, offering sorry little bunches of potatoes, onions and carrots, and in the back of my mind it dawned on me to remember that I was among the fortunate.

Philippe returned to the house in the afternoon. I had returned before him and, wiped out, had dozed on the concrete floor of the front porch.

"So, what are you doing?" he asked.

"I'm pouting," I said. "I'm feeling sorry for myself."

He laughed. "You mustn't do that!"

On the phone in the morning, Philippe had offered me a Brufen brand ibuprofen tablet for my headache. Now, he asked if I had found the tablets in his big cardboard box overflowing with semi-legit and out-of-date prescription medicines. I told him I had; there had been one left.

"But there were many more," he said, puzzled.

David was standing around along with a tall, quiet guy named Magloire, whom Philippe introduced as "friend from my work, the most prudent truck driver in Haiti." Philippe had a discussion with them in Creole, then spoke again to me in English.

"Chrisnel, you know, David's elder brother, he gets headaches often," he said. "His health is very weak. So I told him to take Brufen this morning. There were thirteen or fourteen of them. So probably he took more of them. I told David that in French someone who does that is called a thief. Magloire said he is not a thief, because what he took belonged to his employer. *Quel pays!*"

✳

"I am so pissed off," said Philippe one morning, hands on hips. "My chickens are remaining so small. I don't know when we are going to eat them. Three months already! I think I will make a henhouse, so they won't run around so much."

I was feeling low again, I had money worries, a neighbor's radio had kept me up overnight. The disadvantage of electricity was that people took advantage of it to play their radios really loud. Once again, Philippe cheered me up. He urged me to take multivitamins and gave me a ginseng tablet.

"When I was in Washington I bought some things like this, because they are unexpensive in the States," he said. "And I knew I was going to be working these two jobs, and I should have something like this.

We have to be careful about these things, because we are sweating a lot, we are not really eating regularly ..." He indicated his big box full of medicines. "You see, my house is almost like a hospital."

He then told me a story: "One night I was at a party, and one of these boys who I'm paying for his school and this, he came to my house (not this house). He was attacked in the street. He said he fell, but he was attacked. His wrists were cut with a razor blade, almost to the bone. I never saw that before. He came to my house about eleven, but I didn't get home until one, one-thirty. And he was waiting at the back, but after waiting at the front. And I came, and there was so much blood. I went to the back and saw him, and there was this deep of blood, and he says to me, 'I'm weak.'

"It was late at night, and I had no money, and there was no way I could take him to a hospital. So I just gave him water and sugar, and cleaned up his wounds, and put a—"

He gestured.

"A tourniquet?"

"Yes, like a bandage, so the bleeding would stop. And now he's okay, but ... The problem is that in Haiti, when you help someone and if it goes wrong, you are responsible. You have to pay the funeral expenses, and give money to the family. So if it's someone you don't know, and you can't protect yourself by having witnesses, you have to be careful. It's—" He touched his forehead with a forefinger.

I was already feeling better. "I think you've been through a lot more in this country than I'll experience in a month," I said admiringly.

"Yes," he said. "These things are what make life in Haiti interesting. You are never bored."

I was planning to spend a weekend in Jacmel, about three hours away over the ridge of mountains south of Port-au-Prince at the near end of the southern peninsula. To get there you had to go through Léogâne, and you had to get to Léogâne early enough in the day, and you had to hope for a seat on a *publique* van or to hitch a ride. On Friday morning Philippe said to me, "I am taking out my digital camera because I want to take pictures of these *graffiti*—what is the word?"

"It's the same in English," I said.

"Yes, these graffiti that show the confusion of the situation, before they disappear. Making parallels between Jesus and Aristide and like this. And these leftist democrats in the States, these who don't accept that there should be any mixing between the state and religion—" He gestured to indicate Haiti, where politics and religion and everything else was all mixed together in a big mixed-up mess.

"But it's okay for them if religion and the state are mixed in Haiti," I suggested, "because Aristide makes it look like Jesus was a leftist."

"I don't care if Jesus was a leftist or not," he said. "But problem is that when priest become involved in politics, they are bad priest, like anyone they want to hold onto the power, and usually they are bad politicians—with some exceptions, like Richelieu in France, who was a strong politician. Okay, Ethan—"

"Philippe." The way I said it made Josué chuckle.

"See you, I don't know when. If I am going to Santo Domingo and you are going to Léogâne—"

"Yes, see you on Wednesday, I guess." I squatted on the edge of the porch.

"Coordinate with Junior whether you should take a pyube-lique ..."

I planned to spend the weekend visiting a woman named Wendy Goodman, who worked in Jacmel for an NGO called Aid to Artisans. "What do you think of hitchhiking, as Wendy suggested?"

He shrugged. "Should be okay. Just don't do it at night, when you can be perceived as vulnerable. Don't do with your laptop, don't do with your cash. But otherwise, should be okay." He shrugged again and walked toward his jeep.

"Well, if you don't see me on Wednesday," I called to him, "come looking for me on the road to Jacmel."

"We will look for the birds," he said and waved goodbye.

CHAPTER 6

EATING MISERY

I didn't make it to Jacmel, because the opportunity offered itself to visit Cange, the displaced hilltop village above Mirebalais where Dr. Paul Farmer and Partners in Health had established a renowned hospital. Tracy Kidder's book was still recently published, and my friend Kathy Sheetz had urged me to read it and to meet Farmer. I had not yet read the book, because I wanted to meet the man before I read about him.

I called on Father Octave Lafontant, now in his eighties and retired, at the offices of the Episcopal diocese in Petionville. It was from him that I had first heard the name Aristide, in November 1990. I reminded him of what he had said to me: "*Bon-Dieu a choisi Hitler, mais Hitler a trompé Bon-Dieu.*" God chose Hitler, but Hitler deceived God. I found it fascinating that he didn't remember having said this: what to me had been a life-changing insight was to him a throwaway line.

We talked about Aristide. "*Est-ce qu'il va retourner encore?*" I asked. Will he return again?

"*Je ne crois pas,*" he said. "*Ceux qui l'ont retourné avant, c'est vous les americains.*" I don't think so. The ones who returned him before were you, the Americans.

Would there really be new elections?

"*On ne sait pas encore, parce que les candidats ont peur.*" We don't know, because the candidates are afraid.

I asked what he thought of Bush, whose administration had been instrumental in Aristide's overthrow earlier that year.

"*Le petit Bush, pour moi fait bon travail,*" he insisted. "He had a big problem, which is the problem of 11 September. Until now, bin Laden

103

continue to kill the people. When you are a leader, and in one day they kill 3000 of your people, they destroy two of the most important things you have, you have to find them and do something."

I asked his opinion of Farmer.

"*Farmer fait bon travail,*" he assured me. "*Il fait un travail que personne n'avait fait avant.*" He does work that nobody did before. He reminded me that Zanmi Lasante, the Partners in Health operation in Cange, had been built by his brother. I didn't need to be reminded; my father and the Episcopalians from Milwaukee had first worked in Mirebalais more than twenty years earlier, with Father Fritz Lafontant. The years telescoped and I was sixteen again, reading the inscription Fritz Lafontant had written on March 1, 1982, in Mirebalais, in the French Bible that I still have: "*Dieu a un plan pour chaque homme en particulier. La lecture quotidienne de ce livre te permettra de decouvrir le plan de Dieu pour l'humanité.*" In *Mountains Beyond Mountains*, Kidder writes:

> The enterprise in Cange and the surrounding villages was essentially the creation, from scratch, of a public health system, with Pere Lafontant as the construction boss—amazing how quickly and durably he got things built in a place without electricity, stones, or a serviceable road.

"My philosophy is to go to the real people, those who live far in the mountains," Octave was saying. "They have so little things done to make people happy. We have about 90 percent people that the church try to reach. It can be done with people like your father, like us, *qui acceptent dormir à la campagne.*" People who are willing to sleep in the countryside.

He gave me Fritz's home phone number, and it was by calling there and speaking to Madame Lafontant that I was able to arrange to visit Cange. She told me to wait the next morning outside the Television Nationale d'Haïti building at Delmas 33. I got there early and stood in the heat and traffic chaos for at least 45 minutes, becoming increasingly confused and distressed, and annoyed with myself for not getting more specific information: should I have been standing on Avenue Delmas itself, in front of the TV building, or around the corner on Delmas 33? Mme. Lafontant had told me to look for a white pickup with a drum in the back. But would the pickup be coming downhill from the direction of Petionville, or uphill from the city? And did she mean an oil drum, or a musical drum, or what?

Just as I was summoning the nerve to ask a policeman if I could use his cell phone, a man shouted to me across the road, out the window of a pickup going uphill: "*Machine Zanmi Lasante!* Your name is Eh-than!" He turned off Delmas into the side street, and I hopped in.

Before leaving Port-au-Prince we picked up a grey-haired man named Prosper, introduced to me as one of the founders of Zanmi Lasante, and stopped to fill the tank and to buy drinks and snacks. Finally we were on our way out of town. "What is that boat in the road?" I asked. It was a sculpture to commemorate Aristide's return from exile on October 15, 1994. "In fact this is the Route 15 Octobre that you're traveling on," Prosper said, indicating the road. This part of town was Tabarre, where Aristide had lived. The pickup's radio was playing cloying religious songs in English:

Father, we stand before You today
To glorify Your holy name ...
We're gonna praise You
(Praise, praise, praise Your name)

The smooth paved road gave way to gravel and then, in the middle of nowhere, crossing the Plaine du Cul de Sac, was a Texaco station. "That's called Morne Kabrit," Prosper told me, indicating ahead— Goat Mountain, or Mountain of Goats.

"Why is it called Goat Mountain?"

"Because there used to be a lot of goats."

"There aren't many now?"

"Some."

The road was rough and dusty. A female goat strolled across it in front of us. Every once in a while a pickup passed us, its bed crowded with impassive Haitians. Two small boys ran out in front of the truck and alongside, raising their ragged t-shirts and patting their bellies. We began to climb. We passed a *camion* coming down, then another goat. Prosper tapped me on the shoulder from the backseat. "See that goat?" he said. "That's why it's called Goat Mountain."

Another boy, covered in dust, held out his empty hand. By the road-side were low scrub and rocks, and a very few small trees. A youth wearing a Chicago Cubs baseball cap filled holes in the road with a shovel, hoping for spare change from drivers. On the right, a skinny horse and three children stood in the shade of a tree beside a waterhole. Five or six goats skipped across the road.

"*Kabrit, kabrit, kabrit! Ampil kabrit!*" cried Prosper. Lots of goats!

All this took place at about twenty miles per hour, as the truck picked its way over rocks and around and through potholes. We drove through a village, past a cemetery, peasants on donkeys, a woman car-rying a pile of sticks on her head, a big truck piled high with people sit-ting on full sacks under a large but half-dead tree in front of a church. Three teenagers with shovels filled in a large hole with dirt. The driver stopped and gave them a few one-*gourde* coins. "I don't have any more," he told them. A Mercedes four-wheel drive came toward us.

"German," said Prosper. "Good car."

Later, apropos nothing, or maybe continuing a conversation in the backseat, I heard him say: "In the presidential election, if they don't make a good road through the Central Plateau, I'm not going to vote."

✳

That first evening in Cange was when Ti Jean retrieved me from the guest house and I got a double dose of his and Farmer's views on the ouster of Aristide at the end of February. U.S. complicity in Aristide's ouster "would have been so easy to verify," asserted Farmer. "That's who you should talk to: the people who were covering it at the time." A writer in Jamaica named John Maxwell had covered the story much better than the *Miami Herald*, the *Washington Post*, or the *New York Times*. "I happen to go back and forth across the border a lot," said Farmer. "It's not an open border. How did those weapons get across the border? How could this be so uninteresting to the people who are sup-posed to be telling the truth about it?" Ti Jean had been so disgusted by what one *New York Times* reporter had written after interviewing the two of them and expressing sympathy with the poor that he told

Farmer: "Don't ever bring another journalist here. They just heap calumny on our president."

The most fraught and dangerous issue facing Haiti now was the *anciens militaires*, former members of the feared and hated Haitian Army that Aristide had disbanded. These were the men who had captured Gonaïves, Cap Haïtien, and other towns ahead of Aristide's ouster. They had not laid down their arms and were claiming to be the army again, and that the de facto government of prime minister Gerard Latortue owed them back pay. "That was the most stupid thing," Philippe had told me, "to dismiss the army without any pay or anything. Obviously in any Third World, you have to be careful with the army. But immediately Aristide created 20,000 people who were against him. And really, it was state stealing. Because even their pensions, their retirement, were kept and spent for something else." Farmer said now that the *anciens militaires* had announced their intention to overthrow Aristide's government with new U.S. weapons in May 2003, and that they had taken hostage some Zanmi Lasante staff. As recently as two Wednesdays ago he had run into *anciens militaires* at midnight, returning from a meeting in the nearby town of Hinche.

"All this so-called rebellion really was," he said, "was small groups of heavily armed former military coming in and killing policemen, judges, representatives of the elected government of Haiti. They killed five policemen in Mirebalais. How many policemen could there have been? I'm speculating that they killed more than half of the entire police force in one fifteen-minute period." Against the rebels' automatic weapons, the police officers each had one sidearm.

"In December 2002, we had gone to try and open up an operating room on the border, in a hospital at Belladere," he told me. "It's actually a nice operating room, but it had just been closed for eleven years. I was going for another reason, to do a training with some community health workers in Las Cahobas. And with me was an American documentary filmmaker named David Murdock. Off we went to Las Cahobas, and then to Belladere. And we went to see how things were going in the operating room, and it was very busy, and the Cubans and Haitians were there, and it made me very happy to see the place bustling.

"But I had a patient to see in Cange. So in the afternoon I left, and on the way back there was a patient in the backseat, myself, Ti Jean in the front seat, just the three of us, I think. We saw a group of these former military people setting up a roadblock, which we figured they'd activate at night. One of them had a name tag. It said 'Fletcher,' which is not a common Haitian name. And since our team was coming back later on, after dark, we tried to get a message back to them to have David Murdock hide his camera, because I left him there in Belladere to try to film one of the operations.

"We got to Las Cahobas, sent a message back by the Internet, never reached them and, sure enough, they were stopped at an armed roadblock. And David Murdock fortunately hid his camera. They put guns to their heads, and threatened to kill them, and said they were former military and they were going to overthrow Aristide for illegally dismantling the army, etcetera, etcetera. These are medical people, and they said, 'Well, we're not involved in this. We're just medical people: doctors and nurses.' There was actually one funny line: there was a French guy there who had been working with us, and he said, 'I'm French. I know nothing about Haitian history.' Which made everyone laugh later. I like that line. In any case, they didn't take David Murdock's camera; it was hidden. It was an expensive piece of equipment. And they came home, and they told me this story. And I said, 'Well, I'm sorry that that happened to you, David, but there's been a lot of this recently.' And we promptly forgot about it, because you just do forget about it, to stay sane.

"Well, about three days later there's an article in the *Miami Herald*. It was about these rebels who killed these cops, etcetera, and 'allegedly' threatened a medical team from Partners in Health. And she interviews a guy who's the head of the NCHR, the National Coalition for Haitian Rights, who's notoriously anti-Aristide, right-wing, and he says, 'Well, allegedly they were harassing medical officials, but that's just pro-government propaganda.'

"Someone sent it to me, and I chuckled ruefully, thinking, 'Par for the course in reporting on Haiti.' And I sent it to the American filmmaker, and I said, 'Hey David, how do you like having your near-brush with death dismissed as pro-government propaganda?' Well, he wasn't amused at all. He was pissed, and he wrote a letter to the *Miami Herald* saying, 'I'm a card-carrying journalist, whatever, and this is not allegedly nor pro-government propaganda.' And they published his letter, and you can find them both.[1] The event, and the reporting on it, and the correction by David Murdock—it just stands for the whole sorry, wretched last fourteen years of reporting on Haiti.

"That's what it's been like for us the last three years, because Bush—unelected—overthrows Aristide—elected. Haitians see symmetry: Bush I overthrows Aristide I, Bush II overthrows Aristide II. What incentive do the Haitian people have to vote again?"

"Every time we elect someone, he gets kidnapped," said Ti Jean.

"This is a fucking outrage," added Farmer. "Sorry for swearing. It's been a tough three years."

I told Farmer and Ti Jean that I would write honestly, but that not many Americans wanted to read such things.

"Even if they don't want to read it, he should write it," said Ti Jean to Farmer. "Tracy Kidder is the only one who has written about these things."[2]

---

1 The article, "Haitian government says ex-soldiers mount insurgency" by Jane Regan, was published in the *Miami Herald* of December 21, 2002. In his letter, published in the *Herald* of January 13, 2003, Murdock wrote:

> As we stood in the road, hands in the air, guns pointed at our heads, they lectured us about President Aristide having disbanded the Haitian army. They vowed that they would fight to return the military to power. After this anti-Aristide harangue, they ordered us back into our Jeep, and we continued on our way. The article voiced the views of those who doubted that such incidents were occurring, but I experienced it.

Murdock sent a similar letter to the U.S. Embassy in Port-au-Prince.

---

2 I was to learn that even Kidder was vulnerable to the vicissitudes of American publishing. When the Clinton administration decided not to monitor the 2000 presidential election in Haiti on the basis that that May's legislative elections had been flawed, Kidder sought an outlet for an op-ed piece. An editor at the Wall Street Journal told him: "We'd very much like you to give us a piece on what the peasants think. But we couldn't possibly publish anything that's in favor of Aristide."

"I was pretty taken aback," Kidder told me in September 2004. "*The New York Times* was much more receptive to the kind of thing I wanted to write. I think we

"You were good enough to read that piece in the *London Review of Books*," said Farmer. "First of all, the Haitian military was dissolved by legal acts of the Haitian parliament, after a poll conducted by the Oscar Arias Foundation showed that the majority of Haitians felt that the military should be dissolved. Now why wouldn't they, since the Haitian Army, in eighty years, has never had a non-domestic enemy? They've never been involved in any conflict or war. Only the Haitian people have been their enemy. And the modern Haitian Army was founded by an act of U.S. Congress, in Washington. It was during the American occupation that the army was founded. So not surprisingly, there's not a lot of popular support for an army that has only the Haitian population as its enemy and was founded during a military occupation. But I betcha Oscar Arias would be happy to talk to you about it. I can't believe the sloppiness of journalists who never mention these things, and never want to talk to people like Senator Chris Dodd or Oscar Arias."

I asked why he had written the *London Review of Books* article.

"I thought, 'Poor Haiti, man.' I was watching the spectacle of the dailies every day, with growing anxiety I might add, because it was a very dangerous time, and seeing so much inaccuracy in the reporting. And then, of course, the architects of this plan to unseat the elected government of Haiti knew that shutting off all aid to Haiti, in a country this poor, would probably do the trick with a little push from arming the former military. They didn't arm themselves; they're not weapons manufacturers. Somebody had to be paying for it; they had no money.

"And to watch this all sort of in slow motion, from rural Haiti— because it was in the Central Plateau where all of this was based. And, you know, having gone through harassment of our staff, and losing patients who were murdered by these people, I figured okay, now they've had their way, they overthrew the elected government. Poor Haiti. No English-speaking, English-writing person is going to write about the connivance of the great powers in doing what they've done so many times in Haiti, which is assisting in the trampling of the will of the majority. And the majority of course here, that's the poor majority.

---

have something different now, something much worse. The reporting I saw during the latest coup was very one-sided. What they were saying was that there's only one side to this. And I think there's no question it was a coup."

"Peter Hallward was invited to write the piece. There were two options open to the two of us: one in the *New Left Review*, and one in the *London Review of Books*. And he figured I could write it more quickly since I was down here, in the thick of it. We switched projects. His piece, which is actually much better and more detailed than mine, came out some months later.[3] I was trying to get something out there quickly in English. I knew it wouldn't end up in an American publication. Brian"—Brian Concannon, an American lawyer close to Haitian grassroots movements—"was the one who did all the fact-checking. I took out anything that I couldn't buttress with seventy pages of footnotes."

❋

Two mornings later after breakfast, I sat outside the refectory and watched men working on the top story of Zanmi Lasante's new school. Four men stood one above the other on a two-story homemade ladder, facing outward, handing pails of cement up to a man in a straw hat standing at the top, who dumped them and handed them back down.

As I watched, I struck up a conversation with a soft-spoken young man sitting near me. He was Jean-Michel Robuste, 24 years old, from Les Cayes on the south coast. He also worked on this construction crew; yesterday he had built that metal staircase over there.

"*Dangereux*?" I asked him.

"*Oui*," he cheerfully agreed.

Jean-Michel liked basketball. "Michael Jordan," he said. "Kobe Bryant. Shaquille O'Neal."

"Shaquille O'Neal now plays for Miami," I said.

"*Oui*," said Jean-Michel. "Miami 'Eat. I like *Liqueurs*—*équipe* Kobe Bryant."

"*Oui*, but Lakers are going down now," I said. "Shaquille left, Kobe left, coach left."

"*Oui*. Chicago is down too."

Jean-Michel told me he liked Les Cayes better than Cange, because it was more developed and was on the sea. But he thought Zanmi

---

3 Peter Hallward, "Option Zero in Haiti," *New Left Review 27*, May-June 2004.

Lasante was terrific. "*Mwen renmen Zanmi Lasante ampil ampil ampil,*" he said. I like Zanmi Lasante a lot a lot a lot.

"Why?"

"It's an organization that helps a lot of people," he said. "It gives people health and development."

"What do you think of Aristide?"

"He's a president who was struggling on behalf of the poor masses. You understand? Who didn't take the side of the *bourgeoisie*. The *bourgeois* parties and other parts of the private sector got together and destabilized him and sent him into exile. He's a good president."

"Do you think he'll come back?"

"I suppose he could, but not so long as Bush is president. If John Kerry is president, I think he could return."

I asked him about the *anciens militaires.*

"*Se granmoun ki renmen yo,*" he said. "It's the big people who like them. They've created disorder."

"Who gave them arms?"

"My opinion is that it was the brother of Georges Bush." Jeb Bush was the governor of Florida at the time.

"Who do you want to win the U.S. election?"

"John Kerry."

"Why?"

"He would be better for—for the world. I suppose that a Democratic president would not make wars. Many people have died because of Bush. Look at Pakistan, look at Iraq, same as Haiti. Many people have died because Georges Bush is president."

I found Jean-Michel's views representative on the Central Plateau. Ti Jean ran a program to provide better houses to Zanmi Lasante's poorest patients. I spent a day with his assistant, Wilfrid, walking along the road toward Hinche looking at some of these. Zanmi Lasante paid a local boss, who employed local workers to build sturdy new cement houses with leakproof corrugated metal roofs, painted in the pastels Haitian peasants favored. The indigent patients, suffering from diseases such as HIV and tuberculosis, paid nothing. Sometimes the derelict old house, usually of wood with banana leaf thatching, was torn down;

sometimes it was left and used until it fell down.

Every so often a truck would pass us coming from Hinche. Some were brightly painted *publiques* with seats inside. Others were piled high with sacks, with a dozen or so Haitians perched uncomfortably on top, fully exposed to the sun. At one point we passed some people accompanying a sick woman. Several men carried her on their shoulders in a makeshift litter, shaded with a cloth like a bedsheet.

"Are they going to Zanmi Lasante?" I asked Wilfrid.

"*Oui*," he said. "Zanmi Lasante is the only resource in this area."

The woman at one house, some minutes' walk off the road and down a hillside, invited us to sit down and gave us small ears of roasted corn. We amused ourselves by throwing pebbles, which a skinny little brown *chienne de pays* retrieved and chewed on. Wilfrid threw two rocks at a time in different directions to confuse her.

It was here that Wilfrid wrong-footed me by asking, "What do you think of Aristide?"

"He's not my president," I said. "I'm not Haitian. What do you think of him?"

"If there's any person in Cange who is against Aristide, I don't know him," he said. The woman and her male companion nodded.

"In Port-au-Prince I've talked to many *bourgeois*," I said. "They don't like Aristide."

"The *bourgeois* haven't liked Aristide since 1990. And the *blancs* haven't liked him either. They kidnapped him."

"Why?"

"No idea."

"Who?"

"You know the people already: Bush, Jacques Chirac. They didn't give their reasons. Bush kidnapped Aristide. He was elected for five years. His five years weren't over yet. Commandos came to his house at midnight. It's a crime."

"Bush and others say Aristide is *méchant*," I said. "That he's the same as Duvalier, that he has *chimères*"—armed partisan thugs. "That he killed many people."

"Good Americans don't say that. Americans who are Haitian. Paul

113

Farmer isn't an American, because he loves Haitians a lot. I don't like criminals. But the American people are innocent and generous. They want to give. We like them for that."

✳

I spent four days in Cange. I intended to continue overland to Cap Haïtien via Hinche, on a road everyone told me was nearly impassable. I wanted to do it to prove I could do it, and to stay on the ground. But it was time for Farmer to make his monthly trip to Harvard, and he invited me to ride down to the airport with him. We left from his house around 7:30 a.m. Farmer drove; he said that if he didn't, he got carsick. I sat beside him in the front passenger seat. He stopped more than once to talk to peasants who hailed him. "They're saying I'm too *doux*—soft," he said, referring to Ti Jean and two other Haitians in the backseat. "They say I should get upset and swear more."

"Yeah, that helps," I said.

"This is the land of swearing and getting upset. The last thing it needs is me adding my little contribution in that area."

He told me he had rethought some of the strong assertions in his book *The Uses of Haiti*. "What was fundamentally incorrect was exaggerating the agency of a president," he said. "I hadn't realized just how vulnerable Haiti was to changes within the U.S. government. The world is clearly very fucked up. And it can be cruel, and you and I are the beneficiaries of this system. I get no more confident, as time goes by, that I can figure it out."

I suggested that, regardless, it's preferable to be wounded by experience of the world than to be sheltered from it.

"Yes, of course," he replied. "Because to be wounded is to acknowledge the truth, whereas to be sheltered is to be oblivious. But it's permanent, and it's incurable."

I mentioned V. S. Naipaul, a talented and sensitive writer who had been an early role model of mine because he put a premium on experience and observation, but who had eventually succumbed to the blandishments of his many toadies.

"You just can't be that way if you're living in a place like this," said

Farmer. "Because every day you wake up, you go to the clinic, you do your work, and you see evidence of your failure. Last night at about 11 o'clock a woman and her 13-year-old daughter showed up at our house, just saying, 'I'm hungry. I haven't eaten in two days.' If you've been working on poverty and hunger issues for twenty-something years, and you're not making progress on some fronts, I think it does keep you humble. Knowing that the world is so dented and damaged must be humiliating, if not humbling—one or the other. If you cocoon yourself away from misery, then you can be delusional about how great and praiseworthy you are. But living in a place like this—look at this road. Look at the way these people are transported on these vehicles."

I had always felt a strong, even urgent vocation as a writer, but I struggled with how intangible and seemingly ineffectual my work often seemed. Why write, if it makes no difference in the world, especially given how solitary and isolating it can be?

"Writers unfortunately often do have to cocoon themselves just to do their work," he granted. "They can't be out there having people pulling at their sleeves and saying they're hungry. They have to write."

"But first they have to go out into the world," I said. "The writers I admire the most are the ones who don't just sit in their cocoons and write, but go out into the world. One of my greatest heroes is Greene."

"I was just going to say," said Farmer. "He's my favorite writer. I suspect it takes a lot of discernment and humility, even if you're proud of your writing like I think he was, looking for simplicity and straight-forward prose, but at the same time you have to go out. If you look at his early stuff, though, like *Journey without Maps* with his cousin in Africa, it's really kinda *bwana*-ish. And then the later stuff—people think he got more political, and they're more dismissive of him. I just think he got more informed. Liberation theology figures in several of his later books, and I think he really retained that humility. Also, his characters are really people who are not sure if they're ever going to get it right. They're not confident in their analyses of the world."

"Look at Fowler in *The Quiet American*."

"Yeah, yeah."

"What do you think of *The Comedians*?"

"Well, *The Comedians* is maybe his first political book. And *The Quiet American* came before it, so that's saying something, right? *The Comedians* is where the 'locals'—Africans, Vietnamese, whatever, in this case Haitians—start to come out. And there's a very full-bodied character in there, Dr. Magiot, who is a physician and a Marxist. I think he compares favorably to previous characters who are African or Asian, because they're sort of cardboard cutouts. Even in *The Power and the Glory* or in—" He became self-conscious. "I'm passing myself off as a literary critic."

"Doctors make more money than literary critics do," I joked.

"I make more chickens," he said. "I scored a chicken yesterday afternoon in clinic. I also make more coconuts."

"What do you do with the chickens and coconuts?"

"I eat them! Because I'm going away today, I won't get to eat this chicken. They might save it for me. It's tied up with a little string on its poor little ankle. It's shitting all over my tiny little back porch."

At his house he had told me where he had been on September 11, 2001, and I asked him now to repeat the full story.

"There was a little—there is a little girl, still is, thank God, named Maveline, and she had a treatable childhood malignancy named Wilm's tumor. But by the time she was diagnosed in Cange by a wonderful Haitian-American doctor named Carole Smarth, she already had metastatic lesions in her lungs. So what you can do is just take out the infected kidney, and it's curative. But in this case it was not; she would need chemotherapy. So she went up to Boston for a little while to get chemo and radiation. She ended up being there the better part of a year. "And first her father was there with her, and he's a trip. He almost got me booted out of that apartment at Harvard because I asked him to water the plants, and he had never watered plants indoors, so he just turned the hose on 'em. Second-floor apartment. Anyway, then he kind of went off his rocker and came back here, and his wife, Maveline's mother, went up there. And she's a really wonderful person. I mean, he was wonderful too in his own way, but she is very salt of the earth, sane. And she happened to be in the United States on September 11.

"And Carole Smarth, who was then in New York, came up to see

Maveline. She loved Maveline, and she came up and got them for a weekend in New York. On September 10 they went to the World Trade Center. Carole was trying to show them the sights in New York. And Maveline's mother said, 'I'm not going up there. That's just too absurdly tall a building.' That night, September 10, they came back to Boston. I was leaving in the morning to go to a meeting at the Centers for Disease Control in Atlanta.

"They got in at about one in the morning, Maveline and her mother. Actually, Carole drove them all the way back up from New York. And I went off to a thesis defense, and it finished at about ten in the morning. By then, of course, the planes had already crashed into the buildings. We didn't know about it; we were off in a thesis defense. Later on I went to the hospital. We didn't know: maybe our services would be required. Unfortunately, they were not. When I went back to the apartment, I started thinking: What on earth are my Haitian guests going to think about this horrific event? I also had a Cuban visitor, a scientist who's the daughter of a friend of mine. She had been there for a while too, studying at Harvard. It was the three of them: one Cuban, the Haitian girl, and the Haitian peasant woman. They all got along fine. They spoke to each other in this sort of weird Esperanto.

"I was supposed to be gone. I came back with my luggage. The airports were closed. And the Haitian woman said, '*Pov djab, kounye-a blan-yo ap manje misè pa-yo tou.*' Poor foreigners, now you're going to have to eat your own misery too. I thought a lot about what she said, and there are many ways to interpret it. It was obviously sincere sympathy for us, but the point she was making was that this is the way the rest of the world is: always subject to hazard and danger and violence, and your country's been largely spared that. I didn't ask her, 'Is that what you meant?' Her daughter at the time was five, and she was watching Teletubbies. The Cuban was glued to the TV, and I was too. But I never asked her, 'Is this what you meant?' I know that's what she meant."

We were down out of the mountains now, nearing the airport. "Do I have time to ask you a couple of other things on tape?" I asked.

"If you're quick."

I started fiddling with the buttons on my temperamental minidisk recorder. "So you've done this drive a few times …"

"If I had a nickel …"

We had talked about how jarring it was for him to make the journey between Cange and Harvard every month. "To make that trip as often as you do is probably good for the soul," I suggested.

"I thought you didn't believe in souls," he teased. I had told him that one of the good things about being raised Episcopalian was that you don't get the heavy guilt trip. "Yeah, but the Episcopalians need it," he had rejoined.

"I'm not an economist," he said now. "Nor do I play one on TV. But if you look at the experts, they say that starting in 1980 the indices of economic disparity between rich countries and poor countries have grown very dramatically. This is true within countries, and it's true between countries. But I can't imagine a single more startling leap than from rural Haiti to American affluence. That's got to be sort of the number one, one-stop-shopping trip, right? From Cange to Miami, where I'm going right now. So if the economists are correct, and I'm sure they are, that the gap between the rich and poor is growing, then obviously the gap between my one-day travel between rural destitution and urban affluence in the United States is growing too. And I'm not recounting it that way because it has anything to do with me, or because my own experience of it is significant. I'm just saying, you know, as this continues, this process of widening gaps between rich and poor—it's violent. It's not the violence that you see spectacularly, like a terrorist attack or a war. But it's violent to people, to know that there are some people that are so rich, and they're so poor. It's violent to be hungry when others are throwing away food. That's what I meant about it being jarring.

"Don't get me wrong. I may go to the movies tonight. And I much prefer urban affluence to rural poverty and not having hot water and all that stuff. To say nothing of being even close to people who are hungry. I told you about the woman who came to my house last night at 11 o'clock, whose chief complaint, as we say in medicine, was that she and her daughter had not eaten in two days. But it feels violent to go from such squalor to such excess, you know?"

CHAPTER 7

Meeting Mr. Clean

Philippe's friend Gerald Oriol Jr. belonged to an elite Haitian family and had a business selling potable water. He had muscular dystrophy and was confined to a wheelchair. His legs were twisted and useless; he could move his arms, but not easily or very effectively. When I first met Ti Gerald, at a party Philippe had taken me to, I made myself useful by fetching a second helping of food for him and pushing his Coke to the edge of the table so he could sip it through a straw. I spent most of the party talking to him.

"Are you a Republican or a Democrat?" he had asked me.

"I'm anti-Bush," I confessed.

He smiled. He had a nice smile. "So there is a Nader factor with you!"

"No!" I replied, horrified. "I'm anti-Nader too."

I found Gerald good company: likeable and intelligent and interested in the world. He lent me his copy of *When States Fail: Causes and Consequences* by Robert I. Rotberg. He told me he was twenty-four years old. We met again, for lunch on the balcony at Muncheez restaurant in Petionville. Gerald came to Philippe's house in his pickup driven by his personal driver, whose duties included gently carrying him from the passenger seat to his wheelchair and back. Gerald asked me to help the driver carry him up and down the long staircase at Muncheez. I thought of how vulnerable someone in Gerald's situation must be in a place like Haiti. But he said he preferred Haiti to Florida, where dealing with the American social service bureaucracies was just too frustrating and demeaning.

We talked about the U.S. election. "Who do you think is going to win?" I asked.

"Kerry," he said.

"Really?"

"Yeah, because I think Bush has made too many mistakes. Though I must admit I would still prefer to see a Bush victory. It would better serve Haiti at this point. Currently, the administration seems to be interested in making the transition work. And I fear that the departure of a Republican administration might mean a change of policy and eventual return of Aristide. However, I believe the fact that the stabilization force is officially under UN command will make it difficult for any administration to fully reconsider the United States policy toward Haiti."

"So how do you think the U.S. or the UN or whoever is going to manage things in Haiti?"

"It is tough to provide a clear answer. However, it is obvious that the U.S. will be very much involved in defining policies, even though the UN is technically leading the stabilization force."

Then he had a question for me: "What is your opinion of the coup d'etat?" He meant the 1991 coup, the first ouster of Aristide.

"I wasn't here," I said carefully. "What is your opinion?"

"Although I was only eleven years old at the time, I enjoyed listening to the news, and I tried my best to understand the situation. I think the coup was wrong. I was personally opposed to stances taken by Aristide, but he was popular at the time and had an indisputable mandate from the population. There might have been some irregularities in the election, but he clearly won by a large margin."

"So you think he should have been allowed to serve out his term?"

"Yeah. The army and his political opponents should have compelled him to follow the democratic process. For instance, his movements should have been restricted, and he should have been compelled to soften his rhetoric and positions. There's no doubt that Aristide is difficult to work with, but they should at least have tried."

"The only problem with your theory," I said, "is that surely Aristide would never have agreed to be a puppet."

"Yeah, but they had to give it a shot. They should have tried to control Aristide and at the same time get a handle on the situation in Haiti. Undoubtedly, the opposing forces were not homogeneous or in full agreement. For instance, some members of the army clearly were pro-Lavalas, but probably most were not. It was a tough time, but I still think they had the resources to sustain Aristide."

"To sustain Aristide?"

"Yeah, to sustain him. Unfortunately, the historical path of coup d'état was followed. I think they lacked a clear vision and leadership. Before Aristide, a similar path was followed with many leaders who themselves had oftentimes come to power through coups."

"They didn't see how Aristide was different."

"They didn't see the difference. As hostile and unpleasant as Aristide might have been, we still should have followed a democratic process in 1991."

I asked him about Marc Bazin, the "American candidate" who had polled a distant second to Aristide in the 1990 election. Bazin was now in his early seventies, and the party he headed was a small one.

"Bazin is still an important player in the political arena in Haiti," Gerald said. "In 1990, he probably would have won if Aristide had not been a candidate."

"Where did the decision come from for Aristide to run? Was it his own decision, or was he pushed into it?"

"He had wide-ranging support in Haiti at the time, but ultimately the decision was probably his own. I sometimes find it difficult to understand why people supported him in the first place. I can understand how the masses were manipulated: he was a charismatic leader, and throughout most of Haiti's history they have been ignored by the political class. But I cannot understand why educated people supported him."

"What's your guess?"

"My guess is that people were frustrated with the political class. And this innocent-looking little priest, with his big glasses"—he laughed and gestured, moving his spindly arms up to frame his own eyes— "signified change and hope for a better future. However, even in the beginning he was belligerent. Oftentimes he tried to foment political crisis, and he never genuinely aimed to reconcile Haitian society. Have you ever heard his speech '*Ba-yo sa-a yo merite*'? 'Give them what they deserve.' Inciting his partisans to attack people opposing him. I believe it was filmed. He gave that speech I think a week or so before the coup."

*

I gladly accepted Gerald's offer to use his contacts to get me an interview with Bazin, and when I checked in with him after my ride down the mountain with Farmer, it had been arranged. The morning of the day of the meeting, at Philippe's house, David saw me putting on a long-sleeved collared shirt. He made a facial expression indicating that he was impressed, as if I were wearing a three-piece suit.

"I have a *rendezvous* this afternoon," I explained.

"With whom?"

"Marc Bazin."

He raised his eyebrows.

"What questions do you think I should ask him?"

"He's the *ancien président*?"

"He was a candidate, against Aristide in 1990."

David thought for a long moment. "Ask him if, according to him, since the coup d'état"—he meant not the 1991 coup, but Aristide's departure on February 29, 2004—"the country is doing better or worse. And what advice would he give to the group that has replaced Aristide?"

"David," I asked, "are you for Aristide or against him?"

"I'm not for Aristide, but I'm not for the others either. Both the Aristide group and the group against Aristide do the same things. What they say the other group does, they do too."

"Do you think Aristide is honest?"

"He's honest to the *chimères*." His partisan vigilantes. "He gives them money to kill people. Then he gives the police money to kill the *chimères*."

"Have you ever met Aristide?"

"No. I don't have the power to meet Aristide."

"If you had the opportunity to meet Aristide, what would you say to him?"

"I would say, 'You don't have a conscience.'"

"David, this year's coup d'état—was it a coup d'état?"

"*Oui*. Aristide was supposed to stay in for five years, so it was a coup d'état."

"Who forced him out?"

"The people who are against him. For example, the Group of 184." *Groupe cent quatre-vingt quatre.* The Group of 184 was a "civil society" coalition led by the wealthy businessman Andy Apaid.

"And Guy Philippe?" Guy Philippe was one of the most ambitious and notorious leaders of the *anciens militaires*.

"*Oui.*"

"*États-Unis*?" The United States?

"*Oui.*"

David still didn't like Aristide, though. "I don't think he deserved to be president," he said.

"But he was elected," I said.

"*Oui*, he was elected. But that was because he gave the people *bel pawol*." Beautiful words.

"*Li menti*?" He lied?

"*Oui.*"

"Did you ever support Aristide?"

"Never. I can tell when someone is lying, and I noticed that when he said he was going to do something, he wouldn't do it. He's a liar. I pray to God for a president who will be better than Aristide."

"Will there be one?"

"I don't know. When Aristide was in, there was *grangou*"—hunger—"and no security. Now there's still *grangou*, but there is security. The country needs jobs. If there is work there won't be thieves, because if a man has work he won't steal."

✳

"Sorry I'm late," said Gerald when he arrived to pick me up. "I didn't have any credit on my phone, so I couldn't call you to say that I would be a half hour late. The reason is because I got stuck in a traffic jam. Also, I left late."

"That's all right," I said. "I actually like it when other people are late for appointments with me, because it gives me the moral high ground. Usually I'm the one who's late."

He laughed. "It happens all too often in Haiti. If someone has an appointment with you at eight o'clock, don't be surprised if he shows up at nine o'clock. Usually, I'm the one on time. If I have a meeting at eight, I try to arrive at 7:45."

As we rode Gerald asked, "So, did you meet Paul Farmer?"

"Yes," I said. "I spent several days with him. I came down the mountain with him on Wednesday." I paused. "What do you want to know about him?"

"Is he as radical as everyone thinks he is?"

"I think his perspective is affected by the fact that he lives in the countryside and almost never comes to Port-au-Prince," I said tactfully.

We stopped to pick up Gerald's friend Patrick Michel, who was the general secretary of Bazin's political party, the Mouvement pour l'Instauration de la Democratie en Haïti. As we waited, the French-language Radio Metropole news came on. The lead item was on Iraq.

"I heard there's been a big battle in Iraq," I said.

"Yes," said Gerald. "Apparently there were 300 casualties. But they're claiming there were only 36 casualties."

"Who's claiming that?"

"The al-Sadr people."

"I wonder how many Americans have been killed."

"I think four. Three Marines and one soldier."

Patrick Michel was dark-skinned, garrulous, humorous—someone you could like easily and quickly. Gerald's mention of Paul Farmer prompted me to say to Patrick, as we rode up the mountain toward the affluent neighbourhood where Bazin lived, that all the peasants I had met in the Central Plateau still supported Aristide. "I wonder how that gap can be bridged in the next election, without bringing back up all the problems this country has had over the last thirteen years," I said.

"You can't ask someone who is hungry to make a choice," he said.

"Why not?"

"In Haiti there are seventy or eighty political parties. None of them have a program. In Haiti, as in most countries, such things are decided by the elite. They reach a consensus—political parties, civil society. In Haiti we have a habit of not paying taxes. Any state has to run on taxes. If a party announces a policy on taxes that is fair, it will not be able to get finance."

"Because the people with money won't give any money to it."

"That's right."

The garden of Bazin's house in the suburb of Thomassin, well uphill from Petionville, was lush with hanging plants, small trees, and red, pink and yellow flowers. Other plants flourished on a balcony, and a healthy Chow dog greeted us. The day was overcast and cool up here, and the mountainside opposite was mostly covered in cloud.

"It's a lovely garden," I remarked.

"Yes," said Patrick. "This is Madame Bazin's hobby. She is very good in that. It's amazing. They've been in this house for one year. After two or three months, you can see!"

"It's impressive," I said again.

"And you know, this neighborhood is a very calm neighborhood. You know, Marc Bazin is a man who uses his brain to work. So he needs peace."

We chatted for a few minutes on the porch as we waited. "Marc Bazin is a clean guy, very clean," said Patrick. "Anti-corruption."

"He's Mr. Clean," I said, invoking his well-known sobriquet.

"Mr. Clean," he agreed. He reminded me that, after a successful career with the World Bank, Bazin had returned to Haiti in 1982 to be Minister of Finance under Baby Doc Duvalier, but that he had lasted only four months in that role. "You will not find many government that can live with him for very long time."

Bazin met us on the porch. "*Comment allez-vous?*" he said warmly, and led us into his lounge. Gerald sat across the room so he could see all three of us from his wheelchair. Patrick held the microphone while I interviewed Bazin in English.

"Elections are meant to take place in late 2005," I said. "Do you think that's going to happen?"

"The whole idea that elections can normalize the situation, and make everybody feel confident that things are going to get better, is a bit naïve," said Bazin. "But apart from that, at issue is how the current transition is going to go. For decent elections to take place, we would have to have a decent transition. Which means in my view something completely inclusive, not exclusive. And what we see now is a government that is trying to help itself, not help the transition. For me a transition should be a national affair, not a family affair. The way it is going on now is going to be conducive to further polarization."

"Can you be any more specific?"

"Say we have an election in which Lavalas doesn't participate. Where do you go from there? You're back to square one. What we should have done is really call everybody around the table and say, 'Listen, guys, Aristide is not there. We don't know how he went. Some people say he was kidnapped, some people say that he resigned. Well, let's assume either of the two. Let's see where we go from now. Because if we don't, it's going to reverse and go back.' What we are seeing now is a scenario that is being played without the principal character. Aristide is gone, and the same scenario is being continued, and I have never seen a scenario like that! Where the principal character is out, and the film doesn't end, it just continues. So therefore we should have gone back to the new situation and say, 'Okay, now the principal character is gone, what kind of scenario are we going to write?' That's not what happened."

"You're saying the principal character has to come back," I said. "There has to be a sequel to the movie."

"Or you have to change the script!"

"How could the script be changed in Haiti, especially given that almost all the poor in this country still believe in and not only support Aristide, but see him as their hero?"

"I think that you have to go back to the basics, which is: What kind of country do we Haitians want? There was something bad about Aristide. He thought that he had all the solutions, that he was *the* solution by himself. And even he, if he were to participate again in government, would have to call everybody around the table. I mean, there is no solution without that."

"Could he do that?"

"I don't know. It's something that only he can answer."

"You know him," I said. "You've worked with him."

"Yes, I've known him, and like all Haitians, we've seen that this is a man with enormous charisma, with enormous power on the poor people. He has the capacity to promise a lot of things. But he's not able to deliver. Precisely one of the reasons is that he thought he could do it by himself."

"Is he arrogant?"

"Well, you know, absolute power corrupts absolutely."

I told him about my conversation with Father Octave Lafontant just before the 1990 election. "If Aristide had not run in that election, surely you would have won it," I said. "And how would the history of the country have turned out differently?"

"Well, we would have saved ten years," said Bazin. "In 1990, had I been president, I would have called upon all the Haitians to realize the objectives, the challenges that we have before us. I would never pretend to say, 'Well, you know, I am a saint, the people want me, and then I do as I please.' For the last ten years Aristide has been under the pressure of the International Monetary Fund to restructure the economy, and the deficits have been going up and up and up, balance of payments have been deficit up and up and up. And no dent against poverty. We are getting poorer every year. So when he said, 'We're going to have *la paix*,' you know, the peace in the belly, he just was not taking the means by which he could achieve that."

"Do you think that if you had been president, you would have been able to be accepted by the poor and also keep all the factions of the political class ..."

"We have to assume that if I had been president, it is because I would have had the majority. Or some kind of majority. But obviously the ideal solution for all serious observers, starting with Jimmy Carter, Francisco Peña Gomez, Carlos Andres Perez, the obvious solution was for Aristide to call Bazin and make him prime minister. People told him repeatedly, 'You want the good of your country, you are the popular man, he seems to know what he is talking about, he's a good man basically, he can help you do it.'"

"But Aristide didn't want to work with the elite at all, did he?"

"He had people from the elite working with him: he had Malval, he had all the priests. No, he's an autocrat. He believes he's the Messiah. He had the message, and he was the one to whom God wanted to deliver the message, and that was it. You can't run such a poor country like that, under extreme circumstances."

"As controversial and problematic as he was, don't you think it would have been better if he had not left the country earlier this year?"

"The solution that the OAS [Organization of American States] had concocted was a good one. In other words, let's stay with Aristide for two more years and achieve his constitutional term. In the meantime we have the opposition get in, and we form a coalition government, with an electoral commission that is independent of the current government, which is at that time Aristide, and then stabilize the political situation for the next two years. That was a solution. I agreed to it, I made it known that this is what I wanted, and most of the people in the opposition said, 'No, Aristide has no cause whatsoever. We don't even want to hear about this man, even if he's prepared to cut a deal, we don't trust him, we're not going to sit with him.'"

"Surely that's understandable on their part, because he had alienated so many people," I suggested.

"That's not the issue, Ethan. The issue is, are you in politics? I mean, why should he believe the other guys? If there is a crisis of confidence, it's both ways. But you have to have markers by which you're going to explore how serious the other guy is. If you just start with the feeling that 'I can't trust him,' and that becomes psychological, it becomes magic, it becomes irrational, and then you go nowhere.

"Have a look at the security situation. It's incredible what is going on here at the moment. Large parts of the country are not under the control of the government. You have an accord that was signed between the government and some people. We don't know what they are doing. There is a so-called *comité de suivi*, we don't know what it is. And there is a so-called *conseil des sages*. We don't know if they are *sages* and what they are doing either. And then you have now the CEP"—the Provisional Electoral Council—"which is completely in disarray. And there is another *comité de suivi* that's even to look over the shoulders of the CEP. So institutionally speaking, it's complete chaos.

"And you have all the donors meeting in Washington, doing something that I have never seen in all my life. I spent eighteen years at the World Bank. I have never seen donors give more money than you ask for. That tells me a lot, believe me. So obviously, we are in a very, very difficult situation. And unless you reincorporate the whole political structure into one what I would call *accord de gouvernabilité*, for the next twenty-five years, and get everybody to sign on it, and have—before any election can take place—an agreement on the rules of the game for power-sharing over the next twenty-five years, you'll go nowhere. And in addition to that, there has to be an agreement on the police: what kind of police we are going to have, how it is going to be governed, controlled by whom and how, and reincorporate the Lavalas people within the political system."

Phrases like *comité de suivi* and *accord de gouvernabilité* always sounded great in French, like there was actually some system or plan in place. I asked him about the *anciens militaires*.

"We're the only country where you assume that you can solve problems by putting them under the rugs," he said. "It doesn't work like that. We had an army. It had to be reorganized, not eliminated. I mean, even Germany after the war had the army under control of parliament. In all countries of the world, it is not the existence of the army that is the problem. It's how it works, how it is controlled, and who is part of it."

"There's a stark contrast between the current president of the U.S. and the man who was the president at the time of the restoration of Aristide ten years ago," I noted.

Bazin cleared his throat. "I believe that the U.S. presidents, whoever they are, they want one thing from Haiti," he said. "It is stability. How they achieve that, however, varies with who is in power. Is it Republican, is it Democrat, is it Clinton, is it Bush? The means are different. But the basic objective is always the same."

"Is the main problem boat people?"

"Yes. Boat people, and narco-trafficking, and now terrorism, bin Laden."

"Bin Laden?"

"Yes. Haiti is vulnerable to all creeds, because we are so poor."

"Who's going to win this year's U.S. election, and how might that affect events in Haiti?"

"I don't know. I was in the U.S. last week, attending the Democratic National Convention. I spent the entire week in Boston, and I have been following U.S. politics for a long time. It's so tight. I don't think anyone in his right mind can predict who is going to win. But let me tell you this: if it's Bush, it's going to be a continuation of a policy. If it's Kerry, it's going to be reinventing a policy. And by talking to people in Washington last week, I felt that Kerry had not yet a Haitian policy. He is busy with other things."

"Was the U.S. behind the removal of Aristide?"

"Nothing can happen in Haiti without U.S., for better or worse. But in that particular case I don't know how far was the U.S. involvement. Whether they put the train in motion, whether they engineered the whole thing, is not clear to me. But you are not going to have things taking place here without the U.S. saying yes or no. No way. Each time I think of the situation before February 29, I keep thinking of the Secretary of State, Colin Powell. Colin may have said, at least three or four times, the two weeks before February 29, 'Aristide has to continue in office, because he's the legitimate president. We don't want any coup in Haiti. We have to find a way of reconciling the differences.' That was Powell's words again and again, until two days before the falldown of Aristide. So something happened. And you know Colin Powell. He is not the kind of person to say this kind of stuff without knowing exactly what he's talking about."

"After Aristide left, Cheney said, 'We're glad to see him go.'"

"Yeah, but you don't hear about Cheney until Aristide is gone. So you have to stick to what Powell says."

I asked Bazin what had prompted him to return to Haiti to serve as Minister of Finance under Baby Doc.

"When you are a civil servant with the World Bank, you have all the answers," he said. "And then you go around the world and you tell people what to do. And then here is your country, and people ask you, 'Where are you from? Haiti?' In other words, 'What are you doing here?' At one point, you're no longer credible as an international civil servant if you keep telling people what to do and you leave your country the way it is.

"And that makes a difference between me and a lot of politicians. I didn't get into politics to make money. I didn't get into politics to make a life for myself. Or to make a reputation. As an international civil servant I put together the river blindness program, which is the only internationally recognized success of the United Nations system in West Africa. So I was perfectly happy. I had my *carte de visite* already. So when I came here it was really, 'Okay now, Marc, are you sure you want to die without having even tried to do anything about your home country?' That may sound a bit naïve for Haitian politicians, because there are so many cynical guys around here. But that's the reason why I came back."

"Did you have any misgivings about working with that particular regime?"

"No. Because if you start with the idea that you will wait for the ideal regime, you will die without having done anything."

"What was it like for you around '85–'86, when things started getting really …?"

"Well, when Jean-Claude Duvalier left government, I came back for good. You know, I was four months Minister of Finance, and then I had to go because I was Mr. Clean. So I returned to the Bank, and then Jean-Claude left, and I came back. By being Mr. Clean, I had some kind of name recognition. And people thought, well, maybe this guy can do something for the country. But so much had happened on the ground, with Aristide and liberation theology philosophy, with all the priests, and the discontent of the people, and the aggravating poverty, and the corruption. And there was also the *macoute* problem. It was either pro- or against *macoute*. Like now, either pro- or against *chimère*. That's the wrong way to put it. It's not that simple. So I did not get the proper traction against Aristide. But it so happened that only Aristide could stop me."

"I think you're suggesting that there would have been a groundswell for you."

"Absolutely. Well, you just take the diaspora. I was enormously popular in all New York and everywhere, because people said, well, this guy's going to restore a sense of dignity to us. He's been around, he's known. So many of my colleagues at the Bank took Haitian taxis in New York. 'Do you know Marc Bazin?' 'Yes, yes, he's a good man, he's an honest man, etcetera.' They came back and said, 'Marc, you're really popular. All those guys love you.' But Aristide came around, and he knew how to talk to the people better than anyone else. Only he can say things the way he does, and people follow him. So it was World Bank against popular liberation theology, and the Bank lost."

✻

The mood in Gerald's car as we drove back down the mountain was pensive. "In a country you need a conscience," said Patrick Michel. "You need the person you can refer to when things go bad. Aristide could have been that person for twenty-five years. But, a missed opportunity. All civil society leaders have a part of Aristide in them. They see the difference between who they are and who they would be with power. They don't see that they could be more helpful in civil society."

I asked what they thought of Andy Apaid, the prominent leader of the Group of 184. Alongside *Aristid pou 5 ans* around the city, you saw graffiti saying *Aba Aped*—down with Apaid. I had been trying, without success, to get a meeting with Apaid.

"It's said that he is a U.S. citizen," said Gerald. "I don't think he denies it anyway. I believe he even mentioned that in an interview. So I don't think he wants to be president. He probably wants to be an influential social leader, which actually can be a good thing if done wisely."

"You had the satisfactory interview?" asked Patrick.

"Oh, yes," I said. "He's obviously a very intelligent guy."

"I told you he can be more than a Minister of Finance. He can go macro and micro."

I was thinking that Bazin had spoken like a man who still, if given the chance, would not mind being president. But there was a melancholy tension in all he said: he clearly understood just how intractable the country's plight was, but not only did he peddle World Bank-style notions of economic and political liberalism, he seemed genuinely to believe in them. Bazin's curse was to have been born in the wrong country; he was an American intellectual trapped in a Haitian body. His anecdote about why he had returned to Haiti seemed an admission of this. I thought of what the doctor in Petit Trou de Nippes had told me in 1993: "His campaign was like an American campaign. He made all these ads for TV. Beautiful ads. But who in Haiti owns a TV?"

"I was very interested in what he said about why he came back," I said.

"Yeah, he tells us that joke every time," said Patrick. "But knowing my country, we will never have the chance to have Marc Bazin as president. We'll have K'plim—Evans Paul. I tell everyone that if he is president, I will leave the country."

"It is clear Bazin is not very popular," remarked Gerald. "However, whoever is governing the country should not overlook him, because he is very knowledgeable and has lots of experience. I must confess, however, that he has in the past taken positions that I totally oppose, the most recent one being that it would have been good to let Aristide stay in power for two more years. Another two years of Aristide would have been devastating for the country."

"Aristide isn't really a good politician, is he?" I suggested. "Because political skill is all about making deals and compromises with people who have different interests than you."

"But looking at Haitian history in a Machiavellian way," said Gerald, "Aristide was a very successful politician. Because he remained popular and stayed in power longer than many."

CHAPTER 8

ON THE STREETS

I hired one of Philippe's young pals, Gerard, to go with me up the coast to Montrouis, where we would spend a night before I went on to Cap Haïtien on the north coast. Montrouis was where Josué and David and their older brother Chrisnel were from. Philippe assured me I would be welcome in their parents' home.

Gerard and I rode a tap-tap down Delmas, then walked about a mile north, past piles of garbage and men welding beside the chassis of one of those blue-and-white American school buses that were introduced to Haiti after the 1994 invasion. The bus's engine and hood had been removed, and the words *A Vendre*, For Sale, were painted on the front. Gerard gestured for us to cross the street, and we walked through market stalls, past *ti marchands* crying "*Blanc!*" at my back. One woman yelled insistently: "*Blanc blanc blanc!*"

We pushed our way onto a crowded *publique* and rode up the coast, mountains to our right, the sea visible for long stretches on the left. We passed several locations whose names I knew: Cite Soleil, the famous waterfront slum, which I had visited in 2000; Ti Tanyin, where victims of the military regime had been dumped in mass graves; Cabaret, which Papa Doc had renamed Duvalierville in honor of himself.

Montrouis was a roadside town, and we arrived there sooner than I expected. It was around here that I had snorkeled with Steve Albright, the dentist who wore a toothbrush behind his ear, twenty-one years earlier. The brothers' family house was a short walk uphill from the road. I greeted Chrisnel and their father, who sat by a small stove at the top of the front stairs. I had forgotten to expect Chrisnel here, and

I was embarrassed to have to ask his name again. But he had forgotten mine too, which made me feel better. Paul Farmer had pointed out that my life would be simpler in Haiti if my name didn't have a *th* in it. "Eefan," said Chrisnel. "Is it simply an English name?"

"It's a name from the Bible," I said.

He said he didn't recognize it from the Bible. Chrisnel was very devout.

"It's not a famous name from the Bible," I said. "There are some Bible names that are famous, right? *Comme Abraham* …"

"*Moïse*," offered Gerard. "*Jean* …"

"*Oui*," I said. "Well, my name isn't one of the famous names, but it is in the Bible."

Chrisnel handed me a Bible in French and asked me to show him where my name appeared. After a few minutes, I found the most interesting of five mentions (1 Kings 4:30–31):

> *La sagesse de Salomon surpassait la saggesse de tous les fils de l'Orient et toute la sagesse des Égyptiens. Il était plus sage qu'aucun homme, plus qu'Éthan, l'Ezrachite, plus qu'Héman, Calcol et Darda, les fils de Machol; et sa renommée était répandue parmi toutes les nations d'alentour.*

Ever since a curious friend had looked it up in an online Bible concordance, I had thought that a pretty cool mention: I wasn't quite as wise as Solomon, but apparently still quite wise.

"Oh, *Éthan*," said Chrisnel, giving it a French pronunciation. I asked the origin of his name. It was an amalgam of the words *Christ* and *L'Éternel*. He wrote both words and his name, to show me.

Chrisnel was the third of eight children and the oldest brother, but he was gentle and fragile and had effectively ceded the first son's responsibilities to Josué, who was more robust and confident. He gave me a snapshot of himself. On the back he had written:

I would like that
you remember me
for always.
Louis Charles Chrisnel
to
Casey Ethan

Chrisnel gave up his bedroom to me that night. "*Ma chambre est à toi*," he said. It was small, about eight feet by five or six feet, with concrete walls painted green. On the wall opposite the hard single bed were photos of Club Med resorts around the world; postcards of London and Notre Dame in Paris; the booklet from a Whitney Houston CD; a growth chart showing smiling children of various races, with the heading "*Jésus aime les petits enfants.*" Clean shirts, trousers, and baseball caps hung from a wooden beam above the foot of the bed, and undershirts hung from a rope strung across the other wall. A birthday card with a pencil drawing of flowers and a bird said "Happy Birthday Chrisnel" in English. And there were Bible verses written in French with a pink marker: Proverbs 17:1 and 1 Corinthians 13:13.

We were up before dawn, so Gerard and I could get on the road. I exchanged good mornings with Chrisnel's father as he walked past holding six goats on leads. "*Salue moun yo pou mwen,*" he said—say hi to the folks, meaning Philippe and the boys in Port-au-Prince. I washed my hands and face and brushed my teeth in local water because I had no other option, and asked Gerard where I should go to urinate.

He gestured toward a cactus at the corner of the house. "*Ou kapab fe pipi nenmpot kote,*" he said. "*Se sistem-la.*" You can piss anywhere; that's the system.

On the way to where we hoped to catch a bus, Gerard told me that Chrisnel's mother had asked him for thirty Haitian dollars, or 150 gourdes, about US$4. "David's baby that he hasn't seen yet is sick," Gerard explained. "It has diarrhea, maybe AIDS. She needs to buy medicine. She asked me for thirty dollars, but I told her I could give only twenty dollars, because I needed the other ten dollars for my ride back to Port-au-Prince." All this by way of explaining why he couldn't give me back the 150 gourdes of mine he had been carrying since the day before.

"Of course," I said.

Gerard was a dude who wore a cap at a rakish angle and a religious medal on a chain around his neck. He dug my minidisk recorder and made me turn it on so he could rap into the microphone. The previous morning at Philippe's, looking at a map, I had been impressed when he told me he was from Port de Paix on the northern peninsula. I had never been to the northern peninsula; it had always seemed to me romantically remote, with evocatively-named towns like Môle St. Nicholas and Bombardopolis. Haiti was replete with evocative place names.

"Wow," I had said. "How far is it from Gonaïves to Port de Paix?"

"About three hours. The road is bad."

"Have you ever been to Môle St Nicholas?"

"*Oui.*"

"Is it *agréable?*"

"No, it's not *agréable*. It's poor."

"Why did you come to Port-au-Prince?" I asked him.

"Because I wanted to get out of Port de Paix, and there's no work there." So much for romance.

It turned out we had missed the bus. "Shit," said Gerard in English. He wasn't the most competent or resourceful of guides, but he was cheerful and well-meaning. While he busied himself wishing there were a bus, I took charge by insisting we avail ourselves of the three-tap-tap option.

What ensued was an authentic Haitian road trip. Gerard and I were two of nineteen people in the bed of the first tap-tap, to St. Marc. Then we stood around there, alongside other travelers and locals selling water, biscuits, and greasy fried patties. Gerard hailed passing tap-taps. They were all full or couldn't take us, but it also seemed his timing was off—he always hailed them just after they had passed us. He approached a guy on a motorbike.

"You can negotiate with him," Gerard told me.

"Yes, I can negotiate with him, but how much does he want?"

"He wants 80 dollars"—80 Haitian dollars or 400 *gourdes*. I could afford this, but still. "He can't take both of us on his moto, and I don't want to go alone with him, because I don't know him," I objected.

"We can both go on his moto," Gerard insisted. I wasn't so sure, I didn't want to spend US$11 for one leg of this arduous day-long journey, and I didn't like the look of the motorbike guy. "No thanks," I said. Finally a truck drove past, its large bed empty except for a tire lying on its side and an upright oil drum. At first its driver refused

Gerard's entreaties and drove on, but then he seemed to have second thoughts and stopped again. Gerard waved to me, and we caught up with the truck. He said it would take me to Gonaïves and the driver would show me where to catch a tap-tap *au Cap*. Gerard would turn back here and return to Port-au-Prince, if that was all right with me. I hurriedly paid and thanked him, we shook hands, he jumped down, and I was on my way to Gonaïves.

The landscape was mostly flat and arid, full of cactus and sad-looking rice paddies, and the sun was now high in the sky. I sat in the truck bed and suffered. At one point the driver stopped, some people loaded roof thatching in the bed beside me, and two young boys saw the books in my rucksack and asked for a *livre français*. I had one—*L'Amant* by Marguerite Duras—which I was reading to prove to myself that I could read a whole book in French. I wondered what they would make of the story of a dysfunctional French family whose teenage daughter has an affair with an older Chinese man in colonial Indochina—if, that is, they could even read French.

"Give it to me," said one boy.

"Give it to me," insisted the other.

I offered to tear it along the spine and give them each half.

"No!" said the first boy, laughing. "*Pas bon.*"

In the end I kept the book. As the truck rumbled down the white dusty road and the boys fell behind and gave up chasing it, I felt sad and guilty.

At Gonaïves I paid and thanked the driver, and a 12-year-old boy named Jean Roulin guided me through the streets to where the tap-taps left for Cap Haïtien. "*Au Cap au Cap au Cap au Cap au Cap!*" a man cried, and I climbed on. When the tap-tap was full, the last leg of my journey began: out of town and up the mountain roads, then down to the coast. It was mid-afternoon when we arrived in Cap Haïtien.

✳

I was here to see Doug Perlitz and Andy Schultheis, thoughtful young Catholics who ran Project Pierre Toussaint, a small organization that served street kids. They ran a center behind an Episcopal church where boys came daily to bathe, eat, play marbles, and get school lessons, and a "village" for older and more stable boys outside the city. I had met Doug and Andy in passing at Zanmi Lasante in Cange.

"The rebels came up this street on the twenty-second of February, shooting bullets left and right," Doug told me as we drove to the Hotel Roi Christophe to drink rum punches and watch American football on television. "They killed one of our kids' cousins, a 12-year-old girl." He gestured. "This was all looted on the twenty-second of February. This is the police station, and over here the courthouse. All of this was torched. What does that tell us? Get rid of the police and the court-house. We don't need law and order any more. Might is right!"

I spent a couple of days at the center with Andy. "We've got a little bank," he told me. "The kids sleep with any amount of money in their pocket, and it won't be in their pocket when they wake up in the morn-ing. Kids give me whatever they've got, and I hang on to it, and I have a little ledger where I keep track of it all. It's now got nearly six hundred Haitian dollars in it."

"And they get money from begging and whatever?"

"Begging, and some of the older ones wash cars. Some of them steal. Some of them probably get money from doing not very pleasant things. They're gambling over there." He pointed. "They know if I catch 'em gambling I'll take the money. I'll just take it and put it in the bank, and if I need to buy something for the program I'll use it. Or I'll go out and give it to poor people who really need it. That really drives 'em nuts."

I sat on a table near the entrance to the small building and chatted with Watson, age ten, a grubby little guy with dried snot caked under his nose. He was wearing a light blue t-shirt inside out and backward, with the tag in front, and filthy shorts that probably had been white. "Have you bathed yet today?" I asked him.

"Not yet," he said. "Over there is where we bathe. I had a radio, but they stole it. I had five dollars, but they stole it. Do you know Auntie?"

"Madame Calixte? I've just met her."

"She gives us food, three times a day."

I capped my pen and clipped it on the collar of my t-shirt.

"Are you finished writing?" asked Watson.

"I'm finished writing for now. Later I'll write some more."

After breakfast a Haitian sat on a wooden stool with a bucket full of toothbrushes. Each toothbrush was labelled with a name; when a kid took his, the man gave him a squeeze of toothpaste.

After a couple of days, the kids decided I was all right. "*Blanc!*" they yelled whenever they wanted attention, which was all the time. One showed me a plastic wheel off a chair or something. I admired it and handed it back, and he rolled it up and down the wall.

"*Blanc, gade.*" Look. Another boy played on a plastic whistle.

"*Blanc,*" said yet another.

"*Oui.*"

"Give me five *gourdes.*"

"Why?"

"For food."

"There's food over there." He didn't have an answer to that. Little Watson had found it—it was spaghetti today—and was happily shoveling two handfuls into his mouth.

"*Zanmi,*" said another boy. Friend. "New York?"

"Miami," I said, because it was easier than explaining just how peripatetic my life really was. He pointed at my cousin-in-law's Florida Marlins baseball cap. "*L'équipe* Miami. Florida."

"*Oui,*" I said.

"*Doog-lahs l'équipe Chicago.*"

"*Oui.*"

"*Et Andy?*"

"*L'équipe Boston, n'est-ce pas?*"

"*Oui. Bas Rouges.*"

Andy was a Boston Red Sox fan, despite being from Chicago; the May 2004 issue of *Diehard: The Magazine for Red Sox Fans* was in the bathroom of the house he shared with Doug. He had been with Project Pierre Toussaint five years and had a tinge of melancholy in his countenance and his voice. He was considering entering the priesthood. Two mornings after arriving, still feeling bruised from the long overland journey, I lay half asleep on a bench in the room he used as an office.

"You know how some days you just feel you've had the shit kicked out of you by Haiti?" I said.

"I know it well," said Andy.

"*Love* that music."

"Actually the music, as much as I hate it, it calms the kids down," he said. "They start dancing, and they don't fight as much. They're gonna watch a movie in a minute."

Many of the boys got high on paint thinner, which they bought from hardware stores with the money they begged or stole. Several boys were in the room, with questions for Andy or just hanging around.

"A lot of these paint-thinner kids, they're really screwed up sexually," Andy told me. "Every night it's like a big orgy where they sleep. And when they come here they cause so many problems. You try to give 'em punishments, but sometimes we just have to kick 'em out. Like this kid, when he's not high, he's great." This was a boy of twelve or thirteen in a purple t-shirt that said "Vermont" and had pictures of cows on it. "Like he's not high now, and he's fine. But he just showed me his wiener, and it's got all these bumps all over it. He probably got 'em fooling around."

Doug was thirty-four, smaller and more thickset than Andy. Both were such normal-looking white guys that it was inspiring to meet them in Haiti, doing what they were doing. Doug had been with Project Pierre Toussaint for eight years and was thinking about writing a book based on his diaries.

"This year I've been trying to read classics and stuff," he told me. "I read *Cry, the Beloved Country* by Alan Paton. That is such a great book. I'm reading it and thinking, 'This is just like Haiti.'"

Doug and Andy and several of the boys went out of town one day to the funeral of the mother of one of the boys. She had died of cancer only the week before, in the room where I was now sleeping. I didn't go because there wasn't room in the truck, and anyway, I was still sore and didn't feel able to experience another Haitian road just yet.

"I got emotional several times during that funeral, because it was like a funeral for Haiti," Doug told me afterwards. "I mean, this woman was forty-four years old, dirt poor, no medical care, she had cancer of the uterus, which in any frickin' normal society would have been cured—she would have had a hysterectomy and would still be alive." The coffin had been too big, so men had had to break it up and manhandle the body to get it inside the tomb. "It was one of those moments where you just go, 'Ching! Put that in your back pocket.' It was tiring, it was emotional, but it was a gift too."

He put it to metaphoric use: "We have an idea what we want to do with the project, but all we're really doing is walking in a funeral with a dead body." But even this was worth doing, for its own sake. "If you hold everyone at arm's length it's safe, it's neat, it's clean. But if you do this"—he spread his arms—"you get bloody." I thought of Dr. Magiot in *The Comedians*, who told the narrator Mr. Brown: "I'd rather have blood on my hands than water like Pilate."

I went with Doug to the village for older kids, which was surrounded by a kilometer-long wall. "We built the wall, which we hated to," he said. "It cost us $60,000, but we'd be history without it. The land was given to us. It's amazing to see personalities emerge. Kids come out here, and they're allowed to be who they are. The kids have helped us create it. There's a rabbit project over here. They're raising rabbits." There was also a soccer field and a basketball court, and well-tended flower beds. "Paul Farmer says, 'Raise the bar and you'll be surprised how many people come up to it.' That's something I think is a real tragedy about Haiti: how many Mozarts and Beethovens are there who never have a chance to excel? It's all about self-esteem and confidence. And this is a whole country that has none of it."

✳

Cap Haïtien had been at the center of events in February. Doug said the U.S. Coast Guard had intercepted boat people here, within Haitian waters. He and Andy had not considered leaving. "During the coup the kids were on vacation," he told me. "And they came to the house to make sure Andy and I were okay. I told my mom, 'Don't worry. We're in good hands.' And the fact that we stayed counted for a lot. If we had left, they might have thought we weren't coming back."

On Thursday morning, Andy drove me to the airport.

"Is Aristide blameless?" I asked him.

"No, I don't think anyone's blameless," he said. "Me personally, I think he sincerely wanted to help this country develop. But he got caught up in all the power, and all that power brings. I don't doubt that there was funny business going on, but he didn't have anything to work with. I think he just let it get out of hand. Those people definitely caused a lot of trouble here in town."

"Lavalas?"

"Mm-hmm. They were driving up and down the streets with their guns out, trying to scare people into supporting Aristide. Then again, I don't believe that Aristide said, 'Go barricade this intersection and throw rocks and bottles at schoolchildren.' I believe these people had their own agenda, and their own warped idea of how to show support for Aristide. If he was involved in drug trafficking, if he was involved in the collapse of these cooperative banks, if he was involved in illegal acts, fine. But nothing warranted what happened in February."

And what happened could not have happened without U.S. support: "It couldn't have happened so smoothly. The rebels had no problems in any of these places they went to. They were well armed, they were well equipped, they were well trained. They just plowed through towns and terrorized people. The same thing they criticized Aristide for, they did.

"Right now, nobody knows who's supposed to do what. And they don't have the cars, they don't have the equipment, they don't have anything. Last Saturday there was a huge argument in the market and a lot of people standing around staring. And a truck full of heavily-armed rebels went into the market, and a couple minutes later they came back out with three guys handcuffed, put them in the back of the truck, and drove off. So who do people call when they need someone to break up a fight? They don't call the police, they call the rebels."

The airport was a single runway a few minutes out of town toward Milot and the Citadelle, the magnificent mountaintop folly built by the early nineteenth-century King Henri Christophe to repulse an expected invasion by Napoleon that never happened. Inside the small airport building was scaffolding, plywood, fresh cement. The damage done in February was being repaired.

Andy pointed out to me a short flight of stairs that led nowhere— the building it had been part of had burned down. I thought of the coup I had witnessed in Cambodia in July 1997. When Pochentong airport finally reopened after eleven days, I had gone there for an early morning flight to Bangkok; it was an eerie scene: bullet holes, charred ruins. My memory of it was of a moment when society had ceased to function. But the longsuffering mass of ordinary Cambodians had known from long experience what to do: the families that streamed five to a motorbike with their children and sacks of rice toward the Mekong River, where boat owners waited to gouge them for rides across, had done so with a glum, practiced air.

Andy told me that here, in February, a freelancing pilot had offered chartered flights out for US$1500 per seat and had told passengers not to tell anyone in Port-au-Prince that they had come from Cap Haïtien. Andy and Doug got their mail delivered weekly from Fort Lauderdale through a service called Lynx Air. "We were here to try to get our friends on a flight out, one of the charters," Andy remembered. "As we waited for the plane, we went into Lynx. It looked like a tornado had gone through it. That was probably the most depressing thing: the desperation of the whole thing, the first indication to me that there was really no law and order. I remember going through where we used to get our mail, going through each letter piece by piece and looking for one letter or magazine that belonged to us. I remember I found one empty envelope and one three-week-old copy of *USA Today Sports Weekly*.

"On Monday we walked around in town to see the damage done. The rebels were parading through town and being greeted very warmly. We were visiting the different buildings that had been damaged: the prisons, the police buildings, the mayor's house. Chamblain [a rebel leader] stopped on the street corner and got out and basically said, 'We are here to bring peace. We are here to liberate. If anyone decides that they want to continue the looting, the pillaging, the stealing, they're taking their life into their own hands.' He was obviously very tired, and very to the point. And he got back in his jeep and drove off."

*

On Saturday, August 14, back in Port-au-Prince, walking out from Philippe's house to catch a tap-tap down Delmas, I ran into David. We slapped hands. "Where are you going?" he asked. "Petionville?"

"No," I said. "I'm going to the *manifestation*."

He raised his eyebrows and grinned.

"*Map manifeste*," I added, as a joke. I'm going to demonstrate.

He laughed. "Who are you going to demonstrate against?"

"I'm not telling."

"Take precautions," he warned, now in earnest. "The Haitian police can be *sauvage*. People throw rocks. And sometimes they shoot people."

David ran into one of his girlfriends and stopped to chat her up. I waved and walked on. At the bottom of Delmas I got off and walked around, looking in vain for a *manifestation*. Nothing much was going on, except that a group of young people in matching yellow shirts were sweeping the street near the Roman Catholic cathedral. Their shirts announced, in French, that they were part of some sort of youth initiative sponsored by the Latortue government.

I walked down toward the bay. Rounding a corner I saw, halfway down a long block, above a high wall, a large U.S. flag. In this building in the year 2000, an embassy man had spoken to me (off the record, of course) with bitterness and scorn about how his own State Department bosses had ignored negative reports the embassy was sending to Washington about Aristide, because they undermined the Clinton administration's portrayal of Haiti as a foreign-policy success. That year the U.S. had sent humanitarian aid of around $75 million to Haiti, dealing directly with non-governmental organizations, completely bypassing the government. The embassy man had seemed drained and on edge. I felt pity for him, and for myself in my fruitless effort to distinguish good guys from bad guys. As Jack Wall of Wall House had told me on that same visit, "You hear so much crap around here, you don't know what to believe."

I started walking toward the flag. Abruptly, an SUV full of armed men in uniform stopped in the middle of the road, not more than thirty feet from me. One jumped out and walked toward a car emerging from a side street, aiming his rifle through the windshield. The nearest I had come before this to a rifle aimed in anger had been during the 1997 coup in Phnom Penh. That time the rifle had been aimed at the pavement in front of me, as a warning that if I took another step forward the soldier would aim it at my chest. I had slowly raised my hands and backed away. That memory served me now, as I calmly turned my back on the cops and began walking down the side street. At the end of it I saw a crowd, hurrying away from the rear of the embassy. A boy of about twelve running toward me said in Creole, in a very mature tone: "Don't go there. You'll get hurt." The genuine concern in his voice moved me, and the authority in it preempted my decision. I turned around and went back to the boulevard, turned left, and stood on the steps of a neighboring building with a man who asked me in English: "You are journalist? American journalist? CNN?"

"I'm not with CNN," I said carefully.

"Which press are you?"

Why did he have to assume I was press? "I'm not the press," I said. "I'm a tourist." The only tourist in Haiti. "And you?"

"I work in this building."

"A dangerous place to have your building," I suggested.

"Yes," he agreed with a laugh.

I excused myself and rounded the next corner, catching up with the crowd after a few minutes. I caught a whiff of ganja. Back up rue Pavée we marched, past the covered sidewalks crowded with people selling old English and French books and magazines, booze, peanuts, t-shirts, downmarket brands of toothpaste and black hair products. I weaved among these because I was leery of being seen walking, the lone *blanc*, carrying bulky recording equipment, with the *manifesteurs*.

"What's your name?" I asked one of them.

"Emmanuel," he said.

"How old are you?"

"Twenty-three."

"Why are you in this *manifestation*?"

I heard sirens but could not look around to see where they were coming from, because I had to concentrate on holding the microphone near his mouth.

"I like the *manifestation* for the President Haristide, for come back in Haiti, for come back in Haiti for five years," he said. "This President Bush keep the President Aristide, you know, that's a lot of people Haitian don't like that. I don't like this Bush. He keep President Aristide. Population he say we like President Aristide come back in the Haiti."

"Where do you live?"

"I live Cité Soleil. Seventeen."

"What do you do for a living? What's your job?"

"I work for the"—what he said sounded like "*à peine*" or "a pen." "This military Haitian, he come to fucking keep Boniface, Boniface and Latortue." Boniface Alexandre was the elderly new figurehead president. "He fire me now from my job, he fire me. Not job no more. President Aristide here in the Haiti, I'm work. You know, when President Aristide not here, Latortue, he fire lotta Haitian."

"But what was your job?"

"APN. A-P-N."

"I don't understand." I said it in Creole: *M-pa konpren*. But these guys seemed accustomed to talking to journalists; they spoke to me mostly in English. Several explained all at once who Emmanuel's employer had been, spelling out the acronym.

"Where are you walking to now?" I asked Emmanuel.

"I don't working."

"No," I said. "Where is the *manifestation* going?"

"You going to Bel Air. After you finish to Bel Air, you go to Palace. You go to Palace. You came with the manifestation for the President Haristide come to Haiti, come back in the Haiti for five years. I need the President Aristide in the Haiti. You know, President Aristide say some for the people that's white, some that's black, and the black they're for the Haitian. White man that's white man for the USA. Black fuckin' Haiti. I don't like that fuckin' Bush, keep President Aristide. For while Haiti don't got nothing, he don't got shit. President Aristide he make all the ting for the Haiti. You know, Mister Bush he see President Aristide, you clean fuckin' Haiti. You keep the President Aristide. Go home. For why."

"Why did Bush get rid of Aristide?"

"Bush he see the Haiti clean. He say the fucking like Haristide fuck cleaned Haiti, he say, you come to keep President Aristide for go home the fuckin' not president no more in the Haiti. The popu-lah-tion he say, 'We like President Aristide for president, come back fuckin' Haiti.' I need the Haristide for five years, five years, five years. Too much popu-lah-tion—"

Another guy cut in. "Too much people want Awistide for five years, nome sayin'?" He was stocky with longish hair, like a younger Samuel L. Jackson.

"But lemme tell you sumpin'," he went on. "The manifestation is get behind the Cité Soleil, you nome sayin'? But when the people just keep some quiet—you unnerstan' whum sayin'?—the Pwesident Bush just keepin' the Pwesident Awistide get back in Afwique, you nome sayin'? The people don't like it. We want the Pwesident Awistide get back in Haiti. Because I don't like the situation and cannot make some life. You nome sayin'?"

"What's your name?" I asked him.

"My name is Moïse, man."

"How old are you?"

"I got twenty-five years, man."

"Where do you live?"

"I live in the Cité Soleil."

"What's your job?"

"I'm not working. Before I'm working in the telecommunication, you nome sayin'? But the *gouvernement* of the *de facto* just come in, man. He says, 'Get out.' I'm not workin' now. All right? Lemme show you." He showed me a laminated card with his photo. "That's my name, you nome sayin'? That's my name, that's my first name I got. The telecommunication I'm working, but now I'm not working, man, all right? You unnerstan' whum sayin'?"

"Are you afraid that the police might come and shoot the people in the manifestations today?"

"The police come in the Cité Soleil. I see before the guy just comin', man. He just keep some guy get put him in the prison, nome saying? I don't like this shit, you nome saying? I need the Pwesident Awistide just get back in Haiti. You know? You unnerstan' whum sayin', man?"

Trailed by SUV-loads of armed cops, we marched through the Bel Air slum. We passed the monstrous new tower near the Palace. Philippe had told me about it: "It was started by Aristide for the bicentennial, never finished, it's as fascist as a monument can be. It was made very badly by Taiwanese. From the beginning there were pieces of concrete falling off. And it is *so* ugly." All along the route and on the big square in front of the National Palace called the Champs de Mars, people approached me or shouted as they walked past, and I scribbled in my notebook.

"*Nou mande retou Presidan Aristid. Li te vote*," said a woman angrily. We demand the return of President Aristide. He was elected. Her name was Fredline Zephyr, age forty-one.

"*Moun nan pa gin djob*," said someone else. People don't have jobs.

"*Vive Kerry!*" shouted a woman in a yellow shirt.

"Much people like Aristide, man," remarked Moïse.

We were now opposite the lower, western end of the Palace. Uphill, behind me, I heard a gunshot.

"The Haitian police just killed some people over there," a man said. "Don't worry, man."

There were more shots, and the crowd started running downhill toward the city center and the water. I looked uphill and saw a police vehicle stopped near the upper front corner of the Palace.

"I see one policeman take off his shirt," said a man in a blue sleeveless t-shirt, in English. "You see?"

"*Gen moun tue?*" I asked. Has someone been killed?

"I don't know yet."

Sirens screamed. We stood there for a few minutes, near the wall by the basketball courts. "I don't like the journalist Haitian, man," said Moïse.

"*Yo tue moun la*," said a young guy in a grey t-shirt. They killed someone over there.

"*Konbyen moun?*" How many?

"*Youn sel moun.*" Only one.

The guy in the blue sleeveless shirt told me again, in English, what he knew, which wasn't much.

"Shit!" said the guy in the grey shirt. "*Ça fait mal.*"

I recognized him as Michelin, who had accosted me on rue Pavée before the *manifestation* because his friend Aldy was calling to me from his truck. Aldy drove a tap-tap that was bigger than the usual colorful pickups, more like a full-sized truck. I had said hi to Aldy then and told him I'd meet him again on the same corner and ride uphill with him around one o'clock, when he came back around on his route. But I had missed that rendezvous because of the *manifestation.*

Aldy and I had become friends the day before. After my interview with Pierre Paquiot, the university rector who had been confined to a wheelchair for three months after being attacked by Aristide partisans in seminal events in early December 2003, I had waited to catch a tap-tap uphill, via rue Panaméricaine to Petionville. A woman had tapped me on the shoulder to point out that he was calling to me from a truck. He recognized me as the *blanc* who had ridden his truck downhill earlier, on my way to meet Paquiot. Going uphill, Aldy had insisted I sit in the cab with him and his sidekick, and he had refused to let me pay the five-gourde fare.

Aldy was cheery and garrulous and came across like a brown version of Archie Bunker's pal Stretch Cunningham. He didn't speak French or English, and I didn't fully understand his fast-paced and colloquial Creole, but we got on well. He was twenty-nine years old and had previously worked as a driver for a company called Elio Distributors S.A., but lost his job when the company went out of business after the boss was imprisoned in Miami for cocaine trafficking. Now he drove this truck up and down between the city center and Petionville. He was from Les Cayes on the south coast and said his father's father had been a white Frenchman. His wife had Haitian parents but had grown up in Venezuela and spoke Spanish. He showed me pictures of her and of their four children, including one of his eldest son with Santa Claus. He rented the truck and cleared 400-500 *gourdes*, US$11-14, per day, most of which was eaten up by school fees. On the passenger side of his truck's windshield was a big spiderweb crack. "*Roche?*" I asked him. Rock? "*Manifestation*," he said. It had been a pro-Aristide manifestation, so he assumed it was a pro-Aristide guy who had cracked his windshield with a *baton*.

When Aldy had dropped me off at Place Boyer in Petionville, we exchanged contact details and I said I hoped we would meet again. "*Map prie pou sa*," he said. I'll pray for that. He hoped God would provide him with his own vehicle and that, if He did, we might drive around the provinces together sometime.

Now, in front of the National Palace, as we stood around speculating about whether the police had just killed someone, Aldy drove past again on his regular route in his truck. I didn't see him to wave to, but I recognized the truck by its size and color and by the crack in the windshield.

A crowd had gathered in the intersection near the upper front corner of the Palace, across from the ugly Taiwanese-built tower. A police SUV was stopped there, and several policemen stood near it. I approached the crowd cautiously.

As I neared, I saw a policeman bend down to pick up a bullet casing from the pavement. In the crowd I recognized a *blanc* I knew named Seth Donnelly. Seth was a high school teacher from California who was volunteering with the Institute for Justice and Democracy in Haiti, and one day we had walked together most of the way from Canapé Vert uphill to Petionville, then across to the top of Delmas. At first Seth had seemed like the most irritating sort of knee-jerk lefty, but during that exhausting hike I had come to like him. We shared an interest in C.L.R. James, the great historian and author of *The Black Jacobins*, and he urged me to read *Open Veins of Latin America* by Eduardo Galeano, which I still haven't read but will get around to one of these days. Seth told me now that he was at this *manifestation* as a self-appointed "human rights monitor."

"People are saying a SWAT team killed him," he was saying on a cellphone to someone at the simultaneous *manifestation* in Cap Haïtien. "They got him through the windshield."

151

"It's good to see you again," I said. "Even if it's under these circumstances."

"It's good to see you too, man," he said.

"I thought you wouldn't be here anymore."

"I stayed another week. I think they're gonna blame this on Lavalas. This is gonna be a pretext for stepped-up repression. I think this could be a setup to blame this on Lavalas."

At the corner just inside the Palace fence, Brazilian UN soldiers manned a guardpost. One of them was taking photographs of the crowd through the fence.

"The fucking UN," said Seth. "There's more UN guarding a boo-geois grocery store than making sure shit doesn't happen at a demonstration. I mean, what's that all about?"

Seth filmed the scene with a video camera, as a Haitian with him interviewed bystanders and another translated.

"He was going in the hospital with his wife," said the translator, "and his son was sick, and when they stop him he say that he's a police, and he get outside just to identify himself, but when he twy to identify himself the police in black uniforms just shoot him and they said he has, he had bullets in his head, and was killed down, and we, we was, we have been able to see the blood down, and there was the bullet, and we have seen the impact on the windshield of his car. They put his wife in the car, and they escape with the wife, and they all escape because they twy to have contwol of the situation."

Another man spoke in Creole.

"Awistide was asking them to send people to help him to fight against the tewwowists in the countwy," said the translator. "They didn't, but what they do wight now is like they send all the tewwowists to tewwowize the population. When Awistide ask to have help in the countwy, Georges Bush pweferred to send people in the Dominican Wepublic to be twained. So they say that they fighting against tewwowism, but they kind of the father of tewwowism. I have a message for Georges Bush. He should wemember that his father has been out of the power just because he gave a coup d'état to Awistide. Wight now the Georges Bush son will not be able to be in power just because he give another coup d'état. All that United States are suffewing wight now in tewwowism are because of the policy of United States over all the world. And it's clear that Georges Bush is kind of thweatened. The thweat is clear on the United States, and if Georges Bush doesn't stop, maybe it will be worse evwy day."

When the crowd moved away I saw a pool of blood, already drying on the asphalt.

What was left of the *manifestation* began moving uphill. Someone said we were now heading to the French embassy.

"I agree with you," I heard Seth say to someone.

"What did he say?" I asked.

"He said he wanted Aristide to come back to Haiti," said Seth.

I scribbled in my notebook.

"No match *Bresil-Haïti sans Aristide!*" cried Bel Air resident Jules Francois, 23.

"*Vous ne voulez pas savoir mon age?*" asked a young man in a yellow shirt and long denim shorts named Emmanuel (not the same I had met much earlier, before the shooting). I said I did want to know his age. He said he was nineteen. Unlike most of the others, he spoke to me in French.

"*À bas* Georges Bush! *Vive* John Kerry!" cried the crowd. "Ti Bush! Junior Bush! *À bas* Boniface! *À bas* Latortue! *Vive* Aristide!"

"*Nou pa vle Bresil sans Aristid,*" said Emmanuel and another guy. We don't want Brazil without Aristide. The world-famous Brazil soccer team was coming to Port-au-Prince on August 18 to play the Haitian national team, as a goodwill gesture and a sideshow to Brazil's participation in the UN force. Lula, the left-leaning Brazilian president, was also coming. A couple of weeks earlier I had witnessed Haitians all over Port-au-Prince watching televisions on the streets and maniacally honking and shouting and ululating to celebrate a Brazil victory over Argentina. Haitians loved the Brazil football team. But apparently at least some of them would rather have Aristide, and they saw the UN force—including the Brazilians—as U.S. lackeys supporting an illegitimate regime.

I listened and scribbled as we walked through a market. My eyes on my notebook, I failed to notice until too late that I had stepped on a pile of garbage in open sandals.

"Georges Bush *kidnape* Aristide!" said Jules.

"Writing," said a tall man named Jean-Marie, age 30. He meant "Write," as an instruction or command.

"I'm writing, I'm writing," I said.

"We got so many thing to tell you now. This is some occupation. If Haristide never come back, we will have so much danger in the street. Because Haitian people love Haristide."

"*Mwen ban ou mesage,*" said a guy in a red shirt with a U.S. flag on the left breast. I give you a message.

"*Ki mesage?*" What message?

"*Mesage lavalas-la.*" The Lavalas message, or the message of the landslide, the avalanche, the flood.

We walked past a big heap of garbage.

"*Regardez,*" said Emmanuel. "*Ce sont les fruits du Président Boniface.*" A woman standing somewhere to the side made a remark about me that I didn't catch.

"*Respekte jounalis,*" Emmanuel admonished her.

"*Li pense mwen se CIA?*" I asked him. She thinks I'm CIA?

"*Comme ça,*" he said. Like that. "*Mais ce n'est pas vrai. Vous etes journaliste. Journaliste doit etre ni pour, ni contre.*" But it's not true. You are a journalist. Journalists should be neither for nor against.

We passed the Eglise Notre Dame du Perpetuel, white with yellow trim, with "1882–1942" above the entrance.

"*Je peux vous accompagner?*" Emmanuel asked me.

"*Oui, s'il vous plait.*"

"*Si je vous accompagne, vous ne devez pas avoir peur.*" If I'm with you, you needn't be afraid.

I had spent most of several hours walking through a filthy, dysfunctional city under a tropical sun in the middle of the day, and when I hadn't been walking I had been hearing gunshots and contemplating blood on the pavement and trying to reconstruct how and—even more elusive—why police had gunned down a passerby on his way to the hospital with his sick child. I had had nothing to eat or drink. As we walked through Bel Air in the direction of lower Delmas, I saw a man selling drinking water from a pail in little plastic packets. I went over to him, meaning to buy two or three. I thought of the youths walking with me, that they must be hot and thirsty too. I asked for ten packets; they cost one *gourde*, about three cents, each. I meant to hand one packet to anyone who wanted one.

Too late, I realized my folly: I looked down into the bucket at a dozen black arms reaching, snatching, grabbing. This was not a country where people queued politely; in Haiti, the compulsions of survival dictate that you take what you can get, when you can get it, any way you can get it, like whoever stole $100 from my wallet. I knew this already. But I was the well-meaning but foolish white man, like Mr. Smith of Wisconsin passing out dollar bills to beggars in *The Comedians*. Feeling ashamed and vulnerable, I found a 50-*gourde* note in my pocket, thrust it at the water man, and stumbled away.

"*Nou pat vote Boniface, nou pat vote Latortue!*" cried the crowd. We didn't vote for Boniface, we didn't vote for Latortue!

"*Aristid wa-pwesidan*," said a man.

"What do you mean, *wa*?" I didn't understand.

"*Wa-wa*," he said. "*Wa.*"

"*Comme Roi Christophe?*" King Henry Christophe, Haitian hero and builder of the Citadelle.

"*Oui, oui, oui!*"

✳

That night Philippe and I sat on his porch, smoking and sipping whiskey and listening to gunfire somewhere nearby. "This morning at seven o'clock I was standing waiting for a taxi," he said. "And I thought of an idea that no one—not USAID, or IDB, or anyone—has thought of, to get this country moving. Really, it was the beginning of salvation."

"What was it?"

"I can't remind myself what it was."

"You can't remember it at all?"

"No! Never mind, I would have been persecuted anyway."

I told him about the *manifestation*.

"That was the point of all the destruction," he said, "the week before and the week after he left: to make the Aristide time look like the good old time. And I don't expect simple people to think beyond that. They have no money, no food, no jobs. And no rain this year."

"No matter what he did and how many people he killed," I objected, "he's still the only president who took them into consideration."

I had been thinking a lot about *No Other Life*, Brian Moore's *roman à clef* about Aristide and Haiti. When it was published in 1993, Amy Wilentz had reviewed it scornfully in *The Nation*; how dare a novelist take license with real events that were urgent matters of life and death? I felt differently, and it was the novel's ending that was on my mind now, on Philippe's porch.

The Aristide character agrees under duress to a *modus vivendi* with the army and the elite, but manipulates them into allowing him to lead an outdoor prayer service in front of the cathedral. "Ganae has always been ruled by corrupt presidents, or by dictators," he tells the narrator, a Canadian priest, on the way there. "The people have always waited to be led. They must not rely on a leader. They must learn to make the revolution themselves." At the service he tells the huge crowd:

> Today I go back
> To those from whom I came,
> The poor, the silent, the unknown.
> From today on
> We wait for you.
> As the dead wait for you.
> To bring us freedom.
> Brothers and Sisters,
> You are the anointed ones.
> With God's help
> You will not fail.

Then he walks into the crowd and disappears.

To a cardinal in Rome, the narrator reports: "Father Cantave's name is never mentioned by the government-controlled media. If questioned about his return, civilian and army leaders pretend indifference. Raymond, the premier, recently told *Le Monde* that 'Cantave is now irrelevant. Ganae has moved on to a new stage of democracy.'"

And in the final chapter, the narrator tells us:

It is now ten years since that day when Jeannot seemed to disappear from this earth. There has been no revolution but, to the dismay of the elite and the Army, an ungovernable rage and resentment consumes the daily lives of the poor. ... Nothing has changed. The system is, as always, totally corrupt. The poor are its victims. ... His name is never mentioned among the elite but the mystery of his disappearance sits under the arrogance and privilege of their lives, like a dangerous earthquake fault.

I sketched the story to Philippe. "So it's almost as if he's more powerful absent than he ever was as president," I concluded.

"That's why it's important to bring him to trial and condemn him," he insisted.

"But wouldn't the poor see such a trial as condemning them?"

"It's important for this country to be inoculated against providential presidents. He can't be allowed to become a mythical prophet."

"But if he's brought to trial and condemned, wouldn't he be seen as a martyr?"

"There's a proverb in Creole," said Philippe. "*Mapou tonbe kabrit mange fey li.* When the mapou tree falls, the goats eat its leaves."

CHAPTER 9

"Isn't the world just going nuts?"

When I told a *bourgeoise* that a man had been killed at the *manifestation*, she said, "There are always these stories." I wanted to say: I heard the shots. I saw the blood on the asphalt. I watched a uniformed policeman pick up a shell casing. The only people I saw with guns were cops. But I held my tongue; she was being kind to me, and I didn't have the heart.

"There's always violence at these *manifestations*," the politician Gerard Pierre-Charles assured me.

I needed out. It was not my country; I felt entitled to avert my eyes. But I found Miami maddening. A well-intentioned wealthy woman there asked how I had found Haiti. I told her the truth. "You stayed in good hotels though, right?" she said solicitously, and I was at a loss.

I played part of a minidisk for the station manager at Miami's public radio station. "He's saying they don't want the Brazil football team to come to Haiti unless Aristide returns," I translated. He was incredulous. "What does one have to do with the other?!?" he asked.

I thought: If you don't know, or can't guess, then you've got no business running a public radio station in Miami. The more thoughtful sort of American was always saying how much better public radio was than most U.S. media. Paul Farmer had told me that the NPR reporters who visited Cange looked silly chasing roosters with microphones.

In mid-September, in the midst of a memorably severe hurricane season, mudslides caused by Tropical Storm Jeanne and abetted by severe deforestation devastated the city of Gonaïves and killed about 3,000 people. Survivors in and around Gonaïves were desperate, and flooded roads made access to the city difficult for aid workers. On September 29, *anciens militaires* arrived in Gonaïves offering to help with security and bringing three truckloads of food. UN peacekeepers told them they could enter the city only without their guns. Some got through anyway, and one of the rebels' trucks was mobbed and looted.

"No foreigner has the right to tell us to put down our arms," Remissainthe Ravix, a rebel and former army colonel, told the Associated Press. "We went there because wherever security is needed, we'll be there."

No one knew who was in charge in Haiti. The country had four armed factions, with four agendas: the national police, the UN, the *anciens militaires*, Aristide supporters in the slums. On September 30 several demonstrators were wounded by gunfire near the National Palace, as they marched commemorating the 13th anniversary of the 1991 coup. On October 2, two senators and a former parliamentary deputy from Aristide's Lavalas party were arrested at a radio station after they had criticized the Latortue government on the air. There was widespread violence and disquiet in Port-au-Prince throughout the following week, when I was there again. A friend of Philippe's, a singer named Toupac, was shot dead in Cité Soleil, and Toupac's brother Billy was wounded. Two policemen were beheaded in a mysterious incident, and rumors circulated about something ominously called "Operation Baghdad."

On October 13, a Roman Catholic priest and Aristide ally named Gerard Jean-Juste was arrested after police besieged the building where he ran a feeding program for children, near his parish on the outskirts of Port-au-Prince. "I'm sure he's plotting to feed more children or something like that," Paul Farmer said to me.

✳

I was able to return to Haiti twice in October and November, thanks to a temporary job. Anne Hastings, director of a microfinance organization called Fonkoze, planned to hold a summit of microfinance practitioners from around the world in Thomonde, a village on the Central Plateau between Cange and Hinche, in mid-November.

The meeting was jointly sponsored by Fonkoze and Zanmi Lasante to address the needs of those living in "extreme poverty," which Anne defined as "the kind of poverty that prevents people from having hope-filled lives and effective futures," in which people were "consumed by day-to-day survival." People living in such a situation were not ready for microcredit, very small loans that required repayment. What they needed first was the question Anne wanted the summit to answer. She hired me to publicize it to the media and to Fonkoze's allies and micro-finance colleagues worldwide.

Anne was an intriguing, highly-strung American who had chucked in a successful management consultancy in Washington, DC eight years earlier to move to Haiti to help a Haitian priest, Father Joseph Philippe, get Fonkoze off the ground. Fonkoze had since become by some measures Haiti's largest microfinance organization. Anne was tenacious and intensely focused, sometimes jarringly so—but tenacity was a prerequisite in Haiti if you wanted to achieve anything. Visiting microfinance initiatives in other poor countries, Anne had been shocked by, for example, how good the roads were. "I said, 'How can they have all these things in Bangladesh and Uganda and Kenya, and Haiti is the way it is?'" she told a meeting in Miami in December.

In Bangladesh she had met Rabeya Yasmin of the microfinance organization BRAC, whom she invited to the Thomonde summit. "What if you have a village and it doesn't have any economy?" Anne had asked, and she was impressed by Rabeya's answer: "Every village has an economy. You have to find out what it is." Another spur was a conversation with Paul Farmer, who told Anne: "I'm tired of bringing people on the edge of death from tuberculosis, AIDS, or other diseases to the point where they can become economically active, and then watch them suffer because they have no way to make a living."

Anne pulled off a feat of planning and logistics by bringing more than a dozen of us to the Central Plateau from around the U.S. and the world. We flew to Hinche in a thirteen-seat plane and spent the first evening talking with Paul Farmer and Ti Jean in a group on the porch of Farmer's house.

"This is not a conference to sit around and bullshit about what can we do to improve the place," said Anne. "It's a question of political will and commitment. We have examples of things that work, and now we want to apply them to the Haitian context."

"How do you ask poor women who are sick or just recovering from sickness to go out and succeed in a faltering economy?" Farmer asked the group.

"You cannot—not with microcredit alone," replied Rabeya Yasmin. "They need far more than that. But we do know what they need."

Farmer was at his most unsparing. "This stuff about, 'Well, local resources have to be used,'" he said. "What if the resources have been stripped?"

"If a program is designed carefully and using the experiences carefully, then you are bound to have success," Rabeya insisted.

"What do you do in a situation where all sorts of rights are being flouted?" Farmer rejoined. "If we start organizing like we were a year ago, we'll just kinda get shot. There's supposed to not be an army. We don't have roads. That's another big problem."

"Advocacy should be one of the major activities to do."

"It is an illegal, de facto government that was put in power by a coup."

"I understand that," said Rabeya. "Still, it doesn't matter if they are legal or illegal. Still they are human beings. In Bangladesh also we had martial law for many years."

"We're not satisfied," insisted Farmer. "What is the purpose of public health and public education, if not to serve the poorest of the poor? We're hurtling forward on a planet where there's the privatization of everything. When I was growing up in Florida in a trailer park, you could turn on the tap and drink water. Now everyone is drinking water out of bottles. I'm just so worried about the public part of this. We're raising private money and investing it in everything from banks to hospitals. Can we, and should we, as NGOs, give the state a free pass?"

Rabeya took most of the week to process just how different Haiti was from her country. "The most important basic difference," she told me, "is that Bangladesh has a government, and there is no governance system in Haiti. That makes a whole lot of difference. The four basic characteristics of a state are government, land, population, and sovereignty. I think Haiti lacks two major characteristics: government and sovereignty."

We met in Thomonde for six days. Out of the summit came new Fonkoze-led programs to serve households living with HIV and tuberculosis and families living in extreme poverty that included at least one potentially economically active woman.

"You can't work your way out of poverty if you're starving," Anne told the Miami meeting afterward. "You have to relieve the stress first. And you have to awaken the possibility in someone's mind that there is an alternative future. That's the key."

✳

The summit helped palliate the despair and exhaustion I had been feeling since August. But I knew better than to hope for easy answers or solutions. In Port-au-Prince I sat down with Poloma, an Asian-American woman in her thirties who had lived in Haiti for seven years. Like most foreigners attracted to Haiti, she was a little off-kilter and had an interesting personal story. "I came here to Haiti because I fell in love with this movement, with Aristide," she told me. "And it pains me, everything that's happened, to see it now. Even when I go out, I feel like I shouldn't be partying when everything's all fucked up."

You didn't see many Asians in Haiti. I asked Poloma if Haitians considered her a *blanc*.

"No, they call me *chinois*," she said. "I don't mind if they call me *chinois*, even though I'm not *chinois*. I do mind when they say, 'Ching-chong!' I try to adapt myself as much as possible, but in the end I'm an outsider, and if I want to, I can leave."

"Do you feel like you're a tourist?"

"Yeah, sometimes. I feel like an outsider. But then sometimes I don't. While I was living in Haiti"—she was ambivalent about remaining—"I wasn't interested in going to other countries." Other than Haiti, she meant.

"Why?"

"Because of the struggles of being an outsider. You go through that every day. It's not interesting."

"You seem to have opened yourself up to be wounded by this place," I said admiringly.

"That's my problem with my parents. I don't think they understand that I actually live here, in every sense of the word. It's seeped in. They say, 'It's just easy. Just leave now. You've helped them enough.' I hate that word. I don't feel like I came to help. I don't know if it's a question of semantics, but I feel like I came here to support what Haitians were already doing."

Poloma claimed white people didn't understand the world. As an example, she cited a perfectly pleasant young woman we both knew. This woman, she suggested, would sooner or later—more likely sooner—return to her white world in the States and become a happy white soccer mom.

I didn't know whether to take this personally. "Am I white?" I asked.

"You're white, but you reflect," she said.

"Paul Farmer's white too," I pointed out.

"Yeah, and he's awesome. I mean, I think there's a white mentality. The prime minister has a white mentality!"

I bought Poloma dinner at a restaurant in Petionville and cajoled her into letting me record some of her reflections. "If they really have a real, honest election, there's no way they're gonna win," she said, meaning the *bourgeoisie*. "Lavalas is gonna win. But what they're trying to do is destroy its reputation as much as possible. This you can't get out of. There's no end in sight. The middle class think the poor are too stupid to vote, or something."

"The middle class *need* to think the poor are too stupid," I suggested.

"Yeah, the middle class need to believe it," she agreed. "But the *bourgeois* know that the poor aren't stupid. They know how insidious their wealth is. Every time they try to stop the military from doing something, all of a sudden there's this wave of violence and crime. And people don't say, 'Oh my God, maybe it's the former military!' But Ethan, you see that it's all fucked up, don't you? And there's no end in sight. And Ethan, what if one day someone like Guy Philippe is running this country? What about all the people who suffered during the first coup? I just realized I'm living through a post-coup period, and I never thought I'd have to. Or whatever you call it."

The French Ambassador had recently said that Fanmi Lavalas had no right to be part of the political dialogue anymore, because of its alleged involvement in corruption and drug trafficking.

"God, that's awful, if the foreign embassies are saying that kind of thing," said Poloma. "But Bush got in, so they think they can do anything they want. But you see, they know the popularity of Aristide, and Lavalas is so strong. That's why the moment is so crucial for them to do everything they can to destroy their reputation. It can't be like before. The people voted in who they wanted, and he brought them into the dialogue of the country. He acknowledged their existence, and he acknowledged the horrible conditions of their lives, and the injustices that created those conditions. Who else was saying that? They understand the concept now that if you vote, the person the majority voted for wins. And now you're gonna have an election, and the candidates who are gonna run don't speak for the people, and that person's gonna win? How do you explain that? 'Cause people aren't gonna vote, first of all. Who's gonna vote? It's gonna be *bourgeois*, all pretty. 'Hey, it's not our fault they didn't come out to vote.' Or else they'll pay them to vote. You know what I think is really interesting?"

I gestured for her to pause so my scribbling could catch up to her talking.

"Hey!" she protested. "I just wanna have a normal conversation with my friend Ethan. Hey, but you're flying to Miami, right? When you talk to Marcus you have to be very clear to him that he can't stop what he's doing, because it's very appreciated."

Marcus was a journalist with a radio station called Melodie FM, whose real name was Marc Garcia. I was hoping to catch up with him in Miami the following week. "There are some people out there who are not brainwashed or manipulated by this," said Poloma. "But they're too scared to be vocal about it. Please tell him not to bow under pressure. To keep giving balanced news. But do you know what the problem is,

Ethan? For people who are trying to be fair and balanced, they're accused of being pro-Lavalas."

On our way up to Petionville in Poloma's car we had listened to Marcus's daily editorial in French, straining to catch his argument. "I don't think he's saying it straight, but he's saying about the illegitimacy of the ex-military," she had said. "He's trying to make this comment that here's this force that's trying to say they're constitutional, but everyone knows it's a lame constitution anyway, and you're hearing all this stuff but none of it makes any sense. But you know Reed?" Reed Lindsay, an excellent American journalist who wrote for *The Observer* and *Newsday*. "He told me that Marcus told him he used to be pro-Aristide but now he's not. So the fact that he's not pro-Aristide but he can still report in a way that's more responsible, tells you something, doesn't it?"

We talked about Pakistan, where I had been in February when the rebellion in Haiti began making the news. "Isn't the world just going nuts?" she said.

"Yes it is," I agreed.

"And I can't get myself a decent boyfriend!"

Haiti's current regime was, she said, "more insidious because even though it's in your face, it's disguised prettily. It's more insidious because it's so hidden. But it's more in your face at the same time, because if you understand, you understand. People see it, but they can't say anything. They've been beaten down, so they're just like, 'Forget it.' At the same time, they've been psychologically manipulated. Because even if they understand what they're up against, they can't stand up against it."

February was "hell," she said. "It was the uncertainty of everything: maybe I'm not going to be able to stay here, or we don't know what's going to happen tomorrow. You can see what's going on, what it's all about, but you can't stop it from happening. That whole 'We're students. The police are going after us.' And it was all bullshit. So many people, you can just pay them. Somebody who hates Ethan can just pay people to go out and say, 'I love Ethan,' and do all this craziness."

After February, needing to get away, Poloma had returned to her parents' house in California for several months. "I wish I could be detached," she said. "When I was back home and I saw that film about Jean Dominique, I started crying. And it wasn't even anything happening in the film, just pictures of the streets of Haiti. Because I'd been away for three months, and I already knew that so much had changed."

"You saw the film when you were back home?"

"Yeah. There were three people in the theatre. No, four, including me."

"I think your inability to detach yourself is one of the most appealing things about you," I said.

"Well, it's good for your book," she said in a rueful tone. "People say, 'You're just defending him.' People accuse me of just blindly defending him, like I'm naïve. But I'm like, 'No. Show me some concrete proof.'"

"That's why what the French Ambassador said is so fucked up," I suggested. "Because he's saying Aristide has no standing to stand in elections because of drug smuggling or whatever. But these people do?"

"Yeah. That's why I liked that report from the Council of Hemispheric Affairs. Because they said the only way to have any stability or security is to have several things, and then they listed them, and one of them is that you have to arrest human rights violators, including the Minister of Justice. I struggle with this, because it's not a black-and-white issue anymore. It's not like, 'Here are the good guys, here are the bad guys.' It's much more complicated than that. When I came back and I was trying to process it all, sometimes it was like you were trying to defend the indefensible. Because they would say, 'He did this, he did that,' and what can you say? I want to defend him, but he did so many things. So anyway, your book is gonna have to mention that I have a cute haircut and a cute purse."

"They're both cute," I acknowledged.

"Change my name. Like, give me another name. Like, I've always liked the name Poloma."

"Poloma?"

"Yeah, I've always liked that name. I was gonna name my daughter that, if I have one. But now I'm not. I want people to read it and go, 'Maybe it's her, maybe it's not. Could it be? No.'"

I entreated her to allow me to publish her real name. We argued about this a bit. I felt I went out on a limb all the time by using my real name on everything I wrote or said and that, although I couldn't compel anyone else to do the same, I didn't concede that others were necessarily in more peril than I was. I had fought the same battle with a friend in Pakistan, and lost. "I've made my compromises with this society, and I'm not willing to expose myself in that way," he had told me.

"You remind me of a middle-aged Pakistani man," I told Poloma.

"You do make your compromises," she said. "If you didn't make your compromises, you couldn't live here. Or you'd be bitter every single day. I hate this government, but I'm still glad I have electricity. I just don't feel like the environment is safe enough now to really be outspoken about how you understand the situation, about who are the causes of the situation, who are the main actors of the situation. And I think it's evident: no one is immune from it. You can see that in the death of Jean Dominique: he thought he was safe. Even this stupid prime minister – they killed his chauffeur a couple months ago. I don't even care if you say that I'm Asian, that I've been here a certain amount of years. And you know what? I'll even buy your book, even in hardcover. But not if it's like forty dollars, 'cause it's so damn expensive! And I don't like hardcovers, because they're hard to read, they're not comfortable to read in bed. The Harry Potter, the eight-hundred-page book, was so damn hard to read in hardcover. It was painful."

We met again the next evening, on the balcony of the picturesque gingerbread relic the Hotel Oloffson.

"When you're on the outside, I think you see what they want you to see," she said. "And you also see what you want to see. You hear all the beautiful words, and you want to come and be a part of it. And you don't see the frustration and the isolation of trying to live in another culture. And some of the people that you glorify as the good guys, you come and see that they're not necessarily the image that you had. And not just that they might have done crooked things, but just who they are as a person. You have this image of them as perfect, and they're not, not even Aristide. And it's going to take a hell of a lot of time to make things change in this country. So now when I hear it, I just don't want to listen to it. Unless it supports what I believe."

"What's the essence of Haiti?" I asked her. "In one sentence, what should I understand about it?"

"That it's a place that you can't possibly understand."

"Is that a cliché, or is it the truth?"

"It's the truth. You try to put it in the context of poverty and what it's like to grow up in this context. But then you say there are certain things where you just have to say, 'No, that's wrong.' But then you think, 'Maybe that's just my privileged background.' And then you just don't try to figure it out, because you'd just go nuts."

"Tell me what brought you here in the first place."

"I think there was two things. I was searching for some kind of meaning in my life. And the second thing was that growing up in the States, you were provided for. Even though I'm not from a wealthy family, all my basic needs were taken care of: food, school, a place to live, two parents. I could go to movies. Running water, electricity, a car. Then you come here and you see everything, you hear the stories. It's just like, you hear that poor people exist, right? And then you see the TV ads for 'Give like twenty dollars a month' and you're like, 'Oh my God, that's so Over There.' And me, I know what it's like. I know what it smells like. It's bad on TV. It's even worse in person."

We flipped through Aristide's little book *Eyes of the Heart*. "I mean, like, these pictures in this book, they're so pretty. But you don't smell all the pee and the shit. You don't see how dirty it is. But at the same time, there's so much beauty too. But you don't see it unless you want to see it—unless you open your mind to it and see beyond what's there. Just like when you look at something that's beautiful, and you look closely, and you see that it's not so beautiful. It kinda makes you teary-eyed: like, here are the answers to the criticism. But at the same time you think maybe it's just bullshit. I don't know what to believe anymore. But you want to believe. I think life is a process of trying to figure out who you really are and what you stand for."

Our conversation ended abruptly just before eight o'clock, because Poloma wanted to get back to her apartment to watch *All My Children* on cable. As we were leaving I looked around admiring the Olaffson, remembering how it had been the model for the Hotel Trianon in Graham Greene's great novel of the Duvalier time, where the Secretary for Social Welfare is found dead in the empty swimming pool. "Have you read *The Comedians*?" I asked.

"No," she said.

"What?!?"

"I haven't read it."

"You've lived here for seven years and you haven't read *The Comedians*?" I was incredulous, but also strangely impressed.

"The minute I came to Haiti I didn't read any more books about Haiti," she said. "I mean, living here is the education, right? I don't need to read any of the damn books. When I'm in the States I read everything I can get my hands on. I mean, I read the Bob Corbett [email] list and it freaks you out about the place. And then I come here and I'm like, 'Whatever.'"

✳

I wanted to interview Father Gerard Jean-Juste in prison. I finally reached his lawyer, Mario Joseph, on Friday morning, November 26, the last business day before I had to return to Miami on Sunday. I waited several hours in the lawyer's office, dozing in the heat, while he finalized his application to the judge for Jean-Juste to be released. Finally, around 4 p.m., he arrived with the news that Jean-Juste was to be released on Monday.

On the way across the city in his four-wheel drive to the prison in Carrefour, I quizzed Mario Joseph. "Now that Bush has won the election, the Latortue government can do anything with impunity," I suggested.

"That's exactly right," he agreed.

"Is Latortue *méchant*?"

He laughed. "It's not Latortue himself. It's the system. It's like asking if Bush is *méchant* because he went into Iraq. In Haiti we have to say there's a dictatorial government now. This government has all the characteristics of a dictatorial government."

169

"Is Père Jean-Juste going to be in danger again after this?"

"They put him in prison because they're afraid of him. If they put him in prison, they can kill him too. I also could be in danger because I work with him."

I asked what the charge against Jean-Juste had been. It was complicity to murder, changed from an original charge of disturbing the peace.

"*Complicité à meurtre qui?*" I asked.

"*Personne.*" No one.

I didn't get it. Then again, there were many things in Haiti that I didn't get.

"Why are they releasing him?"

"It's the law."

"But they don't always respect the law."

"The law said the judge can release any people according to this article. And then the file is closed, but any time the judge can call him to ask some questions. But still he is released."

"Is this judge a good judge or a *méchant* judge?"

"He is a good judge, because he applies the law."

"This judge must be very brave then," I said.

"I think he's brave," he agreed.

Mario Joseph was a very dark-skinned black man who dressed casually and spoke French and Creole both eloquently. He was forty years old and came from "a poor, poor family" in Verrettes near St. Marc, along the coast north of Port-au-Prince. He said he had been working with political prisoners since March—since the ouster of Aristide. "Before, I worked with the poor people in the slum areas, like Raboteau and Cité Soleil. I'm a human rights worker." He had two brothers and a sister, and his mother still lived in Verrettes. His wife and daughters lived in the U.S. "Because my work is dangerous. They could kidnap my three daughters, kidnap my wife."

I asked how he had become a lawyer.

"I went to missionary school," he said, "and I got a scholarship from the missionaries, and I became a teacher of geometry. And when I became a teacher, I got a little money and I went to law school. If I had had my choice, I would have been an engineer. But there wasn't a school of engineering in the Artibonite, so I went to law school instead. I didn't have a systematic motivation, but I think it was because of all the things I saw when I was young that I fell into human rights work." His father had beaten his mother, and as a boy he had witnessed the impunity of the Volunteers for National Security or *tontons macoutes* under Baby Doc.

Traffic was heavy, and it took a long time for us to get to the prison. When we did, we hurried in the gate and through the courtyard into a front room of the building, where we waited for Jean-Juste to be brought out to us. The guards were pleasant, even friendly with Mario, and they greeted me cordially. Jean-Juste was a diminutive bald man with a grey beard and a tropical-style shirt that he wore loose. He greeted his lawyer warmly, then sat with me on a wooden bench. I was told I had no more than ten minutes with him.

We spoke hurriedly, in English.

"Do you believe you're a political prisoner?" I asked him.

"Yes," he said.

"Please tell me why."

"A week or two before my arrest, I knew they were going to arrest me. I called the bishop and he said, 'Just be careful. Don't go very far.' And knowing they are going after Aristide supporters, and I am one." According to a 19th-century concordat between the Haitian government and the Vatican, the proper way for state officials to approach a Roman Catholic priest in Haiti was through his superiors. "Instead of doing that, they came directly for me at the rectory. I told them to get out. If they want to get me, they should talk to the bishop, the nuncio, the Pope. They said, 'The hell with the bishop, the hell with the nuncio, the hell with the Pope.'

"Some hours before my arrest, I was talking to President Aristide. I told him I was going to spend a month in Florida to be with the Haitian community. I have some influence to the people. The phone was intercepted. You should ask the American government about that." Jean-Juste had lived in Miami and was well known among Haitian-Americans there. I realized later that he was suggesting that he had been arrested to keep him from mobilizing them to vote for John Kerry on November 2.

"The worst thing is for me the shooting of three of the children," he said. On the day he was arrested, three children had been killed.

Abruptly a guard said our time was up. I asked Jean-Juste if there was one particular thing he wanted to say to anyone who might read my book.

"What I would like to say is for human rights to be respected for everyone in Haiti and a return to the constitutional order," he said. "This de facto government has got to go. It has no place."

We shook hands as the guards began leading him back to his cell. In a low voice I said, "Paul Farmer told me to tell you he says hello."

His face lit up. "Oh! Please tell him if he could come by here to visit, it would be great."

✳

"You're friends with the police officers," I remarked to Mario, back in his car.

"I have a bit of experience," he said. "I worked on a big case, the Raboteau case. So the police know me."

The sky was crimson and black now, as we headed back into the city. Carrefour was notorious as a traffic bottleneck, and as an unsafe area of Port-au-Prince. Because I had had to wait in uncertainty most of the afternoon then hurry to the prison, no one knew where I was at this moment. Policemen in riot helmets carrying automatic rifles stood in the middle of the crowded road, looking menacing in the gathering shadow.

"Those are not traffic police," said Mario.

We listened to the news on 107.5 FM, Radio Solidarité. There was news of a demonstration in Bel Air "for the return of constitutional government," and a report about Jean-Juste's impending release that included an interview with Mario recorded before our prison visit. "*Il est libéré*," he had told the interviewer, and added that Jean-Juste would celebrate Mass on Sunday *chez lui*. I asked how he could do that, if he wasn't going to be released until Monday.

"I'm putting pressure on the system," he explained. He answered his cellphone and spoke into it: "*Je viens de voir Père Gerard Jean-Juste.* Yes, he's fine."

When his call ended, I asked Mario to tell me more about his work. He said he was the only lawyer from the area who had returned to Verrettes and Gonaïves to take cases *pro bono.* "My priority is to work with the poor," he said. "I work with the most vulnerable people." He had finished law school in 1990 and started practicing in 1993. "Right at the start of my career, there was a coup d'etat. Again now, I work with the victims of the coups d'etat. The only explanation for me is that it's a *boulot*"—a job—"that God has given me. *C'est la volonté de Dieu.* Because I'm the first person who became a lawyer in my family. I didn't have any example. I had no one who oriented me toward human rights. It's dangerous, what I do, because this is a non-democratic country. But I'm comfortable. I'm not afraid."

PART THREE

Prologue

Paying Attention and Taking Notes

In January 1995, a New York literary agent informed me that "people's interest in Haiti has peaked." Her name was Lelia Ruckenstein. "But I'd love to stay in touch," she added. "Please tell me what else you're working on." I had mailed her from Bangkok a 125,000-word manuscript that I had written in a fever of urgent purpose during the second half of 1994. Titled (with intended irony) *Restoring Democracy*, it was an honest, if callow and inelegant, attempt to integrate my experience of Haiti with public events, to reclaim personal meaning from the cynicism and intellectual poverty of public conversation, to wrestle with Aristide's problematic significance, to articulate some things I had begun learning. When I wrote it I was not yet thirty, and it was overly ambitious. Rereading it in 2004, I found much of it embarrassingly overwrought. I'm glad *Restoring Democracy* wasn't published.

But the fact that I've been able to include long portions of it in this book is telling. In truth there are no borders and, as Aristide says, hiding the truth is like trying to bury water: it seeps out everywhere. Lelia seemed to be implying that only American people are people. Or maybe she meant only that Haitian people are not people. I do know, of course, that what she was actually guilty of was nothing worse than being lazy and parochial. But that's bad enough, because Haitian people's interest in Haiti had not peaked; Haitian people had to go on living in Haiti and dealing with whatever happened there, whether they liked it or not. Little more than three months after the U.S. invasion of Haiti—the culmination of more than three years of violence, political chaos, excruciating bad-faith diplomacy, and global attention—Lelia's attitude accurately reflected that of most Americans: Well, that's taken care of. On to Bosnia and beyond.

I didn't stay in touch with Lelia Ruckenstein. What would have been the point? After 1994 my personal and writing lives moved in new directions, toward surprising destinations. I concluded that the best I could do was to pay attention and take notes. Meaning declares itself with the passage of time; as a friend told me as I was fleeing Detroit, we see the shape of our lives only in retrospect. Or, as my father once said, none of it means anything unless it agrees with experience. And that's the thing about Haiti: you don't learn anything unless you listen and let time pass.

Listening implies and conveys respect, and respect entails suspension of judgment. Betsy Wall, the daughter of the Canadian missionaries who ran Wall House off Avenue Delmas, called the North Americans she met there "the odds and sods of the world, the misfits. And there they are: to transform Haiti." She urged me to "be still and listen. There's something extremely humbling in listening. If that's all I ever experienced in Haiti, I think Haiti would be more whole, and so would I. Because life is a gift, I have a responsibility to respond. People come here, and they think Haiti is so corrupt. Well, you know what? It's that way everywhere in the world. Haiti is what we all are. And I sometimes think this is why America comes here to try to change things: to try to redeem itself."

Everyone has a use for Haiti. The lefties want Haiti to lead the way in the global revolution. The churchies want it to be all about Jesus. The genteel rightist *New York Times* columnist David Brooks had the temerity and extreme bad taste to publish a column, two days after the earthquake that compelled the occasion for me to complete this book, blaming the victims in "places like Haiti" for lacking "middle-class assumptions." But we're not entitled to use Haiti to flatter ourselves, no matter who we think we are.

From Bangkok in the wake of the tragedy of 1991–94, I gave an essay on Haiti to *Books & Culture: A Christian Review*, whose editor, John Wilson, had recruited me to write for his new magazine after reading a previous piece I had written about Haiti. It wasn't a good fit. John and I had a number of problems with each other, but to me the defining betrayal was when he allowed my translation of a French verb to be changed without consulting me. I had asked Father Octave Lafontant rhetorically, not to say impudently, whether God had chosen Hitler to be a leader. To me his answer, *"Oui. Bon-Dieu a choisi Hitler, mais Hitler a trompé Bon-Dieu,"* carried meaning in precise correlation to its ambiguity, like the Hebrew word *timshel* in *East of Eden*. Best not to translate it at all. But if it had to be translated into English, to me *trompé* meant *deceived*.

To someone at *Books & Culture* it meant *betrayed*, which I found out only after the essay was in print. *Tromper* can mean *to betray*, but in the specific sense of sexual infidelity to a spouse. This meaning might be defensible as allegorical with reference to God, but I don't think that's what the person who "corrected" my translation had in mind. In the English version of the sentence, *betrayed* carries no implication that God might be fallible or vulnerable. The French verb *tromper* implies exactly that, whichever of its several meanings the speaker intends. To me, the sin lay in shoehorning a self-flattering gloss of Anglo-Saxon moralism on Haiti and the world and, for that matter, God, into Father Lafontant's clearly different and greatly subtler—and hard-earned—meaning. It was the religious analogue of the American habit of writing and thinking as if other countries matter only insofar as they impinge on U.S. national interests and policy. It was what I ran screaming away from when I left America in the first place. The man said what he said, and it's not okay to portray him as having said what you wish he had said instead. I never brought this up to John Wilson, because he never offered me an opportunity. At first I felt I simply had to swallow hard, because I was young and in a position of weakness. Then, after our falling-out, he refused to discuss the issues I had with his treatment of me and my work. But my response to *l'affaire tromper* was to say to myself: If that's what it means, or what it takes, to be a Christian writer, all right, then, I'll go to hell.

I decided that being a writer means not having answers or an ideology but paying attention and taking notes, and I found that if you do that long enough, things start falling into place. Meanwhile, every human life spirals back on itself. Like a book read first in youth and reread at intervals, a formative early experience lies in wait, ever ready to yield up new aspects of meaning. At sixteen, I hadn't known what I was letting myself in for. Nearly three decades later a great deal had happened, but little had changed. *Tout moun se moun*: all people are people. *Byen mal pa lanmo*: almost dead is not dead. *Pito m-led m-la*: I may not be pretty, but at least I'm here. Everything I've done and written since 1982 has been in the service of keeping faith with Haiti.

This is why I spent so much time in Haiti in 2004 and why, on January 12, 2010, I knew despite myself that I would have to lay other things aside and return again.

Chapter 10

"I'm Goin', Man"

The day after the earthquake, I was on the phone with my friend Todd Shea. "I'm goin', man," said Todd. And he went.

Todd was a bearded, big-bellied middle-aged guy from Maryland, whose promising career as a singer-songwriter had been derailed by the September 11, 2001 terrorist attacks. He had been in New York to play a showcase gig at the famous CBGB nightclub the next night. Seeing the towers on fire, he had removed his musical equipment and belongings from his van, driven to Chelsea Piers, and asked how he could help. He spent the next week ferrying supplies from stores in Brooklyn and Queens to relief workers at Ground Zero. The experience had led to the discovery of a new vocation, which Todd defined as providing logistical support to emergency workers in the aftermaths of disasters. He worked in Sri Lanka after the tsunami, in New Orleans after Hurricane Katrina, and in Pakistan after the October 8, 2005 earthquake that killed nearly 80,000 people. He had remained in Pakistan and started a hospital in the remote mountain village of Chikar because, he said, it was the first place where people had asked him to stay, he had seen a long-term need even as other relief workers were packing up as the emergency phase wound down, and he had fallen in love with the children. He liked to say that the American public hears "two percent of the story a hundred percent of the time" when it comes to Pakistan. "I want the American people to know the truth, and not the misperceptions," he told me. "I believe that if they had all the information, they would know what to do with it. But I don't think they have complete information. I think that will create opportunities for a better world."

I first met Todd in January 2009 beside a swimming pool outside a home in Pasadena, where members of Southern California's Pakistani community had gathered to meet both of us. I got to know him better during a week we spent together that summer in and around San Francisco, where we both spoke at the annual convention of the Association of Physicians of Pakistani Descent of North America (APPNA). With Todd, what you saw was what you got. "I shoulda been dead a long time ago, so this is all icing on the cake," he liked to say. What you got, besides a force of nature that did life-saving work in the direst of conditions, was a righteous and unmistakably American prophetic voice. I heard that voice loud and clear as we drove from San Jose to Fish Camp outside Yosemite National Park, where people Todd knew from Fresno held an annual Islamic summer camp for their kids. Todd had just spent several weeks bringing relief to some of the nearly three million civilians who had been displaced by fighting between the Pakistan Army and the Taliban in the Swat valley. "We're mostly concentrating at this point on the northern part of Mardan, which borders with Buner," he told me. "So we're in direct line with where people were coming down."

I asked him what the situation was like.

"It's not good," he said. "The monsoon rain season, people are not going back to their homes, they've been living in [other] people's homes for upwards of six-seven weeks, and in camps, and these places are not getting medical services. When they get back, their crops are going to be destroyed by the fighting. We're finding places that we're the first to give them medical supplies, and we're only a small team. Obviously, there should be a coordinated effort. We're trying to do what we can to survey the area, by way of visiting areas that haven't gotten enough aid. There's places that haven't gotten any help, medically at least, and it's ridiculous and it's a shame and it's a travesty. When somebody deploys, there has to be an information resource that's comprehensive, so that duplication of resources doesn't happen, or so that lack of resources doesn't happen. And this is exactly what happens. The UN health cluster and the government on the ground are supposed to be coordinating this."

About U.S. aid to Pakistan, he said, "It's very simple. If these things line the pockets of ministers and feudal landlords and the elite, if the masses don't benefit, there's a danger of revolution-type magnitude. And if that happens, the feudals are likely to lose everything. People will partner with extremists, because extremists are giving aid in areas where none of the above are present. The feudals should give half their land to the people that have been living on it all these years. Isn't it time? Give them hope, for God's sake."

Todd was unsparing, but he was an ex-Marine—at least in the sense that he had been kicked out of the Marines after boot camp at age nineteen for testing positive for cocaine use—who considered himself a patriotic American. "We have built into our system introspection that helped make our country great," he insisted. "Otherwise slavery would never have been abolished, and things like the civil rights movement would have been brushed under by a Tiananmen Square-type of massacre. I want my son to grow up in the America that I believe in, not the America of Elliott Spitzer"—he nursed a special animus against Spitzer, because of a friend's ordeal—"and the Federal Bureau of Islamophobia, and sending people to black sites, and electrocuting people's balls and stuff like that. The very words of our founding documents allow for that introspection, and also allow people to change people's minds and ideas. And there were some other things I read off the back of that Cheerios box, but I can't remember them right now."

"You're very quotable," I told him.

"Hey, someone puts a wire on my balls, I'll tell 'em I planned all kinds of shit."

"It's inspiring to hear you saying things like this."

"Well, I'm no expert in anything. Barely made it out of high school. But I do have a sense of justice and injustice, and I've always gone against bullies. And I've gotten my ass kicked a few times. But I've always been happy with myself for doin' it. And the bruises ain't that bad, really."

Todd's plan for his small organization, Comprehensive Disaster

Response Services, was "to keep growing and expanding to whatever level we can, depending on our donor resources; and, on the other side, to continue educating the American public, and to be an example. Right now many people's reality is rooted in misconceptions on all sides, and that's a dangerous place to be. And somebody somewhere has to take initiative in presenting information that people need to have in order to have a better understanding. In this case, educating Americans about the reality on the ground in Pakistan, the history that they don't understand, our culpability, and our need to do something about it.

"And on the other side, I want to be a part of showing Muslims that America is not out to destroy Islam or kill Muslims. I have not seen any evidence that that is what our intentions are. But I think it's high time we showed Pakistanis the best of America. If you're a true friend, you don't run out on somebody when you don't need them anymore. And if people have an ounce of pride or self-esteem, pretty soon they don't come around anymore. Pakistanis don't trust America anymore. We need to show Pakistanis who we really are. I don't buy into all those conspiracy theories and all that baloney about 9/11. What I do believe is that 9/11 is a direct consequence of Pakistan becoming a vacuum. We didn't just get hit out of the blue. We helped create conditions that caused it.

"Now, that's a far cry from saying that we deserved it. But I'm one that doesn't believe in doing things just because they might benefit you now or in the future. I believe in doing things that are good, and then naturally they don't come back to haunt you. And they automatically come back to you in positive ways. Work for justice, avoid hypocrisy, go out in the world and live the values that you espouse, and I think you'll be okay. Fail to do those things at your own peril."

Todd lamented the U.S. failure to remain engaged in Pakistan and Afghanistan in the 1990s, after the successful war against the Soviet Union. "I believe that it was a direct recognition that in the eyes of the U.S. leaders at the time, they were barbarians, subhuman, not worth it," he said. "And I would submit that they are human beings, that if U.S. leaders had treated them as important in a human way, then society in Pakistan and Afghanistan would be far further along today, because we would have helped them avoid all the things that are happening now. If you remember, at the time, we were loved. Both countries were in such a state of need, and then we just left. 'We got rid of our big enemy, let's get outta here,' and boy, wasn't that a strategic error. When the [Berlin] Wall came down and we were waving flags and saying, 'America, America,' why weren't we waving Pakistani flags? I remember seeing the Wall come down and all that, and I don't remember hearing anything about Pakistan. What kind of idiots were runnin' the show? I'll tell you who: Bush Senior."

"Yeah, but you know who else?" I said. "From '93 on it was Clinton."

"Yeah, well, him too. He was more interested in lookin' up some chick's skirt. He was a good president domestically, but he didn't do shit about Rwanda, he didn't do shit about Kosovo until the pressure was on, and he didn't do shit about Afghanistan."

"And he fucked up Haiti."

"There you go. And that era of prosperity—wasn't it an illusion?"

Driving through Yosemite back toward San Francisco, Todd said: "You can be the most competent, but are you the most motivated and the most committed? And I can tell ya, there aren't a lotta people beatin' on my door to replace me up there [in mountainous northern Pakistan]. I'd be happy to work with anybody who wants to come there."

I asked if he had heard of Paul Farmer.

"He's the guy who wrote that book *Mountains Beyond Mountains*? Or it was written about him?"

"It was written about him."

"Yeah, I was given it by somebody, and it's actually in my bag," he said. "But it's like two books behind your book on my reading list."

"What's unusual about him is that he followed the moral compulsion that he felt," I said.

✳

So half a year later I was on the phone with Todd and he was saying, "I'm goin', man." He was in Washington, DC at the time, on a fundraising tour for his work in Pakistan, but he dropped everything and flew via Fort Lauderdale to Santo Domingo, and went from there by road across the border into Haiti. On the flight to Santo Domingo, he walked down the aisle of the plane and talked to each of the other passengers, until he identified a few people with whom he felt he could work.

"I started figuring out how I was going to fly there, and I saw that the option through JetBlue was to go through Santo Domingo," he told me afterward. "I bought a ticket and went down on the 14th. I thought, I'll go into Santo Domingo, and I'll check the road, and I'll bring whatever I can, and I'll go quickly, so that I can lay a track of information that can start helping people possibly get in this way. I Facebooked a friend of mine, the only person I know who is Dominican. His name is Osmar Torres. I worked with him in a friend of mine's company after 9/11 for a couple years. Him and I have kept in touch over the years, and we're Facebook friends, so I didn't have his current phone number. I Facebooked him and said, 'Hey, call me as soon as possible.' So he called me, and I said, 'Osmar, I need some guys that you know in the Dominican Republic who are honest, straightforward, smart, can speak English—at least one of 'em—and can get some vehicles, and maybe set up for something that might last for a few weeks or a month or so, to get doctors into Haiti.' So he gave me the number of Yuel and Franklin, who picked me up at the airport, rented vehicles, and have been working with me. We instantly put together a team. We went and bought a bunch of supplies, and on the morning of the 15th, I headed to Haiti."

He was telling me this in late February 2010, in the living room of our mutual friend Dr. Salman Naqvi in Irvine, California. Todd had just returned from Haiti to speak at a fundraiser. "Where did you get the funds from, and what supplies did you buy?" Salman asked him.

"I used $2400 borrowing from CDRS funds," said Todd. "We knew that if we did something, we'd get some donations and pay that back. Because that's money that Pakistan donors have given for Pakistan, and we also need money there, obviously. And then I had $2000 from a friend of mine, Dan Panitz, who was the guy who Elliot Spitzer destroyed, who's a reverend. So he gave me $2000 from his side, and a satellite phone that one of his parishioners bought for $1000 or something like that. I came down, rented a couple vehicles, paid for the fuel, bought some medicines, bought some food in Santo Domingo, was able to get a donation of water from a company down there, and just brought all this stuff over into Haiti. Talked to the border guards there, made friends with a guy called Commander Santana, who for four weeks was great, and we never had a problem getting in or out of the border at any time of night in this whole effort—until the [Baptist missionaries from Idaho] were arrested that were trying to bring the kids over. Then the border clamped down at night and was more problematic.

"One of the best decisions that I made is that I scoured the plane from front to back on JetBlue from Fort Lauderdale to Santo Domingo. There were three nurses that were coming, white ladies. The whole rest of the plane was filled with family members of people from Haiti. The plane was full with Haitians and Dominicans going to the Dominican Republic. It was about half and half, I'd say. And then there were these three nurses, and then there was me. I went from the back to the front of the plane, talking to each and every person, getting business cards, giving my business card, talking to people about where they were going, what they were doing, 'What's the lay of the land, what's it like there?'

"So I got up near the front of the plane and was talking to a group of movers: big, muscular Haitian-American guys that were going over to look after some family members in Croix des Bouquets. And that's the first time I heard the name Croix des Bouquets. I also was armed with some information from you. The only real information I had before talking to those guys about the lay of the land on the ground in Haiti was from you: where possible border crossings were, where things were, what distances were from here to there, how difficult things may be. At that point, no one was really sure if the road into the city was damaged from that direction. It was all unknown. So we had to try to figure that out. And it wasn't until I actually took the road myself, and got into Port-au-Prince, that I realized that the road was fine. And quite to the contrary of Pakistan, it was a road that, from Santo Domingo to Port-au-Prince, was mostly paved and a very good road.

"So, on the plane I was talking to these movers. And a guy in the row in front of them turned around and started talking to them and me. And within about a minute of listening to him, I said, 'That's my guy.' A guy named Oliver Kernizan, ex-U.S. Marine and Army. He's Oliver, but it's actually Olivier. But he goes by Oliver in America, I guess. He works for Air France, and his wife was four-five months pregnant, and he's got his family obligations at home and stuff like that, but he came over to help his country. So we got to talking, and I just really hit it off with him in every way, and decided right then and there that we were gonna partner together. We didn't actually go over together; we met up the day after. Unfortunately we couldn't find each other, because his phone wasn't working for a while; there were some problems with the networks being down.

"We got into Croix des Bouquets, but the guy that we had come to turn medicines over to was not there. We went to this town square; there were 75 to 100 people laid out on the basketball court. It was nighttime when we got in. There were a lot of injured people there. And I was trying to call Oliver, couldn't get him, and so I said, 'Wow, these people here look like they need help, so I'll give the water and food, the supplies I've got, over to them.' So I was asking who was in charge of this joint, so I could turn these things over. And a gentleman there told me that the town magistrate was in charge, and that he was coming back in an hour or two. So I said okay, and I told Franklin and Yuel that we'll camp here for the night, we'll sleep here, we'll turn over these things to this guy when he comes over, so he can use 'em to help his people and do whatever he wants, then we'll go back to Santo Domingo and get more stuff, and I'll try to establish contact with Oliver, and then we'll go from there. In the meantime, Dr. Ayesha Mian was putting together a team with IMANA"—the Islamic Medical Association of North America, which eventually deployed about 200 volunteer physicians who worked with Todd—"that we later picked up on the 16th, drove over, dropped our stuff off, and on the morning of the

17th opened up our clinic. It was the quickest that IMANA had ever responded.

"But I very quickly got a lesson in some of the problems in leadership in Haiti. There seems to be a very large importance placed on who's in control and going through proper protocols and channels, and if that's in any way not adhered to, even unintentionally, then people get very angry with you. I didn't have that in Pakistan. Pakistan was just the opposite: people were happy that you were doing something and taking the initiative, and happy that they didn't have to take responsibility within the government sometimes."

"That's problematic too sometimes," I suggested.

"Absolutely," he agreed. "But in this case it was a situation where we had the things, and our intentions were correct: to give them to someone in charge. That person wasn't there. A Haitian Red Cross medic came up to me and said, 'There's one doctor over here, and he's dealing with a patient who just had a baby and is bleeding, and she has a broken leg.' We went over and saw her. She was very ashen, and very much looking in shock to me. I can't clinically diagnose shock, but I can tell you that what I would think shock would look like would look like this lady. She had a compound fracture, she had a bone sticking out of her leg, and she was bleeding from her uterus."

"That bone had been sticking out of her leg since the earthquake?" I asked.

"Yes. And she looked very ashen, and the expression on her face was very lethargic and distant. She just didn't seem like she was in very good shape. So I went over, and I said to this guy that they said was a doctor, 'They're saying it's an emergency. I've brought some supplies, and I don't even know some of what I've got, because I went to a pharmacy and I asked them to give me a little bit of everything, and I put it together very quickly.' I said, 'You can look at what we've got. And if you need something for this emergency, please take it.' So we got the stuff, and we were laying it out so that the doctor could see what was there. And about fifteen minutes into that process, this guy comes in, with an entourage of three or four guys. Actually kinda sleazy-lookin', the bunch of 'em, to be honest with you. And he came over, and he was raisin' hell in Creole. Obviously intensely displeased with me and this situation. And of course a crowd began to gather. So I said, 'Whoa, whoa, whoa, settle down.'"

Todd stepped to the side and tried to explain to the man that he was here to help, then asked to address the crowd through a translator, to help clear up any misunderstandings. But emotions were running high, and it didn't go well.

"And then of course, my Dominican guys, Yuel and Franklin, were sayin', 'Todd, we need to get outta here. This is Haiti, man. You're in Haiti.' And I said, 'I don't give a shit where I'm at!' And they said, 'Todd, you know, his guys are kinda fannin' out into a perimeter.' And I said, 'They can do whatever the hell they wanna do! I don't give a shit!'"

Policemen tried to intervene, but then the Haitian Red Cross, "who were mostly young people," refused the supplies. Todd believed that the magistrate had threatened them while he had been talking to the police.

"So to make a long story short, we got all the rest of the stuff, gave it to the mayor, gave him our blessing, packed up and drove off. Went back to Santo Domingo. And slept in Haiti at the border. Not because we couldn't get back into the country, but because we were so tired at that point, we just slept out under the stars. That was my first night in Haiti."

Todd could be reckless and intemperate at times, but he got things done. Afterward my friend Pete Sabo, who had traveled with me to Pakistan and spent about a week in Haiti with Todd helping organize a makeshift pharmacy, told me: "I have to say Todd was always dealing with something, didn't require much for himself. Just a shady place to recharge."

*

Dr. Salman Naqvi was a member of a group of Pakistani-American friends who had organized themselves into a board to support Todd's work in Pakistan, and who did the same for the operation he set up in Haiti. "Todd was there, he'd already rented a truck and filled it with supplies," Salman told me. "So we said, 'We need to do something.' So Laila Karamally and I, we started to talk to different people, and I started talking to my hospital and sending emails to friends. We sent a mass email, and Laila got a reply from somebody in India, saying that 'If you guys give water, we will send you money.' And they wired five thousand dollars. They were Indian Shia Muslims, and they said, 'As long as you have a banner and say this water is for Imam Hussein's sake.' And I think we said, 'Why not? Sure! We're getting water, the Haitians will get water, not a problem.' Our basic aim was to inform as many people as we could and get funds. I wanted to go but couldn't, because of my passport. I became a citizen on January 8, and it takes six weeks for a regular passport, and at the time I didn't know that I would need a passport urgently. So since I couldn't go, Farzana [his wife, also a physician] said that, 'I'll go.' And we decided that both of us can't go together, because of the kids."

Two Southern California journalists, Yvette Cabrera of the *Orange County Register* and talk show host Leslie Marshall, were especially supportive of the initiative and helped spread the word by interviewing Salman.

"As Pakistani-Americans," he told me, "we can empathize with what the Haitians are going through, because we have gone through it already, and this is their time of need, and we are there for them. We assembled a team, doctors and nurses from Orange County and the Pasadena area. And we made it very clear to the volunteers that 'You have to rough it over there. You may not have water, you may not have anything, and you should be willing to sweep the floors, even if you're a surgeon.' We contacted Dr. Faisal Khan, and he started to assemble his team over there. Farzana came back from Haiti, and she spoke so highly about the setup over there. She said, 'It was much better than what I expected.' The devastation was much bigger than what she expected. I was kind of getting desperate, and really didn't know what to do, and the travel agent said that he had sent somebody to the passport office, and they didn't even know if I existed. I was depressed that my passport was gone and I would not be able to make it. And Sunday morning, around 8 a.m., Farzana came and said, 'Your passport is here.' And I said, 'Okay, I'm going.'"

"It arrived on a Sunday?"

"It arrived Saturday. I didn't know about it. I think the kids got the mail and left it. So at 8 a.m. I found it, and at 10:30 I was at the airport. My doctor friends were covering me; they were very gracious. And Majjida's niece, Sara Khan, desperately wanted to go, so she also flew off with me."

"She's a physician?"

"She's an internal medicine physician, yes. I think flights had just started going to Port-au-Prince. We got out, and there was a huge crowd outside the metal gates, and people were trying to take our suitcases and trolleys and help out, and we saw Todd over there waving at us. That was a relief! He said, 'Here's an orphanage I'd like you to go to,' so we hopped into the van, and they dropped us at the orphanage with some medicines. I and Sara and, I think, two interpreters."

"Within an hour of landing, they were at work at an orphanage, helping some kids," said Todd. "Sara was a breath of fresh air, too. From the beginning she was all into doing whatever it took, and she's still there. She doesn't want to leave Haiti."

"She's been sending text messages saying, 'This is the best thing,'" said Salman. "She said, 'I've found myself finally.' An interesting note on her. She wasn't getting permission to go from her mother, who was in Pakistan. She didn't want her to go; she heard Haiti was in a bad condition."

"So she went without telling her mother?"

"No. She said, 'I'm going with Salman.' She calls me *mamu*. *Mamu* means uncle. So then she said, 'If you're going with Salman, you can go.' Then I wasn't going, because I didn't have my passport. But she just told her, 'He's going with me.' So when we were at Miami airport, her mother called and said, 'Where are you guys?' And she said, 'I'm at the airport.' And her mother said, 'Where is Salman?' Sara was like, 'Here he is, talk to him!' I told Sara, 'What would you have done if I had not been here?' She said, 'I would have thought of something!' At the orphanage we set up, my first patient was a two-week-old baby.

The last time I saw a pediatric patient was in medical school, which was twenty-five years ago. But things come back very quickly. And we took the books and things like that, to look at the dosages, because the dosages are very different. That day we saw probably a hundred, hundred and fifty patients, and all of them were children. So we picked up our pediatrics pretty quickly!"

The location Todd had found to establish a clinic was a derelict amusement park called Bojeux Parc, which had a giant smiling cartoon character looming above the entrance. That was where Salman and Sara started working the next day.

"A lot of patients were coming in the morning and waiting, and we were seeing them in a subacute area and treating them," said Salman. "But those who were really sick, we were sending them to an acute site, which had more acute medication, IVs. There were a few doctors and nurses there. And if somebody needed surgery, there was an OR. It was a nice setup; it's like a proper hospital there. In the afternoon, Todd arranged for us to go to the mountainous area. And the day after that I went with the 82nd Airborne to downtown Port-au-Prince, near the Presidential Palace. That was an experience. There were two Humvees in front, and two Humvees behind us, and our truck; we were three-four doctors and three-four nurses and social workers. The soldiers were basically guarding and controlling the crowd, and we saw three hundred and fifty-plus patients. That was some experience, because those were probably the sickest and poorest of all the patients.

"There were patients who had diabetes or hypertension; they had lost their medication, they didn't have medication. They brought one patient to me saying, 'Her pulse is very high.' It was around 130. Normal is around 70, 80. And she was feeling palpitations. I took her blood pressure, which was 260 over 120. Normal blood pressure is 120 over 60 or 70. And she was still smiling and talking. Usually in the U.S. if you get a patient like that, you'd go straight to the ICU and put them on IV drips and all that. We didn't have that stuff, so we loaded her with some p.o. [oral] medication and said we'll repeat the blood pressure again. And we checked her again, and it had come down a little bit, but it was still very high.

"So I told the soldiers, 'We need to take her to the hospital.' They said, 'We can't do that; can she walk there?' Ultimately she said, 'No, I don't want to go anywhere.' So I gave her three months' supply of medication and said, 'Take it. But if you can go to the hospital, go to the hospital.' We saw so many patients like that. They just don't have the medications anymore. A lot of skin diseases. A lot of diarrhea and dysentery. A lot of vaginal discharges of different kinds, because of poor hygiene. Whatever medications we had, we used them. And if we didn't have them, we were writing them prescriptions, but we know that they just can't afford to fill them.

"So you do whatever you can at that time and try to substitute the medications, or just talk to them. Just talking to them was at times enough, because a lot of patients had post-traumatic stress syndrome. Their complaints were pain in their stomach and dizziness, and that happens very commonly after earthquakes. We were seeing it in Pakistan [after the 2005 earthquake]. The earth shakes, and they get that false sense of dizziness, as if an earthquake is happening. A lot of them had that problem also. This was an experience I will never forget. And naturally I did not want to just leave and come back, because of the feeling that you're leaving, you know."

At Bojeux Parc there had been a few tense moments, because of complaints and misunderstandings involving a few of the volunteer physicians.

"The bathroom got stopped up every now and then; we got a little short on food every now and then," said Todd. "So there were minor inconveniences, that I don't like hearing complaints about at all."

"There were physicians who had worked twenty hours, they were exhausted and tired," said Salman. "I think it's our fault. Next time we have to tell them, 'Stock up. Take your stuff, so that in case there are things not available, you don't have to depend on the food that's provided. You should have something ready for yourself.'"

"Here's the thing," said Todd. "I had all the time in the world to take care of them and give them everything they wanted, make sure that all the food was there, fix the showers, make sure the toilets weren't clogged up. But if I had done that, I would have neglected the Haitian children. My deal on the priority list is that our doctors have their survival needs met, but they're willing to tough it out, because what we're doing, with limited people, limited resources, limited time, is trying to maximize our efforts for people that we came there to help. Now, I think that 90 percent of the doctors that came fully understood that and didn't cause a problem. I'm rather terse about it when it comes to my time being utilized to help children and people. A few people thought that I was little more than a chauffeur, arranging transport back and forth, not realizing that operationally speaking I was dealing with everyone from the army to local officials to our local partners on the ground, other NGOs, and planning out and orchestrating strategy, to help very poor and very devastated people. There was a neurologist who came. The day after arriving, not even having been there a full twenty-four hours, he said, 'I'm a neurosurgeon. I refuse to treat another vaginal infection.' And I said, 'Well, you can get the F out of my compound, because I don't accept that here.'

"If they had been more in tune with what I was doing, maybe they wouldn't have bothered me with such mundane crap. Now that they're back home, I think some of them probably regret complaining about not getting a slice of pizza or something. I made a comment in one of the meetings that, 'When you go home, in the weeks and months as you reflect on your experience here, you won't remember that. What you'll remember is what you were able to do for the children. And if you had to suffer a little bit and even feel maybe just a little pang of what they're feeling every day since the earthquake, and even before, maybe that reminder will be helpful to you to understand what they're going through, much like Ramadan and fasting are supposed to remind you of the hunger and suffering of others.'"

I asked Todd about the lack of coordination among international agencies in Port-au-Prince that I had been reading about in news reports.

"Haiti has been problematic early on because of the airport and the gridlock," he said. "And the UN agencies, especially the World Food Program, have been very bureaucratic. Tents and food could have been put out faster in many different ways, and it wasn't done. I don't know who to blame that on, but it didn't have to be that way. What I noticed, when I went to the airport, was that there weren't many flights getting in. And there was that aid, that I really could have used, piled up, obviously waiting for somebody to pick it up. But it's always sad to see people right on the other side of the airport wall, and no sense of urgency at the airport or within the UN bubble. And I see things sitting that could be used and are needed right away. But in criticizing the UN and larger agencies, I would have to say that the foot soldiers in the UN, the people that do the grunt work, are amazing, dedicated people that have a real sense of what should be done, and they're probably just as frustrated, if not more. If you have a bureaucratic system in place where dictates from the top down are the way that things work, and if information can't work its way up to become part of the decision-making process, then I don't think you can be as effective. I think you have to listen to your people on the ground."

At a reunion of the first team the Southern California group had sent to Haiti, I sat down with Salman's wife, Dr. Farzana Naqvi,who had been the team's leader. "Our team took everything in their stride," she told me. "You would expect people to be anxious or irritated or whatever. But nobody was like that. It brought me a lot of memories of 2005, when I had gone to Pakistan. In many ways, it was exactly the same thing that I was seeing, in terms of the destruction: I would compare it to Balakot, which was a city that was totally demolished [in Pakistan]. And again, you felt that sense of desperation there. But life had gone back to normal, and that's what I saw in Haiti too. The shops were open, people were in the marketplace, there was music going. The people were trying their best to move on. It was very difficult, but they were trying their best. The kids are the cutest, both places. In Pakistan, I was seeing patients in this tent city; we used to drive there to see patients. And all the kids would flock and come to be seen, and also to see me. I was like the local attraction! Even in Haiti, in the outskirts and the suburbs, you saw that people were trying to put their life back together.

"They used to come all dressed up to see the physicians. It was so sweet: you saw the kids with their lace socks and their little pompoms, and the young women all dressed up. The locals explained to us that they dressed up in their Sunday best! Somebody said, 'Oh, you had a problem with language in Haiti, which you didn't have in Pakistan.' But that's not true, because they speak a different dialect. So even in Pakistan I had an interpreter, who was such a lovely young man. And in Haiti I had this wonderful interpreter, a really bright young woman. In fact all the volunteers, who were running the pharmacy for us and being interpreters, they weren't being paid. They were just volunteering. Such a bright young group of people. In Pakistan my interpreter was so bright, and after that he did go into nursing. So sometimes the worst situation brings out the best in people, and I saw that.

"One of our drivers [in Haiti] had a pawnshop. He lost everything: lost his business, everything was totaled. And these were people without big bank balances; this was his living. So I asked him how he was doing, and he told me every day was a headache. And I thought he meant for himself. But he was working for this church, and they were trying to help people leave Port-au-Prince. They were trying to leave, and they needed money for that. He was sifting through the applications and trying to arrange funds for them. So his headache was not that he had lost everything; his headache was how to help other people who he felt were worse off than him. You see this amazing spirit in people; that's the grace that you see. Of course, you have the other element too. When we were with the 82nd Airborne, they said where they were when they were doing the food distribution, there would be fighting, and the machetes would come out. You see both sides of human nature."

"You have a nice life here in California," I said to Farzana. "There are many other physicians living nicely in California. They didn't go to Haiti; you did go. What's the difference?"

"I guess we all do what we have to do," she said. "I wanted to go; I went. I have a lot of friends who are physicians, and you want to do the best that you can. And sometimes you do succeed, and sometimes you don't."

"Why did you want to go?"

"They needed physicians there. I got a call, and I was told they needed a physician, and would I go. So the fact that I was needed was, I think, the reason I went. If somebody needs you to do what you are able to do, I think that's reason enough to do it! I saw a lot of patients, but what I really remember are two. And I didn't do anything professionally as such for them. One was this baby that was about a month and a half, and the grandma had brought the baby's mother to me. We had to go through the interpreter to really figure out what was happening. The mother was raped. And she was mentally handicapped, so she wasn't able to take care of the baby. And she then got diarrhea and was dehydrated, and she wasn't able to breast-feed the baby anymore. The bottom line was, they had this baby, the mother couldn't breast-feed, and they didn't know how to feed the baby. Though the mother was my patient, and I was concerned about her maybe having a sexually transmitted disease, and I was thinking about contraception, and then they explained that, you know, it was just that one act. So they finally brought the baby, and we were able to get enough formula and oral rehydration solution to help the baby. Then there was another little girl, who had a bad laceration. I couldn't suture it, because it was one of those really deep hand lacerations, where you need a surgeon to do the various layers. But we were able to get the surgeon to her, and then when she was in pain, I was able to hold her. And I felt I was able to do something for that little one. I remember that. So sometimes it's not even what you do, but just that you're there for someone."

I asked Farzana about Pete Sabo, my friend from Seattle who had traveled with me to Pakistan, and who had spent a week at Bojeux Parc.

"Have you noticed whenever people talk about Pete, they always have a smile on their face?" she said. "He has that effect on people. Wonderfully giving, very hardworking, so quiet. I think sometimes we take him for granted. People like that are usually taken for granted, because they give so selflessly. And unless you're looking, you even miss out on how much they're doing. I thought he gave so much. I was very impressed."

"Were you changed?" I asked her.

"I don't think you go without coming back changed. It was really hard to talk about it. It took time to process, and that's why I think it was a good idea for us all to meet tonight. When we were there we were all so hyper. I think it's like a coping mechanism. Because honestly, you're seeing such destruction, and everything. But I was not depressed, not now, not when I was in Pakistan. Because otherwise you can't function. You have that adrenaline running; everybody was on a high. People say about discomfort, this, that, and the other. Honestly, you have no sense of that."

"Are you still on a high?"

"No. Because then you crash. It always happens. I came back and there was too much happening, and Salman was leaving. I didn't even have time to think. I came back late Thursday night, early Friday morning, and Salman left Sunday morning. And Saturday was our daughter's eighteenth birthday. I hadn't unpacked my suitcases—can you imagine? Whole day Friday I was trying to get things organized, and Saturday was the birthday. So Sunday morning I unpacked mine, and I packed his at the same time. It was, 'These are the anti-malarials. This is your antibiotic. *There* is the stethoscope and the books, and *there's* the sleeping bag.' Half the things were repacked. Asim went with us to the airport, and then we went straight to Majjida's house to plan the fundraiser. And then Monday I was going back to work. In a way it was good, because I didn't have time to think."

"How long have you been back?"

"About two weeks. You slowly get back into mainstream life. Going back to work helps, because it's the routine. You want to hang onto a little of what you felt, but I don't know how long that stays. Some of it stays. And you *hope* you can hang onto it. Because I'm somebody who's impatient; that's my biggest problem. So I get irritated, I get impatient very quickly. And you see how people face things, and the strength and the character that you see in people. I saw it in Haitians, and I saw it in Pakistanis when we were there. And you want to have some of that."

Chapter 11

In the Ruins

On January 12 I had been minding my own business, when I got an e-mail from a friend with the subject line "major quake in Haiti." There are times—a lot of them, these days—when you get walloped by the realization that life can't go on as normal, or rather that normal life never was what you had been hoping it would turn out to be. I was settling into a graduate program in South Asian Studies at the University of Washington. The winter quarter had just started; Tuesday, January 12 was the second meeting of my weekly seminar class. After that day I sleepwalked through the rest of the academic year, lugging around a heavy lump in my chest.

And all around me college students sported hastily printed T-shirts, retail establishments solicited Red Cross donations at point of sale, church groups and school kids jumped on the bake-sale bandwagon, large numbers of mobile phone users zapped small dollar amounts through the ether. More than half of American households "gave to Haiti," as the expression went, after the earthquake. Given such an outpouring, how could one feel churlish? And yet, how could one not?

Boy Chokes to Death in Hot Dog Eating Contest for Haiti

SAN PEDRO—Police are investigating the death of a 13-year-old boy who choked on a hot dog during an eating contest to raise money for Haiti at the Boys & Girls Club of San Pedro.

Noah Akers, a Dana Middle School student from San Pedro, was among about 120 elementary and middle school students participating in the fundraiser for Haiti on January 28. ...

Noah suddenly began choking during the event, and a male staff member performed the Heimlich maneuver while others called 911.

Paramedics ultimately had to use an extended pair of forceps to remove the hot dog. ... Noah was removed from life support on Monday.

That story was reported by KTLA News in Los Angeles. This one was from *The Onion*:

PORT-AU-PRINCE, HAITI—Less than two weeks after converging upon the site of a devastating magnitude 7.0 earthquake, American anthropologists have confirmed the discovery of a small, poverty-stricken island nation, known to its inhabitants as "Haiti." ...

"That an entire civilization has been somehow existing right under our noses for all this time comes as a complete shock," said University of Florida anthropology professor Dr. Ben Oliver, adding that it appeared as if Haiti's citizens had been living under dangerous conditions even before the devastating earthquake struck. "Of course, there have been rumors in the past about a long-forgotten Caribbean nation whose people struggle every day to survive, live in constant fear of a corrupt government, and endure such squalor and hunger that they have resorted to eating dirt. But never did we give them much thought." ...

"I've vacationed just miles away in beautiful St. Kitts many times," Oliver added. "Never did anyone say anything about this Haiti place."

For weeks I spent long hours at my desk writing e-mails, making phone calls, passing lists of needed supplies from Partners in Health in Boston to Todd Shea in Santo Domingo, even at one point fielding a call out of the blue from a New York City rescue dispatcher who needed advice on directing his men from one part of Port-au-Prince to another. I don't know how he got my number. I referred him to my father in Colorado Springs, who knew the city better than I did. I did what I could, but I felt stranded in Seattle. I certainly wasn't needed in Haiti, but for my own sake I wanted to be there. At the same time, I feared the emotional effects of seeing the loss and destruction for myself. But I knew that was self-indulgent and timid; if Todd Shea and Salman and Farzana Naqvi, and my other friend Dr. Shahnaz Khan from Florida, and many others who had never been there before, could go to Haiti, why couldn't I? The answer was that I could, so therefore I would.

In the meantime Todd had been scheduled to be in Michigan in late January, to speak at a fundraiser for his Pakistan work and at a student event in Ann Arbor. He pleaded with me to fill in for him. So at the Islamic Association of Greater Detroit in Troy, Michigan on January 23, I told the mostly Pakistani-American audience how much it meant to me to be there in Todd's stead, especially given that the reason he couldn't be there was that he was in Haiti, saving lives as he had done after the 2005 earthquake in Pakistan. I quoted from the Quran (Surat Al-Hujurat 49:13): "O mankind! We have created you from a male and a female, and made you into nations and tribes that you may know one another." And the effort and eagerness of the young volunteers moved me also to say this: "We all know that America is a nation of immigrants. As an American whose ancestors came here in the nineteenth century from Ireland and Germany and France, I want to thank you for contributing not only your talents and material resources, but also your impressive children, to help build a new, improved America in the twenty-first century." The gift I accepted in return from the Pakistani Michiganders was a generous measure of solace and encouragement in a bleak time.

For several days after the earthquake I had wondered if Paul Farmer was in Haiti, whether he might have been killed or injured. Then I saw him being interviewed on *60 Minutes*. "It's very upsetting," he said. What spoke more eloquently than his understated words was his demeanor: bland, deadpan, simmering with things left unsaid. He must have said other things in that interview, but those three words and his face said it all. What do you say, when you've said it all before, and an unforeseen cataclysm gives you a rare and fleeting chance to reach tens of millions who had never before been paying attention? "It's very upsetting."

❋

In March I had a week free and a scheduled speaking engagement with the Pakistani American Association of Tampa Bay, so I seized the opportunity to spend a few days in Port-au-Prince. At gate E6 in the Miami airport, waiting for the 1:35 American Airlines flight, were several groups of what in Haiti I've heard called "same T-shirt people": *Global Health Outreach* and *Haiti Christian Outreach* and *Haiti Newhope Mission*. Jarringly, most of the people at the gate were white. I wasn't on any of the same T-shirt people's missions. I guess I was on a mission of my own, though. The most visible group was in bright red: *2010 Haiti Mission Trip*, with a logo of a stethoscope shaped like a heart. The potential problem for me was that their shirts were the same color as the one I was wearing, and I had specified to Ti Gerald Oriol that his driver could recognize me by my bright red T-shirt.

On the plane I sat next to a structural engineer from Nebraska named Jay, who told me the death and destruction caused by the earthquake had been so great because cinder blocks in Haiti are only one-third as dense as in the United States. He opened the conversation by asking if I had been to Haiti before. I said yes, and we fell to reminiscing. "When I first came here I didn't have a phone, and I felt like the Apostle Paul," he said. "That was a good lesson. I had to learn to rely upon God. I needed that lesson."

Jay was a congenial seatmate for my first flight to Port-au-Prince since the earthquake. "That's the other thing," he said. "When you'd fly in, you'd almost inevitably sit next to some old Haitian lady and help her fill out her forms."

"Yeah, I've done that," I said.

"It used to be so smelly on these planes in the summertime," he said happily.

Off the plane we were driven in a bus along the damaged tarmac to an unfamiliar warehouse-like room at the far end of the airport. My bag had somehow missed the connection in Miami, so I had to come back for it the next morning. Outside, Ti Gerald's driver found me in the crowd and led me to his truck, where Gerald himself waited in the passenger seat. I reached through the window and gently held the hand at the end of his skinny, fragile arm, and he gave me the alert, intelligent smile that I remembered. It was good to be back. Until the earthquake I hadn't known when or even whether I would return to Haiti, and I hadn't stayed in regular touch with Gerald, but when I had written to him on very short notice he had been glad to hear from me and invited me to stay at his own house. In 2004, Gerald had been only twenty-four years old and already an impressive and memorable guy, an old soul. I reflected now that he was still not quite thirty. What a thirty years it must have been. He had been just ten when Aristide swept to power in 1990, and ever since then he had been living Haitian history and paying close attention.

Gerald's driver, Yovens, was tall and thin and very quiet, and it was moving to watch him gently lift Gerald from the passenger seat and situate him in his wheelchair whenever we arrived somewhere. Yovens looked a little like Kareem Abdul-Jabbar. Sometimes I helped him carry Gerald and the chair up staircases. Another driver filled in on weekends. "I enjoy going out with this driver," Gerald said.

"He doesn't talk much," I observed.

"He's not much of a talker," he agreed. "But he's very dedicated."

Gerald lived near the airport in a walled compound called Village Tecina, named after the construction company his father had helped found. "It's one of the rare examples of Haitians coming back and working together to build a truly modern enterprise, not just a family business," Gerald told me. "Thirty-five years ago, a group of Haitians that were in the United States and were studying, some of them architecture, others engineering, others accounting, decided to work together and create a company that would serve the construction sector in Haiti, while putting ethics, professionalism, and excellence at the forefront. And through their efforts, they have become a major business firm in the country, very well established in Haiti. Most major businesses in Haiti are family-owned enterprises, and here is an example of a modern firm with people from different backgrounds, but with a common goal to serve the country and the construction sector. They've lasted more than thirty years, and they've been able to grow the company. They've faced many challenges, especially during the embargo period. But they overcame all these difficulties and kept the company growing. So it has been a really positive example, not only for me personally, but for all the children and grandchildren of these founders, and now we're like an extended family. And when people talk about modern firms in Haiti, frequently they will bring the construction firm up in conversation. It's called Tecina, which stands for technique, industries, and agriculture." Tecina's headquarters, in a different location, had been destroyed in the earthquake, and Gerald's father had been buried in the rubble but had survived.

What Gerald rather quaintly called the village was an unusually tranquil oasis with large trees, a swimming pool, well-tended little lawns, and a shared generator. Here, on low ground, as opposed to uphill in Petionville and beyond where many other elite Haitians lived, they enjoyed the advantages of plenty of water and proximity to the airport. After a day out on the streets, it was a refuge.

Driving into the compound past a pair of tennis courts, I said to Gerald: "I didn't bring my tennis racket. Maybe I'll bring it in July."

"I remember reading in your Pakistan book, you played a lot of tennis," he said.

There was a ramp that curved steeply down from an upstairs bedroom of his parents' house to their driveway, which Gerald went up and down on the motorized scooter that he used to get around the compound. "Do you always go down the ramp backward?" I asked him.

"Yes, because once I was traumatized," he said with a laugh. "The brake didn't work, and I almost fell off. So since then, I decided to go backward because I think it's safer. I don't think the scooter was made for such a steep ramp."

"Is there any sense in which life is getting back to normal?" I asked him that first day.

"Well, we have a tendency to take an abnormal situation and normalize it," he said. "If you go to the city you see tents, you see tarps, you see houses being built, people getting on with their lives. Once you go in the public parks, you see the makeshift lottery banks, you see the guys playing checkers. I think for some people this situation is not worse than when they were in the *bidonvilles*"—the poor neighbor-hoods as they existed before the earthquake. For some people it's actu-ally better, because they don't pay rent; they get free water delivered by NGOs."

Gerald himself had been at the UN building just before the earth-quake. "I left it an hour before it collapsed," he told me. "One person who was in the meeting with me actually died."

"At what point did you become aware that there had been a terrible earthquake?"

"I was in my vehicle with my driver, and I really thought that I had a flat tire. Seconds afterward I realized that, obviously, it was an earth-quake, because I saw the electrical poles shaking back and forth, and I saw some walls crumbling in the streets. But in the area where I was at the time, it wasn't terribly damaged. It was only when I started seeing people walking with wounds, and people screaming, that I realized that it was more serious. At that moment, I called home to find out how my daughter and my family were, and it was difficult to get a connection, because all the telephone lines were down. But I persevered, and finally I got through to my mother, and she told me the family was okay. And at that moment I called a few friends, and other collaborators living in poor communities throughout Port-au-Prince, and they told me about the devastation in their neighborhoods. And this is when I realized that the situation was really serious and devastating and affected many, many people. We spent the whole night at home, outside of the house. We listened to a few radio stations to find out how things were in the streets, and in the morning I took an early shower, and I took a pickup truck, and I visited several of the neighborhoods in which I work.

"It was an overwhelming and heartrending experience. We saw people lying in the streets. It was really terrible. We organized a mass burial with some community leaders. We collected cadavers in the streets, children and adults; we dug a hole in the local cemetery and buried the corpses. We must have organized a burial for hundreds of people. I don't remember the count, but it was a lot. We provided transportation to hospitals for people that were still alive but injured. We also sent them to the UN log base that was transporting people to

Martinique or Guadaloupe to ensure that the wounded people were able to receive immediate health services. But during my visit in these neighborhoods, I also realized that the Haitian people really were fighters, that they were truly the heroes. They were trying to remove people that were under the rubble, trying to help out friends, trying to help out neighbors, or trying to help out total strangers. Some of them spent hours digging with their bare hands, helping out, and I realized that the Haitian people really were tremendously courageous and were able to build great solidarity in the face of unprecedented catastrophe.

"For instance, one of the first calls I made was to a good friend of mine. His name is Joacyn Marseille. He was almost hysterical. His daughter was injured. The family house had collapsed, and she was found under the rubble. When I called him, he was carrying her to the hospital. And then maybe five or ten minutes afterward, when he arrived at the hospital, he was actually crying, because he couldn't find any available doctors at the hospital. There were so many injured people that his daughter was not being attended, and she was suffering and crying and begging for help. And he couldn't find any help, and he almost went crazy. But he was also a very courageous guy. On the next day, when I came to the neighborhood, he didn't ask, 'Let us go look for medical aid for my daughter.' He said, 'Let us go bury the dead in the neighborhood.' And when we finished that, he helped other injured people in the neighborhood go with me on the pickup truck to medical facilities. We only went out with his daughter three or four days after the earthquake, and this is when we were able to send her, I think, to a UN facility, and she was transported to Martinique. She spent six months in Martinique, and when she got back, she couldn't speak Creole anymore, only French. This was very, very touching, because his daughter obviously was in pain. She had a broken leg, and she had a wound in her back. And instead of thinking only about his daughter, he thought about the whole community. It was a very touching experience."

I asked him how things were going now.

"With the absence of direction and leadership from the government, the NGOs are not doing an effective job," he said.

"Why?"

"Well, the NGOs pretty much focus on Port-au-Prince. It would have been an opportunity for people to rebuild their lives in provincial towns. But the emergency period wasn't well planned. Everybody was like, 'Hey, Port-au-Prince is where all the journalists are,' and since everybody wants to get their logo on national TV, the NGOs pretty much centered relief efforts on the capital."

"Do you think it's that cynical?"

"Well, maybe I am being cynical. But sometimes that's the way you have to view it. They started to focus on Port-au-Prince and never stopped. Also, they could have cleared the rubble in the *bidonvilles*. But they didn't." In an already severely deforested country, people were cutting down trees to tie tarps for shelter. "People are clearing the few remaining green spots that were left in Port-au-Prince to provide space to erect shacks," said Gerald.

"So these tent cities are becoming the new *bidonvilles*."

"Exactly."

An election had been scheduled for February. "But obviously it got postponed," Gerald told me. They were now talking about holding elections in November.

"What do you think of Aristide saying he wants to come back?" I asked.

He smiled. "At this point in time, I don't think it's a good idea. He can stay in South Africa for a while." Then he asked me what I thought about Aristide. "You must be clear," he insisted. "I want a clear answer. Because last time when I asked you, I remember thinking, 'Hmm, that's a very political answer.'"

I must have given him an answer this time, hopefully a clear one, but I can't find it in my notes. What I can find is this:

"You've admonished me to get over thinking about left and right in the context of Haitian politics. Someone like you, from an elite family, is saying the things that you're saying, and doing the work that you're doing in poor neighborhoods. That seems to me to represent a very different relationship between social classes than Aristide portrayed when he was aspiring to be the leader of Haiti's poor people, in the late eighties and early nineties."

"People have a lot of misconceptions about Haiti," he said. "It's like a book: They want to see a protagonist and an antagonist. As for Aristide, he is unfortunately a divisive figure, with very passionate partisans and foes alike. He can be quite dubious, as exemplified by his riddle-like speeches. You have to really analyze them, to determine whether or not they are coded. Like if he says, 'We want peace in this neighborhood,' he might be saying, 'Guys, go burn the tires.'

"When Aristide got elected in the 1990s, he had large, large support. And people really believed that he would be able to deliver positive change in Haiti. Obviously, he had many enemies in the country, as well. Because he also, unfortunately, used a form of divisive politics. And I think this is what brought his demise. He has lost a large part of his support in Haiti, and many people now realize that he didn't really have a vision and sustainable development plan for the country. Instead, I think he used the political process for his own personal agenda. It is regrettable, because he had such a large support within Haiti, and the people really were willing—were looking forward to volunteer and collaborate. Aristide had support from people from various backgrounds. And he had the opportunity to bring people together like no other president. I think that he could have asked the people to do just about anything he wanted, at one point in time. People were celebrating, people were giving out hands to clean the streets, to undertake whatever social work was asked after he was elected. I remember at the time, in my community, some people came by the village to ask for some financial support to purchase brooms and other materials to clean the streets. This was a great initiative, and it was being done all over the country, or at least in Port-au-Prince, where he had his strongest base. But unfortunately, he didn't live up to his promise, and that's where we are at now. We are living the results of the unreasonable, the destructive politics of not just Aristide, but almost all successful politicians in Haiti. When I mean successful, I mean in terms of being elected."

Gerald was willing to talk about Aristide, but there were other things he was more interested in talking about.

"Let's talk about basketball," I suggested.

"I've always liked basketball," he said. "In my youth I used to be a big fan of Michael Jordan. It was amazing to see the moves, the hoops that he could make. Sometimes you wondered if he wasn't superhuman." He chuckled. "And now, I look at basketball as a possibility for a better Haiti. Basketball obviously is an economic opportunity for youths, because if they manage to develop talents to a high level, they can play in professional leagues abroad. But basketball is also an alternative for youths, because as you know many youths in Haiti do not have a structured environment to guide them as they grow up. And many of them, unfortunately, join the ranks of gangs, or do not develop to their full potential. Basketball is a team sport; you have to be able to cooperate with your teammates to succeed. And this serves as a way to develop friendship in communities. Our personal experience is that Haitians really love that sport. It's actually, in my opinion, the second sport behind soccer.

"So we try to promote basketball by installing hoops and repairing courts in disadvantaged neighborhoods and in schools. And also, we try to organize, once a year, a tournament as a way to promote cooperation among communities, and also as a way to transmit positive messages. Every time we organize a major basketball tournament, while the music is playing in the neighborhoods, it becomes very crowded, and there's huge attendance at the games. So during the halftime, we take the opportunity to talk about disability to the crowd. And sometimes we invite people with disabilities to perform some activity, like a play, or a dance performance, or just talk about their personal life, as a way to raise consciousness among those that are attending the games. Hopefully one day we'll even organize some special games for people with disabilities."

"You could have wheelchair basketball."

"Yes, exactly."

"I know there have been some Haitian players in the NBA. Do you want to see more?"

"Certainly! For the individual it will be an economic opportunity, and surely for their families as well. But also it will in many ways encourage other children in Haiti to pursue their dreams and to really fight hard. And they will realize that there is no such thing as being doomed, that they can improve their life and condition through hard work and discipline."

"You said that basketball is an appropriate sport for Haiti. What do you mean by that?"

"Well, basketball doesn't require much investment. What you need is a hoop and a ball, and a small court. It doesn't have to be a regular-sized court. You can put the minimum infrastructure in just about any neighborhood. I've actually seen one location in a provincial town, in which they made the rim with the cover of a toilet. And the kids were playing with a cheap plastic ball and shooting hoops in the toilet. Obviously, we don't want them to do that. We would prefer the kids to have access to a minimum of infrastructure. But it's an example to show you how little is needed to play basketball."

"Why did you begin doing this work?"

"I have been lucky in life. My origins, and also my family and friends, allowed me to outgrow my personal disability, my personal challenges. It motivated me to help other people in need. I started out in the private sector, working in the water industry. But I felt that this wasn't enough for me, and that I had to pursue more socially-oriented goals. I have been politically active, too. This compelled me to also go beyond what society might have set limits on. And this allowed me to get in touch with poor and disadvantaged communities, where the majority of the people live."

"Have your political motivations turned into more social motivations?"

"Definitely. One cannot be immune to the level of needs and the level of poverty in these communities. Right now I would say I am beyond political, really. I feel like I have a direct stake in these communities. And the people in the communities where I personally work really have become part of my family, at least my extended family. And I see them almost every day; I talk to them every day. And I feel their needs,

I understand their concerns. And also I see hope in their eyes, and this gives me much motivation to work harder with them."

In shared vulnerability, Gerald had found common humanity. He was very much an activist and self-appointed spokesman for disabled people, but he assertively and eloquently resisted being pigeonholed as such, and he himself defined the terms of his advocacy. I wondered what he thought about Sister Joan Margaret, the legendary nun who had run St. Vincent's School for the Handicapped for forty-nine years. "Did you know Sister Joan?" I asked him.

"No, I never met her. But I heard many stories about her."

"She was famous."

"Yes, she was. She really, in many ways, helped set off the disability movement in Haiti. I only got involved in disability-related work in 2003, when my sister asked me to write an article about my upbringing. I could send you the article." Gerald honored and appreciated Sister Joan as a trailblazer, but I sensed there was an ambivalence in his admiration, because he felt there were more and other things that still needed to be done. I asked him to elaborate.

"*St.-Vincent* really has provided a lot of services to people with disabilities in Haiti, and when people with disabilities were in the shadow, in darkness, only *St.-Vincent* provided a lighted candle," he said. "But I also think that we need to ensure that special schools or programs specifically targeting disabled people have an inclusive strategy too. I don't believe in working only on disability issues. It has to be inclusive. Because when you go to a special school, frequently you're only surrounded by children with disabilities, or adults with disabilities, and you live in an artificial environment. To allow these children to feel complete, to feel whole, to allow these children to have a successful life, they need to live in a natural environment. And a natural environment includes a diversity of people. And it will serve as a positive experience for other children and other adults with no visible disabilities."

I tagged along with Gerald as he did his day-to-day work around the city, and one day we stopped at the Western Union office so he could wire or receive some money. "You would think that companies that are based in the States, like Western Union, would have a policy on accessibility," he complained.

"But they don't, because they're in Haiti and there's no law that says they have to," I said.

"But soon there will be," he said confidently.

"You told me that just going in and out of the bank helps raise awareness."

"Yes. People do not often come across persons with disabilities at the bank to check their personal account or to withdraw funds. They see people with disabilities either begging in the streets or maybe at home, secluded from day-to-day activities. It serves to raise questions, in a positive way."

"So do you see yourself as a kind of ambassador for handicapped people?"

"Maybe the term ambassador is too big or too broad. But I do try to contribute to raising awareness about these issues in Haiti, because I understand that personally I was very lucky, and unfortunately I'm probably one of the few people with disabilities in Haiti that enjoy an inclusive and rewarding life. And I think that, because of my personal story, my personal experience, I have a duty to help bring down cultural barriers, so that they too can get their chance in life."

"What kinds of cultural barriers?"

"When people see a person with a disability, they usually believe that that person cannot be productive, that person needs to be permanently assisted. As a result, many parents of children with disabilities choose not to send their children to school, or give much more attention to their other, healthy children. And I think that's a shame, because when you ponder and you realize that about ten percent of the population in Haiti suffers from a form of disability, you will understand that true development cannot materialize if we do not develop an inclusive mindset, a new paradigm where people with diverse backgrounds have equal opportunities."

"Your parents must be unusual people."

"Disability was not really brought up in conversations during my childhood, and my parents never really viewed me as someone with disability. They viewed me as a normal child with some special needs. And they've always strived to help me see life in a positive way, in which, through hard work and discipline, you can be successful in life. My parents never viewed disability as an excuse for failure. If I didn't succeed at something, it wasn't because of my physical deficiencies. The way I see it, the only disability in the end is a terrible attitude."

"You told me once that you used to live in Florida," I reminded him, "but you prefer living in Haiti because it was too frustrating or humiliating to deal with the bureaucracies in the States."

"I've gone back and forth to Florida for many years, and I've thought many times on moving permanently to Florida," he answered. "I've looked at disability in the States, and personally, although there is a lot of progress, I also saw that it's part of a bureaucratic system, and it's not something I want to get into. In Haiti I've been able to accommodate myself, so that I don't even think of disability. It's only really when people ask me about it that I think about it. But the really fundamental issue for me was that I felt that I was really more useful being in my country than abroad. And if I could pursue my academic goals while being in Haiti, I should be in Haiti. And I don't regret it. It's not an easy environment, as you can see, but I love being in Haiti. And the people really inspire you to work harder. To be frank, I don't see myself as a person with disability at all. If you are suffering from a medical condition, and you can overcome these medical problems, and it does not affect your lifestyle, you are no longer disabled."

"What's your goal for disabled people in Haiti?"

"They should have access to all social and economic opportunities, not only because they are entitled to from a human rights perspective, but also because it will be good for the country. If we are able to resolve some of the issues with regards to disability, it will serve as an opportunity for progress and development in Haiti, in which the needs of all citizens are fully considered. And disability affects all sectors in Haiti, both rich and poor. Indeed, it's a common issue that affects all citizens, all families in Haiti, in some way or another. So I think we can all be united for that common purpose, and it will serve the country. If we do not consider disability issues it will backfire in the future, because we will develop a society that depends on assistance, in which people with disabilities are constantly provided services, and this will be costly for the country. But if we invest in disabled people too, if we allow them to be productive citizens, if we empower them and allow them to get training, allow them to have access to education, allow them to be citizens of the country, they can serve a major role in the country. They can be very beneficial to the economic development of the country.

"And personally, I don't think we have the resources to develop a society that depends on assistance. Let me give you one example. It is said that there are a hundred thousand people with disabilities needing access to education. But instead of developing special schools for special children, if we develop an inclusive mentality, most children with disabilities can attend regular schools. And that will cost less money than building separate schools, having separate teachers. And it will also be beneficial to—to all people! And children only develop discrimination as they grow up. When they are little, they don't hold prejudice in their heart. So it would be better if we do it that way to ensure that we uproot discrimination. I try my best to bring up disability in all my activities. Disability is connected to all issues in Haiti: health, education, the economy. And as we try to solve disability issues, new opportunities will arise in Haiti. Let's say, for instance, that the country puts accessibility for people with disabilities at the forefront of reconstruction efforts. Well, Haiti might become a tourist destination for people with disabilities from other countries!"

✳

Each day during this short visit we went across the city to Canot, a dry and previously empty hilltop above Canape Vert, where earthquake victims had created a new community from scratch out of tents and makeshift shacks. "The government didn't want to clear the rubble in the *bidonvilles*, or at least the authorities didn't encourage the NGOs to do so," Gerald told me. "So the people obviously had to find alternative places."

To get to Canot we crossed Avenue Delmas at Boulevard Martin Luther King and drove up across the big hill that went up towards

Petionville. As always there were graffiti on the walls, carrying on the political conversation:

We want Titid back

Ansam nou fort 2010

"You meet all sorts of people in Haiti," said Gerald. "There is a mosque in Haiti, did you know? It's in Delmas 2. I don't know if it was damaged during the earthquake. On your right is the prime minister's office. Now a tent city." Driving up Canape Vert past an empty lot behind corrugated iron walls, he said: "There used to be a public school there. We built a basketball court at that school. And we also organized a disability awareness campaign there."

Through his Fondation J'Aime Haïti, in partnership with the nonprofit arm of the Voila cell phone company and the U.S.-based Sporting Chance Foundation founded by Major League Soccer player Seth Stammler, Gerald had established at Canot a temporary school in a large tent. "Locally we've tried to organize by providing direct relief to the people," he told me. "We started out by organizing mass burials, and we provided transport to medical centers. But we realized that we needed to provide long-term substantive activities to the communities. And one of the pillars of a coherent society is education. Most of the schools in Port-au-Prince—probably 80 percent—were shut down after the earthquake. Some collapsed; others, their staff were no longer available. So we decided to launch this program in Canot, to provide 240 kids in the neighborhood the opportunity to complete their school year and to participate in extracurricular activities that will help them cope with the earthquake. Once the regular schools open, we will send our kids back to their original schools."

"What were you telling the parents in yesterday's meeting?"

"We were telling them that they have to take this program seriously. That even though the program is totally free, they should expect a high level of discipline. And that, to ensure the kids have a successful school year, they must actively participate in the program. They must ensure that the kids study at home, they must ensure that the kids get to school on time."

One of Gerald's friends in Canot was a middle-aged neighborhood leader named Édrice. Édrice walked with a limp, from an injury in his youth that had never healed properly. He spoke no English and little French; in order to appreciate what an interesting personality he was, you had to be able to communicate with him in Creole. I could do this, but often I lost the thread of his conversation because he had a way of lapsing into sermonizing and metaphor.

At the end of one day, riding back from Canot to Gerald's house, I told him I had had a good interview with Édrice.

"You were able to understand everything?" he asked.

"Most of it," I said. "I might ask you for some help."

"Because sometimes Édrice can be very—metaphorical," said Gerald.

"Édrice has a lot of charisma," I remarked.

Gerald laughed. "Yes, he does. He always makes use of proverbs. He'll start saying a proverb, and then expect his audience to complete it."

Gerald arranged for me to get a taste of Édrice's daily life by spending a night with him and his family in their plywood shack. All that remained of his original house was the foundation, parts of a couple of walls, and a toilet.

"Édrice is a strong and key collaborator for the foundation," Gerald told me. "He is a local leader in his community. And also, I would say, a model citizen for Haiti. Although he is from humble origins, he has shown a great determination to help people that are facing serious economic difficulties and social problems. And he has been an active participant in relief efforts. Actually, not just relief efforts. Before the earthquake he was already a local leader, helping his community by managing the potable water system, raising awareness about social issues, like disability, in his community. He's a good friend of mine, and I've learned a lot from him."

"You come from an elite family," I said. "Are you able to work comfortably with each other?"

"I don't think there is such barrier," said Gerald. "For the past several years I have been working in these communities, and I've found amazing people there. This has enriched my life. It has given me more goals, and more hope for my country. Materially speaking they may be destitute, but spiritually, morally, they are rich people. And the fact that they are destitute on the material level doesn't create any barriers between me and Édrice and other people in these communities. At five o'clock on January 12, they were the first rescue teams. The Haitian people. And contrary to what you may have heard, there was very little looting and violence. It was all about collaboration."

Décentralisation had become a buzzword among many Haitians who believed the country's post-earthquake future lay—or should lie—anywhere but Port-au-Prince. The concentration of national institutions in a single city, and the consequent hollowing-out and impoverishment of Haiti's other towns, had happened as a matter of deliberate policy of successive rulers, from the French colonists more than two centuries earlier to François Duvalier in the 1960s. "Decentralization means opening up the doors of power and reducing the authority of the central government," Gerald said. "But at present, if you open the doors of power and decentralize, can you find the human resources?"

On the day I stayed overnight in Édrice's shack, I spoke to a young man named Jean-Baptiste. "We want decentralization," he told me in Creole. "I have family *au Cap*"—in Cap Haitien, Haiti's second-largest city, on the north coast. "There were more than ten people in a house, even before *douze janvier*. One of the things that the state did to concentrate everything in Port-au-Prince was to shut down Customs in the provincial towns. Decentralization would be good for the country. Maybe there would be a good university *au Cap*. With that, I myself wouldn't come here, which by the way is not a beautiful place. It's not beautiful because there's too much *bidonvillisation*. We could plant here, but houses are here instead. You see where people are living? It's not feasible to build houses there. Once you build houses there you put your life in danger, and you cut down trees. It's a situation where you encourage deforestation. Whenever someone builds a house, thirty people follow him. You're putting the environment in danger. I think that even the international aid must consider decentralization. It would be good for the country, because right now we don't have a country, we don't have eleven departments, we only have the Republic of Port-au-Prince."

Édrice gave me a walking tour of his neighborhood, including a cistern that had been installed by a French NGO in collaboration with CAMEP, the water utility, to provide potable water through a public tap. "There were posters, and debates about what they would do with the water," Gerald told me later. "It's real, local politics."

"I'm the one who directs it," Édrice told me. "We sell water for 50 *centimes* for a five-gallon bucket. With the management, we are able to clean up the neighborhood. We pay the vendors of the water, and then we do development with the money we collect."

As dusk fell, he took me to a meeting of a committee that set neighborhood priorities. "We work in close collaboration with the authority, Édrice," the committee president, Jude Toussaint, told me.

"What is the biggest problem for this community now?" I asked him.

"Our biggest problem currently is the food question," he said. "And GOAL [an Irish NGO] doesn't cover the area fully. When GOAL gives it, distribution is very slow. So sometimes Édrice makes other arrangements. And when Édrice finds other arrangements, he divides them with the committees from various areas, but they're not able to cover the whole neighborhood. We can understand that after the catastrophe, the government might be affected, but regardless, up until now the population has a certain *inquiétude*. People have big problems. They can block the sun, but they cannot block the rain. When it rains, water invades their tents. And the bathrooms are insufficient. There are no showers at all. There are no medical services. The water that the people drink is not treated. All the houses fell down. Right now we don't have a problem of tents or plastic; it's really a problem of sheet metal and wood, because there's going to be wind and rain, and today if they came with 100,000 tents, it wouldn't be any solution. So today we need wood, sheet metal, and plywood. We also need assurance about food, drinking water, bathrooms, and showers."

I asked him about decentralization.

"The solution is not taking the people from one location and putting them in another location."

"Do you have confidence or trust [*confiance*] in the Preval government?"

"Throughout the world," he said, "trust is not something you receive spontaneously. It's based on your results and your attitude toward the people. So at this point we won't say that we have trust or we don't have trust, but we would like to have trust. All that is needed is for the people's expectations to be met." Then, in French, he asked me: "You're a journalist, a writer. What do you think about the reconstruction of our country?"

"What do I think?"

"What do you think?"

I preferred not to be asked what I thought; I was more comfortable doing the asking. "I hope," I said, "that the international community, especially the United States, has the intention to continue to notice Haiti and its problems. But Americans are very distracted. They have their own problems. They don't think a lot about Haiti. The earthquake was already two months ago. Six months, eight months, twelve months afterward, I'm afraid they will forget Haiti."

✳

"I would say you met three amazing people," Gerald said when he picked me up the next day.

"Not counting you?"

He laughed. "Not counting me. Fritz and Marseille and Édrice. Although they are from humble origins, they are very rich inside. And very honest. When I meet people like these guys, it gives me a lot of hope and a lot of motivation to pursue my work."

"I felt that pretty strongly when I was in the *bidonville* with Édrice," I said. "That here are people living in the ruins. Literally, living in the ruins from the earthquake. And they're building what they can build, and little by little they're clearing away the rubble, and they're building the new temporary houses that they have to build to live in, in the meantime. And that's the opposite of the destruction. That's the life that's coming out of the destruction, right?"

"Exactly," he agreed. "That is something we have to accentuate. Sometimes people think that Haiti is hopeless, and there is so much discouragement because of past social turmoil. But hope should be in our heart forever. And we should work to improve the situation. And fortunately the most important people always have some hope, and these are the Haitian people."

Chapter 12

MAN OF THE SOUTH

I survived the spring quarter in my South Asian Studies program and daily Urdu language classes, kept up a draining speaking schedule on Pakistan, got married, spent a week off the grid in Hawaii recuperating with my new wife, returned to Seattle, and set about planning a longer trip to Haiti. And then, at the end of July, word began coming out about severe flooding in Pakistan.

It was some days before the scale of the flooding was apparent to those of us who weren't there. The monsoon rains came late and suddenly to Pakistan in 2010, and the flooding started at higher elevations, then gathered force throughout the enormous Indus River system. The people of the Swat valley, nearly three million of whom had fled a full-scale attack on local Taliban forces by the Pakistan Army the previous summer, were devastated again, their fields and orchards destroyed and the valley floor stripped clear of topsoil. Entire villages downstream were wiped out without a trace. By the time the flooding peaked a few weeks later, 20 million people had been affected, two million had been left homeless, and 20 percent of Pakistan was underwater.

The American public scarcely noticed. My first contribution to the effort to rectify that was an article published on the Huffington Post, titled "Pakistan Floods: Why Should We Care?" I quoted Todd Shea, who took every opportunity to point out that Pakistan had been our crucial ally in pushing the Soviet Union out of Afghanistan in the 1980s. But at the time of the floods the cooked-up "Ground Zero mosque" controversy was current, and a troubled young Pakistani-American named Faisal Shahzad had recently tried to blow up Times

Square. Todd had taken to wondering aloud why the tagline on TV coverage of that incident had read MADE IN PAKISTAN, whereas when he had approached Anderson Cooper, Geraldo Rivera, and Dr. Sanjay Gupta at the airport in Port-au-Prince, they and their producers had politely taken his business card but—at a time of wall-to-wall Haiti earthquake coverage—had apparently seen nothing newsworthy in two hundred Pakistani-American doctors volunteering in Haiti through the Islamic Medical Association of North America.

My article had been prompted by a Seattle friend asking me to recommend organizations she and her husband could donate to toward flood relief. But that friend was British, thus less susceptible to a national climate that had rendered Muslims the only group in America against whom it was considered permissible, even fashionable, to be bigoted. It was easy to blame "the media," or to point to post-Haiti "compassion fatigue" or the fact that Pakistan was much farther from the United States, or to note that a flood is a slower-moving disaster than an earthquake and the immediate death toll in Pakistan was much lower than in Haiti. But I felt it was impossible to ignore what the first decade of the twenty-first century had done to Americans' capacity to look at Muslims and see suffering humanity.

Paul Farmer had written a powerful book called *The Uses of Haiti*. We had different uses for Pakistan. If Haiti met our need to have someone to pity, hence the self-indulgent overkill of Americans' response to the earthquake, Pakistan fulfilled our need to have someone or something to fear. Many of the online comments on my article ran along these lines:

> Every year, the United States sends billions of dollars aiding Pakistan from [sic] their own people who are trying to bring down the Pakistani government and turn their country into a brutal dictatorship run by thugs that claim they speak in the name of God. Our thanks? Nothing but demands for more money that we cannot afford.

> In return for the help we have provided, Pakistan allows people who are actively trying to destroy our country to operate, train and plan inside their borders. Those that are not directly supporting al-Qaeda and similar groups passively do nothing to stop them.

So, like many others, I just have a very difficult time caring.

(Then there was this: "Many of these comments outline political reasons [for] lack of support for Pakistani people. Me, I'm just broke this month.")

I had been planning to return to Haiti in July but had to delay my trip until late August, in part because of the floods. Before, during, and after that trip, I tried to get my head around the weird coincidence that the two countries I cared most about, other than my own, had been devastated by horrific natural disasters in the same year. Both disasters were natural, to be sure, but they hadn't happened in a geopolitical vacuum. And our responses to them said little about Haiti and Pakistan, and all too much about us.

✳

"Is this Boulevard Harry Truman?" I asked Pierre. We were driving out of Port-au-Prince to the southwest, en route to Les Cayes on the southern coast. Pierre-Henry Dennery was one of Gerald's father's partners in the construction firm.

"I think so, yeah," he said. "I call it different. I call it Bicentennaire, because for the bicentenary of Port-au-Prince, that area was built by President Dumars Estimé [in the late 1940s]. And it was a beautiful area. At that time Rafael Leonidas Trujillo, the president of the Dominican Republic, came over here and liked it so much he said, 'I'll have to do the same thing in Dominican Republic.' And he built Malecon. And from there the Dominican started their renovation, and they left us behind. And with Jean-Claude Duvalier being ousted from power, and people having this idea of becoming democratic, and it went into anarchy, and all these things have been inhabited, people moved into shacks ..."

"So do you think Trujillo was good for the Dominican Republic?"

"I cannot answer that. I didn't live in Dominican Republic. He was a dictator. How much bad did he do to his people, I don't know. How much good did he do, I don't know either. These kinds of dictators have the tendency to do for the countries, but really for themselves. They build all kind of businesses for themselves. The country benefits from that too, but the good thing that happened to the Dominican Republic is that they continued their political line. They didn't get into battle between parties or between politicians. Here we don't have a culture of political parties, but it's really personal. You see, there were about fifty-two candidates for president."

"What was it like after Duvalier *fils* fell, that time between '86 and '90?"

"It was a time of hope, a time of feeling of renewal, of change. Everybody thought they would *change* everything, but they didn't know how. The fact is that nobody here had been really prepared for doing that change. How to do it, nobody knew. And he was not really overthrown by a revolution. He was ousted from power, and he was replaced by a temporary government that was mostly from the army. It was like he was still there. So whatever the people had in their mind that they would change, that was not happening. The people and the government had different ideas. So we wasted twenty years."

"Because of that time, or because of the Aristide time?"

"Because we didn't know what to do and how to do it. Because of *dictature* for thirty years there were no parties, no political culture. All people, their mouth were shut off for so long. So when they thought they would change things, in fact it was complete chaos. Do the photograph," he added, indicating the street scene outside the car window. "That's what happened. The image that's projected of Haiti is this. Because that's Port-au-Prince. But Port-au-Prince is only a small part of Haiti. When you'll be in Les Cayes you'll see different things: more at ease, more peaceful, cleaner, quieter, more secured. And they don't project that image of the country, unfortunately."

I had arrived in Port-au-Prince the day before with my friend Pete Sabo and Ben Owen, a student who had approached me after a talk I gave in February at Seattle Central Community College. Ben had a lot of ideas and questions and enthusiasm; he had been to Central America and South Africa and was voracious in his quest for more experience of the world. He had jumped at the chance to go to Haiti when I invited him. He had borrowed an HD video camera from a friend and was planning to make a documentary film about our trip.

When Ben asked Gerald what he could do to help Haiti, Gerald said, "Well, there's so much to do. It really depends on your field of expertise. But one thing we need is, we need real ambassadors abroad. Whatever you decide to do, I think it's important to protrude the good image about Haiti. I think maybe that was what was achieved by Jamal and his sons coming." This was my Pakistani acquaintance Jamal Haider, a Silicon Valley software guy who had brought his two teenage sons to Haiti in April, and who had stayed with Gerald. "I think his son even wants to write a book about Haiti."

"Ibrahim?" I asked. "He's the writer."

"Yes. He interviewed several kids."

Pete and I had spent six weeks together in early 2009, traveling overland from Mumbai to Karachi. He had spent a week in Haiti in February 2010 with Todd Shea and the California group led by Dr. Farzana Naqvi, quietly turning boxes of unorganized medical supplies into a usable pharmacy. He wasn't a medical professional, but he worked as a molecular biologist in a lab at the University of Washington and had sewn up his own leg after a kayaking accident off Vancouver Island, so he knew his way around medical-type stuff. In his job he supervised grad students and lab staff, but people, including me, sometimes got on his nerves; he didn't suffer fools gladly, and he generally preferred to be left alone to do his own thing. He was a low-impact kind of guy, in both personal manner and way of life, and a gentle soul. He was one of the most self-contained and self-reliant people I knew, but at the same time a reliable and generous friend.

Pete had seen a lot of the world and knew how to travel light and with minimal fuss and bother. He was a good and tactful amateur photographer and a quiet, reassuring, supportive presence in meetings and interviews during our trips. He trusted me to make most of the arrangements, and he could be so quiet for long stretches, contentedly hiding behind his camera, that I sometimes forgot he was paying close attention. He occasionally took me aside to suggest a line of questioning, but he didn't hesitate to ask a question himself if he wanted to know the answer. Often it was a question I should have thought to ask.

I had done most of my previous traveling solo, and being in charge of a three-man trip was not something I was used to or welcomed. Pete had hemmed and hawed about coming until pretty much the last minute, and a three-person trip was inevitably more complicated than a two-person trip, no matter who the three might be. I had fretted about this and came to understand how my father had finally tired of leading groups of assorted Episcopalians to Haiti. But Pete and Ben both pulled their weight and were good company, and each brought a fresh perspective to Haiti.

Our timing had been lucky in arriving at Gerald's house in the Village Tecina compound the previous afternoon. In Haiti it was always advisable to be lucky, and to seize opportunities and invitations when they came your way. This was how Haitians survived, those that did survive; history had taught them to be resourceful and enterprising. So when Pierre had told us he was going to Les Cayes the next morning and invited us to join him, we had not hesitated to accept.

I had met Pierre briefly in March. "The earthquake is an opportunity *maybe* to change things for real—*maybe*, if everyone wants to do it," he had told me then. He was a slim, light-skinned man in his sixties with a scraggly gray beard and a friendly and humorous manner, in shorts and sandals and flapping shirttail. He was funny: "They are predicting that by 2020 we will become a dessert. A desert," he corrected himself. "A dessert is what we eat." He was officially retired but kept busy with his business interests and his duties as president of the Chamber of Commerce for Haiti's Southern Department. "It's very hard to get people together here," he lamented. "They are all so busy in their little line of business." He sometimes thought about doing a bit of writing.

"Now is a good time for you to do your writing," I suggested, "because you're sort of retired; you've got time."

"I'm sort of retired," he allowed, "but I have got so many concerns in my mind for the Chamber of Commerce. Not so much for the station. The gas station, I am a partner to a guy who is a tenant. He doesn't own the gas station; we lease from Texaco. But he has been a tenant for so long, I became his partner. So I have to give him reports on things sometimes. He is in Canada. But it's not a big problem. The plantation is a problem, because there are always problems to solve. The Chamber of Commerce is a problem because it's for free; it's pro bono. All the members of the board do it for free. But they're not available. They're all doing their business. I am retired, and I am the only one who is left available for everything."

Pierre had a businessman's awareness of Haiti's economy. "There is a big problem for the youth in this country of unemployment," he said. "And it is very difficult to create employment, because the conditions are not there. We used to have so many access to credit. But after the earthquake, access to credit has been reduced because so many banks have lost their buildings, their employees. And it's riskier. Insurance doesn't insure houses. My insurance told me no more insurance for buildings. If somebody has a piece of property now, whether it's a car or what, you better be careful protecting it. Because we don't have the credit availability that you have in the States."

"What about insurance even for a car?"

"For a car there is a mandatory one. The state forces you to have it. But it's kind of ridiculous. You don't really honor it."

I had never been *aux Cayes* before. Pete sat in the front passenger seat with his camera. Ben and I sat in the back, and Pierre drove. We made it through the perpetual traffic bottleneck of Carrefour and past Léogâne, epicenter of the earthquake, then turned onto the road that went southwest over the spine of the southern peninsula and down toward the coast to Les Cayes.

"An interdepartment road—it's treated as a street!" Pierre exclaimed. "Because all the housing beside it faces it, and their front yard is right by the road. There is no barricade, there is no fencing. I think if they want to treat this road as a national, interdepartmental road, they should have those houses facing the other side or sideways, and have streets going into there. But they have never thought of that, and I think it's a big problem. Because you always have a risk of some kid or some child or some drunk person coming right in front of your car."

"Have you talked to anybody about this?"

"I may have talked to myself, or to one or two friends. But that's not in anybody's mind."

"Well, if you don't have a stable government, then you can't do things like that, even if you think about it."

"Not even stable," said Pierre. "They don't have the vision for that. I can see it, I can feel it, because I have lived other places. I have lived in New York, I have lived in Miami, and I have seen how those highways are built. In Miami they even make sound barriers between the road and the houses. Here you have the houses, and most of the time the people think of the road as a market." He gestured through the windshield in exasperation. "You think this guy is in that much hurry, that he has to cross the road in front of the car? What hurry he has? No hurry. He just decides, because that's his yard."

We talked about the earthquake. "So a lot of the deaths were because of the poor construction," said Pete.

"Yes, poorly done, for many reason," said Pierre. "Lack of technical care, also. They build houses themselves with a foreman, without engineering supervision, without even a draft plan. And care is not given enough in the way that they mix the concrete. And when they pour it, also, they don't vibrate it. Nobody vibrates, except some companies. I am part of a construction company, Tecina, and we use vibrators. But most people don't do it. And they might put too much water in it, because this concrete is being carried up, in buckets, and the person who handles the bucket doesn't want a very heavy thing, so he mixes it with too much water. And the material itself is most of the time white sand that they have in Port-au-Prince. And that white sand, it's limestone, it's not really river sand. So it's good for masonry, but it's not *that* good for concrete. If you mix it with river sand, it's much better. If you leave it by itself, you should do a better job in mixing that concrete. They say that in other countries, when you have level eight or more on the Richter Scale, houses or buildings will be damaged, but they won't fall. They won't kill people."

"Like in Chile," said Pete.

"But here, they fell down. We were not used to that at all. Some people were outside in the yard, they went into the house. Some people were in the house, they went outside. And some people were outside and they stood by the wall, and the wall fell on them. People didn't know what to do."

"Where were you?" I asked.

"I was in Camp Perrin." Outside Les Cayes.

"So the earthquake was felt out here," I said.

"Yeah. The earthquake was felt here up to Petit Goave, the town we are going to hit pretty soon. And up to Jacmel also. The day after the earthquake I came back [to Port-au-Prince]. I had to go around. All this fell down. I had to go through here. That's the Bay of Petit Goave. We are still in the northern part of the southern peninsula."

"How do you feel about the UN presence here?" asked Ben.

"My feeling is more calculated, more civilized, more understanding, than most people. Haiti is part of the United Nations, right? So whatever move the United Nations makes here, it does it with our consentment, our acceptation, our willingness. Some moves might be forced upon the country. Their being here definitely helps, because the security situation was very bad. So they are helping, or they have helped, fix it up a lot. What will that give into result later, I don't know. Because all of this money that is being spent to keep that army here, it is deducted from what they call aid to Haiti. Now, what is being done to correct the problems, to fix the causes of these problems? I don't know. If they don't invest in educating people, in *forming*, I mean in educating technicians, teaching trades to mechanics, electricians, plumbers, so and so, so that these people can work and make a living, how are we going to change the situation?"

"Do you think the UN could be permanent here?" I asked.

"The UN has in mind to stay for many years. When they came, they came with the idea that they would stay at least ten years. But ten years might not be enough! Haven't you noticed that for Iraq? You are noticing that same thing for Afghanistan now. For Pakistan. You stay there for ten, twenty years, if you don't go to the roots of the problems, what do you solve? *Arabie Saoudite* has financed more terrorists than the other countries. Okay? And *Arabie Saoudite* is a *partner* of the United States. And Afghanistan and Pakistan are a big, big, big problem."

"Yeah," I said. "Like you say, if you don't solve the root of the problem, you're just ..."

"Buying time," said Pete.

"Yeah, you waste money," said Pierre. "You waste money of the tax-payer, and you waste time, and things become worse."

"Do you see that in Haiti, with the UN?"

"I see it with the whole system. From the national people, from the international people. From the whole system, we are not addressing the right problems."

"What's the right way to address the right problems in Haiti?"

"Education is one thing. And economy is the other thing. If you don't address the economy, you don't create employment, you're not going anywhere. Because if you create employment, people are working, the social problems might be solved. If you just install a socialist state, or a populist government, and you hire people, and you don't teach them, you don't train them in anything, that's not going to solve anything. Teach someone to fish, rather than give him a fish every day."

"Did Aristide give people a fish, or did he teach them to fish?"

"He taught people to hate. I voted for Aristide in 1990. And I thought that he was the right person to try to change things. But the guy was an opposition person. He *stayed* an opposition man, even when he became president. Rather than being a president of the country, he stayed on his own side, and saying things like '*Roch nan dlo vinn konn doule roch nan soley.*'" The rocks in the water will come to know the pain of the rocks in the sun. "In other words, people who had a nice life should know what the pains of the poor people are. He should have reversed his thinking. As a president, you should try to look for a better welfare for everyone, rather than looking to make these who are rich pay. He was a populist, he stayed a populist. He has been president two times, and he stayed a populist. He missed completely his mission. It's really unfortunate, because that guy could have done *anything* for this country. He could have taken this country from zero to ten, from zero to one hundred. He was not able to think the right way, and he didn't do it."

"Some people would say that he had many enemies," I pointed out, "and he had to protect himself and fight against the elite and the business people and the army."

"Yeah, that's right," Pierre agreed. "François Duvalier had the same problem. The difference with Aristide is that he was chosen by about 65 percent of the population. At least you could say he was democratically elected. François Duvalier was *almost* that way, but not completely. The army put him in power. So at that time, you have at least 50 percent of the voters who are against you; you don't have enough popularity. So you either build something from that basis, or you become defensive. That's what happened to François Duvalier; he became so defensive. He arrested many people, he killed, so and so and so. So then what do you do? The government has no time left to do things; it only has time to defend itself from the opposition."

"So the difference is that Aristide really did have most of the people behind him."

"Yeah, he had the people. But did he teach the people? Did he train them? When you are putting people against people, you don't create the right environment for development. So if you tell me, 'Look who beside you is eating well, then you should know what to do,' that means you are putting up the mass of people against the richer people. The richer people are the ones who create employment, who create business, who build things. So if you put them against each other, where do you go? Préval is almost like Aristide, but Préval is much, much, much better than Aristide." Rene Préval, Aristide's handpicked successor as president in 1996, had returned to office in 2006, in the first election after the U.S.-sponsored second coup against Aristide in 2004.

"I've heard that Préval was personally devastated by the earthquake, that he was paralyzed," I said.

"I heard that also. I don't know if it's true. The guy might be cynical. Definitely he was lost. Someone even told me that he was on the point of leaving Haiti, going to the Dominican Republic by the border; they had to convince him to come back."

"That's not very good leadership," I ventured.

"No. Definitely not. But the guy is a shrewd politician."

"Is Préval in any sense controlled by Aristide?"

"At one point he was. I don't know if he has achieved to get away from Aristide's control."

"Do you think the young people will be disappointed that Wyclef can't run for president?"

The big recent news was that the famous singer Wyclef Jean had announced his candidacy in the elections now planned for November 28, 2010, three months away, but the Provisional Electoral Council had declared him ineligible, because he didn't meet the residency requirement; he had grown up and lived in New York. "I respectfully accept the committee's final decision and I urge my supporters to do the same," Wyclef had said on CNN on August 22, just four days earlier. I later was told through the *teledjol*—the rumor mill—that friends of his believed he was relieved by the council's decision.

"Yeah," Pierre replied. "But if they can accept that he has not lived in Haiti for five years, they will have to swallow it. In Haiti, people swallow a lot of things."

✱

We stayed four nights with Pierre at his house in Camp Perrin, in the countryside outside Les Cayes. He was a man of the south, a booster. He had a lot of time—or made a lot of time—to show us around, and he did it with gusto and verve. "I would say if you go inside one country, that would give you a better idea of what the country people think, rather than Port-au-Prince," he said. "There is no big money here, but it is more touristic-oriented. They are more politically active in the north, and I would say they are more violent. The Haitian Revolution in 1804 took place in the north; it didn't really happen in the south. And in the north there were people that were from African tribes that were more warriors. You might hear from them criticisms that are tougher. We [in the south] are not part of the reconstruction plan, because we don't have anything to reconstruct. But have some things to build. This is a country that is relatively speaking special." On this point he meant specifically the local area *en ros camp*, the upper part of Camp Perrin, where he lived. "You see the style of construction.

Many of the people, they live overseas, they come here for one or two month in the summer."

On walls everywhere around Haiti, besides all the graffiti, these days you saw ads for the two wireless carriers, Digicel and Voilà. Digicel's color was red; Voilà ads and merch were an eye-catching lime green. Both colors had become ubiquitous on walls around Port-au-Prince and other towns, as well as on sun umbrellas and shirts worn by guys selling cell-phone minutes on the street.

"Are there laws that control which walls you can paint?" I asked Pierre.

"There are laws, for people who are willing to abide by them."

On walls in Bas de Camp, the lower part of Camp Perrin, was written:

PA KA TANN

POU WOUT LA FET

We can't wait for the road to be built. Like a lot of Haitian graffiti, it was ambiguous. Was it an exclamation or a demand? And to whom was it addressed?

"The river sometimes comes out of its bed," Pierre explained. "It goes through the downtown area. It floods all buildings here. That's why they put up that wall. That's why they're rebuilding the wall here, because it's at risk, it's risky. They asked the people living here now to quit the area, because it was too risky. But nobody would move out. What happened, they raised their floor, or they put barricades in front of their houses."

"Where would they go if they moved out?" I asked.

"They would go uptown. They would go to Ros du Camp. You have to understand, this is a commercial area. So the people live at their place of business, you see? The store is there, they live behind it. Or over it. Is it a question, is it an exclamation, I don't know. Probably it's the second thing: 'We cannot wait.' I don't think it's that much political. Of course, everything here is political. So much so that we don't do the right things. Everything is being so political. Haitians always come around to talking about politics. That means there is a void. Americans don't talk about politics."

"But now they do," I said.

"Now they do, but they didn't used to."

Driving along a road outside of town, Pierre said: "I am going to show you the smallest airstrip that you have seen in your life, unless you count some hidden ones in Afghanistan or Pakistan. This is the airstrip of Port Salut." The roads here were being widened and regraded, and there were trucks and heavy equipment moving around, and dust in the air. Even the road from here to Jérémie, on the far western tip of the southern peninsula, was being improved. Pierre said that when it was finished, it would take only three hours to get there from Les Cayes. This meant that Jérémie, where I had never been and which I had always thought of as almost impossibly remote, would be only six hours' drive on good roads from Port-au-Prince.

It had long been lore that most of Haiti's national highways had not been repaved since the 1915–34 occupation of the country by the U.S. Marines. Haiti was roughly the size of Maryland, but it felt a lot bigger than that. From Port-au-Prince to Mirebalais, twenty-five miles away on the Central Plateau, took more than four hours. From Port-au-Prince to Petit Trou de Nippes, where the Colorado Haiti Project worked halfway along the north coast of the long southern peninsula, took all day, and if the river was high you couldn't get there at all. We *blancs* who came and went could joke about the roads and congratulate ourselves for enduring the hardship, but for Haitians they were a brutal fact of life. But one of the most startling changes in post-earthquake Haiti was that the main highways were being repaved and widened. Port-au-Prince to Mirebalais now took less than two hours. I was to be told that it was being done by an Italian company, at President Préval's initiative with money from the European Union, that the best methods and materials were being used, that it cost $1 million per mile. It was not an unmixed blessing—fatal accidents were more frequent, trucks and motorcycles roared past the Zanmi Lasante compound at Cange, and people living along the roadside were being displaced—but the new roads seemed sacramental of a new sense of hope and purpose. It was easy to be pessimistic and cynical about Haiti, but the new roads challenged me to revisit that longstanding habit. With better roads, what might be possible? How might the provincial towns and their hinterlands be developed? What crops could be brought to market with less waste and more profit to farmers?

I allowed myself to begin believing that I might be witnessing an incipient change for the better. Many other things had to change in order for the expensive new infrastructure to be meaningful. But why shouldn't they? As Paul Farmer and others insisted, if Rwanda could emerge from the depths of hell to stability and relative prosperity, why couldn't Haiti? The first step, necessary but not sufficient, was to believe that it was possible. I had learned that it was wise to be sober and cautious, to begin with where Haiti was actually at rather than indulging in unrealistic hope. But what about realistic hope? Too, I detected in myself the self-indulgence of personal nostalgia. None of us wants the landscape of his youth to change. But it always does. And if our world must change, surely it's better if it changes for the better.

"Tecina made the paving of Port Salut," Pierre told us. He was taking us over the hills to the other side of a peninsula that juts south into the Caribbean west of Les Cayes, to visit some friends of his who ran a small hotel. "There is a MINUSTAH running," he said, indicating a white man jogging in the road. MINUSTAH was the acronym for the UN force. "There is no war here. What else you have to do? You have to run, keep in shape, go to the beach."

On the way back to Les Cayes and Camp Perrin, we heard beautiful music coming from inside a large church beside the road.

"Could we stop for a minute and just listen to the singing?" I asked.

"Yeah. You want to record it?"

"That'd be nice," said Ben.

"You could even go to the church and sing with them," said Pierre.

"We would be interrupting," I said. "If three *blancs* show up ..."

"Just say you just converted."

We stopped the car and stood outside the church for a few minutes.

"You don't get to see stars like this in Seattle," said Ben with feeling.

"Did you watch the stars in Camp Perrin last night?" asked Pierre.

"It was cloudy," said Pete.

"If the sky is not bad, when you are in Camp Perrin, lift up the head. Look at the sky. You see *all* the constellations. In Camp Perrin sometimes I put my lights down, and then I lift the head to the sky."

Pierre had asked me if I felt comfortable driving in Haiti, and I had gamely said yes. He considered my offer, but wisely declined it. Driving in Haiti wasn't for the fainthearted.

"All these people driving motorcycles, most of them don't own it," he told us. "They rent it for let's say 250 gourdes a day, and they drive it, and they take two, three, five people on that motorcycle with hundred-pound bag of rice, plus two people and a baby. And what can you expect from them? They are just trying to make a buck. Some of them are peasants who sold a piece of their land, come to town, and going to make a fortune. Can't even pay for the repairs on that motorcycle. Someone who sells you a motorcycle for seven hundred, eight hundred dollars, he's going to make ten times that amount from selling you parts. You see the left turn signal?" He was indicating the truck in front of us. "That means to him I can go. I can overpass him. Heh heh! He's not turning left. He's just telling me, 'You can go ahead.' I blink to him, he says, 'Okay, go ahead.'"

"I'm glad you understood what that meant."

"I had to conclude that. I was following a truck once, and I wanted to overpass him, and he kept his left turn signal on. So I never passed him. For ten, fifteen minutes I said, 'My God!' Then I realized he must have wanted to tell me, 'Go ahead.'"

The next day he took us to see what he called his plantation, much of it overgrown, with antique stone buildings in various states of dilapidation. In one of these he stored corn; in another he was preparing to raise chickens. "My grandfather and my great-uncle used to run it, and used to live here," he said. "When I was a young kid, I would come here, spend a week with them, eat the coconuts, drink coconut water, drink sugar cane juice, and I would have a great time. I would help them sell some of that rum. One day my grandfather asked me, 'Pierre, what do you want to be?' And I said, 'I want to become a doctor.' And he said, 'Wow. I have a wasted grandson.' Because in his mind I should have been an agronomist. He thought I was interested in agriculture, and when I told him I wanted to be a doctor, he said, 'Okay, you're wasted.' And it happened, life, I decided otherwise. Instead of studying agronomy I studied management, but I got to the point that I bought some of that plantation. It's still owned by family, but I bought part of it, and I'm managing it. I have become a farmer." He chuckled.

He showed us an old mill. "I have to have this tree cut, because this is going to break everything," he said. "These are like savage trees, and no matter that you cut it, it reappears. And it breaks down everything, all the walls. There are places in Haiti where they do rehabilitation, mainly in the Citadelle and Sans Souci." The famous fortress and palace of Haiti's early independence, built near Cap Haïtien in the early nineteenth century. "These places were declared world *patrimoine*. World patrimony, right? And they funded rehabilitation of these things, because it's a very expensive process. So people like me, if we own colonial-type things like this, it's not easy. We are left alone, except that a few years ago I was visited by a presidential commission that was doing some inventory. I think they had some celebration in mind. They wanted also to rehabilitate those kinds of buildings, but they told me they would first make an association of buildings' owners, and through that association try to rebuild these things. Nothing has been done since then. This country has the habit of letting things go because something happens. A few years ago when four hurricanes hit Gonaïves, there was so much flooding that all efforts were concentrated toward how to save Gonaïves, and everything else was abandoned. And the same thing happened about the earthquake. The government was notified that an earthquake could happen. They didn't know when, but could happen. They knew about it, but they were so busy taking care of Gonaïves and other things, that the earthquake hit and killed so many people, and destroyed so many houses and so many families. So ..." He trailed off.

"So Haiti's never quite ready for the next unexpected event," I suggested.

"No. Haiti is never quite ready for that. We have a post-disaster institution that's supposed to help in that situation. When the earth-

237

quake hit I was here, driving my car, so I didn't really feel the earth-quake. That was January the 12th. The next day I drove to Port-au-Prince. And that same night, I was getting to Port-au-Prince, I saw *La Cocina Mobile*, a caravan that came from Dominican Republic. A mo-bile kitchen that came to give us help. That means our neighbors were ready for things like that; we were not ready. And we have to pay the consequences. We are always rebuilding here. We're always rebuilding roads, rebuilding hospitals, rebuilding schools, after hurricanes, after floods. Never build well enough, and never project enough, to do more proper roads, more proper schools, more proper hospitals, and more proper housing. It's a lack of education, lack of training, lack of vision, lack of *formation*, I think. Right?"

"Right," I agreed.

"We cannot go this way. There are bees in here." We went in another direction. "You see? The water would come down here and drop into the wheel and turn the mill. And whatever water would not go to the mill would continue going in here, toward Les Cayes. But with people cutting trees to make charcoal, to sell to people living in the cities, to sell to people who have dry cleaners, to sell to people who have bread factories and who have some industries, this creates deforestation. And that deforestation allows the water to flow down to the sea when it rains, without being retained. So you have less sources of water avail-able to fill canals like that. So plantations that used to be provided water are not anymore.

"I have that big dilemma. Other people think that this should be preserved as historic. Okay, not only it costs a lot of money, which we don't have. Second, in my mind this was in the old time a center of production. It was producing sugar cane, alcohol, things like that. And I think in my mind it should be *again* a center of production. Whether I do poultry here, I do corn, I do sorghum, whatever. And I'm plan-ning to have a pig farm here. Of course, while renovating these things, I would try to keep the old style. I think it could be preserved, yes, but be used for production. Because that's what we need in this country. Production, production, production."

He complained about local peasants who allowed their cows to graze on his land. "Are you in competition with the peasants, in that sense?" I asked him.

"Yes, in a big sense. Because they're too many for the small pieces of land they have, and they don't own enough land, but they have animals that they raise. It's a kind of saving for them. Because when they have pigs, they have cows, they have goats, whenever they sell them for any celebration, for a baptism, for a wedding, they make money out of it. And where do they raise them? On my land. I wouldn't mind, except that when they raise it on your land, those animals eat your corn, eat your beans. It's not fair."

"How much land do you have?"

"About fifty hectares of land. Which could be in the mind of some people a big piece of land, but that's nothing. Whenever they tried to do agrarian reform here, they had probably the wrong ideas how to do it. They took land for some people to give very small portions, half an hectare of land to some individuals. What can you do with half an hectare of land? We should be in a situation where we regroup small landowners to have larger spaces, where you can really put this in maybe an economy of scale situation."

"Could that be done in a way that everybody agrees to?"

"I am in the process of helping making some association. For example, we are thinking of founding an association that would be called Association des Producteurs Agricoles et Agroindustriels. If it happens, we would put our means together. People who have tractors would put them at the disposal of others who don't have. We would try to plan the plantations we're going to do: at what time, and how, and we would try to plan at what time we are going to sell it, so that we don't make too much of one thing at one time. And this is the kind of things that would help, because people would be more reunited, which is not the case now. We are supposed to have a *konbit* culture, where people get together to help each other. But this is not done on a large scale, and we are all individualists. Everyone is on his own, and everyone is losing. I was recently traveling, and people in Italy, they make cooperatives to sell their wine: the grape growers together, and the olive growers together. In Martinique and Guadaloupe they have a cooperative called

Banamart. Banamart takes care of all the *fig banane* plantation, and this is the way."

"There's nothing like that in Haiti?"

"No, nothing like that. We have been recently visited by Banamart, twice, and they are interested in starting some *fig banane* plantation here, and having us farmers do the same thing together with them."

"Here in the south?"

"In the south. It's a very technical way of growing those bananas. So we're thinking of that. And first thing they said, we have to have an association."

✳

Another day Pierre took us to see a research farm in Camp Perrin run by a woman named Monique Finnigan. She was a Haitian who had married an Irishman, and she and Pierre worked together in the Chamber of Commerce. "The same way a university is good for developing an area, because that's where research is done, that's where ideas are made, this place is a good technical place to improve and to move forward," Pierre told us. "Generally people don't understand that; they underestimate what kind of ONG this is. Here they dry up mangoes. You'll probably see that. They make water; that's where I buy my treated water. They make all kind of things with corn and beans. They grow all kind of plants. Bamboo, mango. I'm going to take some water."

We stopped at the building where the farm sold five-gallon plastic bottles of potable water, so Pierre could buy some and return his empties. I was glad this was on his agenda for the day, because we had run out of drinking water at his house. The five-gallon bottles were a staple for Haitian households that could afford them. Generally people didn't turn them upside-down and dispense the water from water coolers, as in offices in the States; here people usually just set them on the kitchen floor or counter and tipped them over to get water. We always filled our personal water bottles from these whenever we left the house for the day. Pierre paid for his water, and we put it in his car. Then we toured a refrigerated building where mangos were processed and dried, then sat down in another building with Monique Finnigan.

She was a tall and attractive middle-aged woman, known as Mousson. With her was an agronomist named Eliassaint Magloire. Later, Pierre told me that he was a descendant of Paul Magloire, Haiti's military ruler from 1950 to 1956, who ousted President Estimé in a coup. One tended to run into scions of Haiti's famous political families here and there. I had enjoyed dinner in 2004 with Estimé's daughter, Regine. Through my French friend Philippe I had met the great-grandson of Vilbrun Guillaume Sam, the president whose dismemberment by a mob had precipitated the U.S. invasion of Haiti in 1915.

"The name of the NGO is ORE, which means Organization for the Rehabilitation of the Environment," Mousson told us. "Which I always say is a very pretentious name. Because we were so enthusiastic when we started, so we thought we would actually be able to rehabilitate the environment around here. We were created in 1985 as a foundation, and we were mostly on agricultural and environmental protection, because we found that the two are linked. We've developed two main programs: high-value fruit trees, and staple crop seed production. The first one came as an alternative to help solve the deforestation."

"The first one?"

"The fruit trees. Because when we started, there had been a reforestation program all over Haiti, and you couldn't see the new trees. Millions of trees had been planted, but they were not there. Because of course when you plant a forestry tree, small seedlings, after a while people just pulled them out of the ground, because they were clearing to plant food. People cut trees down either to clear land to produce food, or because they need the money, cash money, very quickly: charcoal, planks, poles. So we thought, 'Okay. What type of tree will people leave on the ground, and still that tree will produce an income?' And of course fruit trees were the answer, fruit trees that can make money for the farmers.

"So we first started to work with fruits that had a market already, like mangos. And then we included avocados and citrus. Both the latter ones were more for the local market. But every choice was made thinking of what would be the economical impact for the farmer. We started in '85 and now, since 2000, exports have started of mangos.

The market already existed; we just said, 'Okay, let's link farmers to this market.' For avocados, we introduced some varieties from Florida that were out of season for Haiti. So it extended the production period. And of course all fruits have a very big impact on food security and nutrition in Haiti. During the mango season or the avocado season, the signs of malnutrition diminish. If you can extend the period of production, then you extend the availability of nutritious food for the people. Avocados, the varieties introduced, people like them. They're not the best choice for export, but they are very good for the local market. And for the citrus, it was to diversify the type of citrus that people could find on the market. We had what we call the *chadeque*, which is like a grapefruit, and there was some sweet orange. We expanded and introduced new varieties that people could market. All that we were interested in was that whatever new variety, it should be interesting for the local market. Except for the mango. But we did propagate some varieties of mangos that are also doing very well on the local market."

"You're a nonprofit organization," I said. "How does it work?"

"We are technical assistance to farmers," she said. "We provide farmers with the fruit trees, the seedlings. We are financed by different funding agencies. We started with the Canadian embassy, and then USAID for a long time. In fact, USAID is one of our biggest funding agencies. And then the European Union. IDB. Anyone interested in our programs. What we don't do, we don't change because there is a new trend. We've kept those two programs: the fruit trees since '85, the seeds since '87. And we've been keeping at it. Staple crop seed production is one activity that we do on a commercial basis. But as an NGO, we keep reinvesting in the same activity and for research. There is a lot of research that you have to do to maintain the quality of the seeds you want to provide for farmers. But not many funding agencies are willing to fund research.

"Many people have been telling us, 'You should be selling the trees.' But if you wait for people to have money to invest in a tree, then you maybe plant a thousand trees a year. We produce about 50,000 to 100,000 trees a year. People say we should be working with the poorest people. The poorest people sometimes don't have the land. The poorest person cannot afford to even spend two *gourdes* on a tree, because those two *gourdes* will buy a piece of bread for his kid. It's that tight. So yes, they will invest in producing food, because traditionally they know how to do it, and they know what result to expect. But a fruit tree—usually the fruit tree grows by itself. But to buy and plant and care for a tree, this is a long process. And it took us time to prove what we said at the beginning: 'You're going to make money out of those trees.' Now, all over Haiti, people are talking about fruit trees, planting orchards. But that wasn't the case when we started."

"You've been doing it for twenty-five years," I said.

"Yeah. I think in agriculture you cannot have like they do now: the longest program is eighteen months. When you get two years it's like, 'Hoo!' you get so lucky. But in agriculture, when you have innovative techniques, it takes time to prove that the technique works and to bring the results so people can understand and benefit. Then it becomes their own: they change it, they adapt it. But it's theirs; they don't need you anymore to tell them, 'This is how you have to do it.' It takes time. And maybe the vision we have is more like what the Ministry of Agriculture should be doing. Like an extension program, always improving and giving technical assistance to the farmers. Unfortunately, I don't think they have the vision. And we are caught into doing all the steps: the research, the production. And the whole thing was to get to the marketing. Because when production started to come out and be of substance, not just some new fruits that you could see in the market, then we actually started to set farmers so they can organize themselves to sell."

"Cooperatives?"

"It's not a co-op. It's more like an association. Co-ops are a little more difficult; they have rules that you have to follow. But just a free association, for marketing purposes. It was just to say, 'Okay, how do we get mangos to the market? How do we sell them to the exporters?' But now this association exists, and they try to expand. They started in one locality, and now it has expanded to the whole South Department. Some of them have been certified organic, and they are in the process of being certified fair trade. This is a long process. And then the end market was processing the fruit. That's why you visited the fruit-drying unit that's here. A very important program too is the production of improved seeds for maize, beans, sorghum, some tubers like yams and manioc, sweet potatoes. And bananas recently. We are still doing most of our activities as being funded, receiving funds from donors, but we try to have some activities that generate enough funds that when funding disappears, we can still work."

"I have a friend who works in Pakistan," I said, "and he speaks about that a lot. He says, 'We can't rely on the international donors forever.'"

"No. They try and help. But politics always gets in there. We start funding, and they say, 'No no no, we stopped because you've had a coup d'etat.' So it doesn't matter if your fields are sown and you need to continue your production. Even if you see a lot of people out in the streets, farmers still will take care of their crops. They're not going to say, 'Oh, I'm not going to weed because we're on strike.' They're still going to do it. But when the funding stops abruptly like that, sometimes you lose."

"You yourself have been involved in it the full twenty-five years?"

"Yes."

"That's been an extraordinary period in Haitian history."

"I know!" She laughed.

"There was the embargo in the nineties. How has that whole twenty-five-year period in politics affected your work?"

"It was a challenge every time. We stayed here, and we continue working. In the city, if there's a strike, you live the consequence of the strike. But when you are in the countryside, there can be a strike too—they can block a road—but they're not going to stop you doing all the field work. They're not going to tell you, 'No, you can't go and harvest your field.' Life continues. You can have your political views and make a statement. But still, whatever needs to be done will be done. And we've gone through all kind of things. First, they said the trees we were grafting were communist trees. And then we became the de facto military allies. And it all depended on who was in charge and what agenda they had. But we survived them all. And sometimes it was like, you know, not easy. But we never thought that a bad political situation would make us stop whatever we were doing. Because what we were doing was part of the livelihood of people. To us it was an essential activity. And we were lucky that every time, as you said during the embargo, if they had restricted what funding would be for, we would qualify for this little slot. They would say, 'Oh yeah, you can be viewed as humanitarian aid.' But the sad thing was to see that the general overview in the country was getting worse and worse and worse."

"Maybe I will say something," Eliassaint Magloire, the agronomist, said suddenly and quietly. He had been sitting silently, and I had been wondering if he was going to speak at all. "He is a guy who is not very enthusiastic about talking," Pierre said afterward. "But when he starts talking, he would put out some hard truths."

"Let's say that when we started," he said now, "we designed a seed project to cover the South Department, so that we produce all the corn seed. But for political reasons sometimes, you can have hundred kinds of seed here, but you can't sell it because the government received some seed from Argentina, and they just dump it in the market. Let's say that we knew that there is an opportunity of market for Haitians to produce concrete, that we consume a lot in the country. And we designed a project, after the seed production, to produce enough concrete for distribution in the country. Because we import about ten thousand tons from the States and Dominican Republic. But for political reasons we cannot find the money in the country to build the facility to produce it in the country, instead of importing it. So when you look at what happened in the country, we can see that politicians play an important role. Because our farmers lose the market. And what we need for farmers to survive, it's the market. We are not in control of the market. Dominican Republic is selling *everything* here. About a million eggs every day. Even in Les Cayes area, every weekend they come to sell chickens in the market here. So we are not protected by our government. It's the same thing happening in rice. Before eighties, we were self-sufficient in rice production. Now, we are importing 390,000 tons of rice. Meaning that rice and fuel make our *balance économique*, our commercial balance, negative."

"We've lost so many of the products that we used to be able to produce in Haiti and put on the market," said Mousson. "It's becoming really crazy."

"Because of political instability?"

"Political instability, and I would even say political will," she said. "Because for people who want to make money, it's easier to import than to organize the production. We never used to have so many processed produce in the supermarkets that came from Venezuela, Brazil. We don't understand that our population of ten million people, it's a market. But they know it. Clinton said—he was defending the producers. Iowa? Was it Iowa?"

"No, Arkansas," said Eliassaint. He pronounced the final *s*.

"Arkansas." She pronounced the *s* too.

"That's his state. His own state."

"For rice! Most of the rice imported in Haiti, it's from the States."

"Arkansas," Eliassaint said again.

"But he said publicly recently, like his *mea culpa*," said Mousson. "He feels like he's done something bad for Haiti. Of course, I can understand: a country is giving you the taxpayer money, so they want some of that money to go back to their country. But it has to be some kind of balance, so you don't destroy the country you come to help."

Pierre had told me that international organizations had dumped rice in Haiti after the earthquake. "And the people here, they couldn't sell it," he had said.

"I always say, if there is a Third World War, Haiti will lose 50 percent of its population," Eliassaint said now. "Not because of the war; because of food situation. Because we produce right now for 40 to 50 percent of what we need. What we gonna do for the rest of the people, when they cannot find food?"

"Since the earthquake, what have you seen on the ground?"

"We have a small humanitarian program that's specific for after the earthquake," Mousson said. "Because people started to ask what was happening, e-mails, and then they started to want to help. And the best way to help was, you know, to provide money. I said, 'Don't come if you're not coming in a structured group.' Because when you come you have to find a place to stay, meaning tents. You don't just come with your little backpack and think you're going to be okay. Port-au-Prince was so chaotic. You would be overwhelmed and not really be able to help, because you have to provide for your own food, and all the logistics and everything. So private people started to send money.

"So I said, 'Okay, we need to set up something.' The first step was to do what we call the evacuation. Why the idea came is because I have satellite television. We felt the earthquake here. I was sitting exactly here. And Eliassaint was sitting there. And then I felt my chair, and my first reaction was, 'I don't have a dog.' You know, scratching itself under my chair. So I looked, still, and I go, 'What's going on?' And I could see Eliassaint doing the same thing, trying to find out why was this thing moving. And we realized, and we just ran outside the building. And there were two other people that were there, in the office, standing, looking, and I said, 'Come out!' And they came out. That was the first time I felt an earthquake so strong here. So I thought this was happening here, in Les Cayes area. And then I was on my computer, so I am getting ready to close the computer, and then of course I am on Yahoo News: 'Earthquake in Haiti.' I said, 'Wow! That fast?' And to me it's here, and they already know? They didn't have anything yet, just the graph. And then I said, 'Let's look to some other places.' And then they have a map of Haiti, and the thing's, like, right on Port-au-Prince. And I said, 'What? It was in Port-au-Prince, and we felt it that strongly?' And then I tried to call Port-au-Prince. Of course no numbers would go through. There was a second [aftershock]. And then when I went out for the second time, I said, 'Oh my God.' I realized this is something big and huge. But I had no idea about the extent. I was just like, 'Okay, I need to find out about my people.' No phones. People could call me from Les Cayes area for a while. So I received phone calls from people in Les Cayes. They said, 'Did you feel?' I said, 'Yes. Do you realize it's on Port-au-Prince?'

"People who live in the rural areas send their kids to school or university to Port-au-Prince. And many people go to Port-au-Prince to find jobs. So everybody knows at least one person who's in Port-au-Prince. And I suddenly realized I could go and watch on TV what's happening. I started to watch, and things started to come on about this and that, and some images—all the dust. And people couldn't reach their families. So they all said, 'We need to go.' And that's how we got the idea of helping people to go to Port-au-Prince and bring back survivors. We all did it. The local bank did it, and other organizations. We did it maybe longer time, because we had the money. And I said, 'Money is to be used; let's do that.' Because I knew that this was going to start to be a nightmare there.

"And then, when I saw the first dead bodies starting to line up the street at every corner in Port-au-Prince, I said, 'Oh my God. We can't leave the survivors that are from Camp Perrin; we can't leave them there.' So trucks, buses, whatever was available, we paid for it. And then, when we started to have all these people, we made a census. I'm part of the civil protection committee in Camp Perrin. We found that in Camp Perrin it was about nine thousand people that came here. And of that, more than three thousand were school kids. And I think there were over six hundred people who died, that the people reported, that were from Camp Perrin.

"Our focus was, how do we help the majority of people? We didn't have enough money to care for all these people, but we made a proposition that we could help all these kids go back to school. School reopened very quickly here, in the south in general. So we said okay, this is one way to get the kids from Port-au-Prince to just go back to some kind of normalcy. The Minister of Education in Cayes did a survey of the schools, the whole department, and the result for Camp Perrin was that a hundred percent of the kids had been reintegrated into the school system. Which was for us a big success. School fees are one of the priority expenses for each family. If they haven't got the money to pay for the school this year, they panic. So we were saying, okay, best way to help is to at least pay for the school fees."

"That frees up money in every household for other things," I suggested.

"They don't *have* any money. That's the thing. The Red Cross, English Red Cross, using our own survey, they did a sampling—When was that? End of June, July? —to see how many people went back to Port-au-Prince, and they came up with 20 percent. Usually the father went back to Port-au-Prince to look for a job. And most of them left the kids in Camp Perrin, because they had families or friends that were willing to keep the kids. And women who were in trade before, who did some trade, they commute. They try to go back to Port-au-Prince, they buy supplies, and they try and set themselves up. All these people left Port-au-Prince, and we all thought, 'Oh, that's good, because that will enable whatever's going to happen to happen in Port-au-Prince.' Because you get people out of the way. And we all said now it's an opportunity to keep those people out of Port-au-Prince, by creating jobs in the provinces. And it never really materialized."

"Could it possibly still materialize?"

"It could, but people are stuck in Port-au-Prince, and everyone wants to have his name on something that 'We are here! We are doing something in Port-au-Prince!' It's true. In the first month, end of January—we, the whole people of the south, there was a meeting—we outlined a project that could start immediately and help get the people busy, get them jobs, get them money so they would be self-sufficient. And you need to do it for minimum three years, up to five years. Most of them were related to rehabilitating infrastructure—irrigation canals, because there are not a lot in the south—all the reforestation programs, I mean now actually implementing them, until there are trees that are tall enough that you can see a difference. We were looking at projects that could employ people, fast, without any specific skills."

"I would say yes, it's still possible," said Eliassaint. "This is a long battle. Everything is in Port-au-Prince. All the good things are in Port-au-Prince, all the bad things also are in Port-au-Prince. But we want the decentralization at every level. A lot of people go to Port-au-Prince for the university. So we need to decentralize, put some good universities in the provinces."

"A lot of schools were destroyed in Port-au-Prince," said Mousson. "Schools and universities."

"So you could build new schools and universities in Les Cayes."

"Yeah! There is space. There are already some universities in Les Cayes. But there was enough space. People were getting ready, saying, 'Okay, we can have *that* one,' you know, talking to *that* university, saying, 'We have the space.' Some places, they even have the buildings. The question will be to reorganize. But I think people think that if they leave Port-au-Prince they're going to lose some opportunities, because they're not right there, you know, attending—I mean, meetings? Oh, my God. They've made all these 'clusters.' And all these clusters are meeting, now, once a week. It used to be three times a week. We receive the minutes and the agendas. I say, 'Are you crazy?' It's like, 'Oh, you're going to lose opportunities!' I said, 'What opportunity?' I'm not going to do a project around Port-au-Prince. There's enough people trying to do something. I think it was a blessing: survivors, please, let's start something. It's not that you're going to abandon Port-au-Prince. It's going to take so long to rebuild Port-au-Prince. In the meantime, what do you do? You don't pile people more into Port-au-Prince, in those camps. It's awful."

"Tent cities," I said.

"Yeah. You know, I went, because I wanted to see the Palace and was taking photos. So I was there. I could see it. And I could just not believe it. I mean, right across from the Palace, in April, these people had never had *any* visit from *any* official person. In April. And they were not lying. The guy was telling me, and everyone else from the little tents was saying, 'That's true, he's telling the truth. We see foreigners, journalists, and some private people.' We had a tent that we put up here, just to try to see the size of it. You enter it, and you come out sweating. Of course tents were needed at the beginning. But we hesitated so long. What decision, you know: 'Do we do tents? Do we do tarps? And we don't want Port-au-Prince to become a slum, by building all these little transition homes.' I'm sorry, but it is already. Give them something that's decent. And the women that are commuting. You know why they're commuting, most of the time? Because they go and get the husband's clothes, so they can wash them here in Camp Perrin. Because of course in Port-au-Prince, how do you wash clothes? How do you organize yourself?"

✳

On our last evening in Les Cayes, we ate seafood and drank Prestige beer on the beach at sunset, near some wooden fishing boats, looking across the water at Ile à Vache, the Island of Cows.

"You've written two books, and you still haven't fixed Pakistan?" Pierre asked me.

"No," I admitted. "I haven't fixed it, or even figured it out."

"Are you going to do better than that for Haiti?"

Chapter 13

MAKING THINGS WORK

"An American was shot," Gerald told us back in Port-au-Prince.

"Oh really? How? Where?"

"Up the hill, near Petionville."

"Was he robbed?"

"I don't know the details. I think he was a Haitian-American."

"What else has been happening in the world while we were away?"

He laughed. "Actually, I haven't been paying attention." Then he remembered one thing: Préval, who could not run for president again, had met with former president Leslie Manigat and Mme. Manigat, who was a presidential candidate. "He's been meeting with all the candidates. But this is the first time he's gone to meet a candidate. Usually the candidates come to meet him."

"What does it benefit him to do that?" asked Ben.

"I think it's a way for him to show that he's fully invested in the electoral process," said Gerald. "And that he's doing his utmost to make the elections credible. And that he's more than looking forward to stepping down at the end of his term."

It occurred to me that, with Préval out of office, the new election might mark the true end of the Aristide era. I posited this to Gerald. He pointed out that Préval had his own candidate that he was promoting, and that Yvon Neptune, who had been prime minister under Aristide, and Lesly Voltaire, another of Aristide's ministers, were also running. "The mayor of this area is also running for president," he added. We were in Gerald's car, in the perpetual traffic jam at the intersection of Delmas and Martin Luther King.

"I think the era of Aristide will really end when the situation improves in the country," he said.

"When's that going to be?"

"I'm always optimist," he said. "During the Préval term we were able to have some stability, but in terms of social and economic development it was a disappointment, even before the earthquake. I hope that we'll have greater stability under the new president, and that some of the investments that were promised after the earthquake will materialize. There is no reason for things not to improve. Unfortunately, politicians are too concerned with keeping power, rather than focusing on the country's problems. There is no sense of urgency, people are just living day to day, the public authorities have no plan of action. For instance, everybody is just hoping that we'll get through the next hurricane season. Absolutely no leadership. One thing I think the authorities did, they've stored food in some warehouses in provincial towns."

"So we're just sort of waiting for the hurricane season now?"

He laughed. "Yeah."

"The thing I keep getting is that Aristide had such support and popularity, that if he wouldn't have been so bitter, he would have been able to achieve great things," said Ben.

"But Aristide had always been a divisive figure," said Gerald. "If you listen to his speeches, even if you don't believe in intrigues and think that he was very honest when he spoke, the words he spoke were many times very divisive. At a certain point in Aristide's administration, the gang members had more power than the ministers. They could go into public offices and demand money. This situation ostracized him, but it also served as a safety net for him. Because whenever there was political tension, he could use those gang members to burn tires and intimidate people. When he came back in power in 1994, his political power became so intertwined with the gang members that he couldn't govern without them. But in a sense, this is a result of years and decades of irresponsibility by our political leaders. Because if these gang members, many of them still adolescents, had had a minimum of stability and guidance at home, there would have been no reason for them to participate in these destructive activities. Unfortunately, gang-related activities were their only source of income."

We passed a graffito spray-painted on a wall in English:

OBAMA
WE NEED
CHANGE

"What we really need is a new type of leadership in Haiti," said Gerald.

We sat down a few times with Gerald and others for formal, recorded interviews, but most of our conversations took place in his SUV on the way to and from his work in Canot and other neighborhoods. Getting there and back through the potholed and now rubble-strewn streets of Port-au-Prince was just part of what he did every day, so we did it with him. The city had only a few traffic lights, and too few street signs. Some new red signs had appeared, sponsored by Digicel. "Sometimes it's hard to identify streets, because there are no street signs," Gerald mused. "So it makes more sense to say next to the supermarket, or next to the gas station. It can be funny getting directions in Haiti: 'You'll see a hole in the street, and after that there's a huge pile of trash. After that, you'll see a slightly damaged wall.'"

Ben was tickled by a billboard on the airport wall that showed a very suave-looking, square-jawed young brown man smoking a cigarette. He called him the Haitian Marlboro Man.

"You see how they advertise smoking in Haiti?" said Gerald. "Smoking is a cool activity, smoking is good for health." A group of men and women were working along the airport wall, all wearing identical yellow T-shirts. "This is part of a cash-for-work program," Gerald told us. "This is a USAID-funded program. The pay is about five dollars per day to clean the streets. But it is usually highly ineffective, because there is little supervision. I guess it's a way to put money in people's hands, but I disagree with the policy. It's good to give people work, but the job has to be meaningful. Something substantial has to be achieved."

Everywhere we went, there were political graffiti to read and try to decipher. Or rather, what needed deciphering was not any given slogan—they were usually phrased bluntly—but the overall political landscape. Who exactly had spray-painted which slogan, and how seriously should it be taken? Anyone with access to enough cans of spray paint could make any statement many times over, all around the city or indeed all around Haiti. VIV PRESIDENT PREVAL. WYCLEF AYITI RENMEN-OU. ABA OKIPASYON. Long live President Préval. Wyclef, Haiti loves you. Down with the occupation.

"So who are the people who write 'ABA OKIPASYON'?" I asked. "Are they Lavalas?"

"Not only Lavalas. If you want to have popular support, you cannot support the occupation."

"What's *okipasyon*?" asked Ben.

"The UN occupation," I told him.

"The politically correct term is 'stabilization,'" said Gerald with his grin. "I think these spray paints should be banned. There are certain products that we shouldn't import."

"Spray paint, styrofoam, and plastic bottles," suggested Ben.

"Yes, we'll make a list."

One day we stopped at Sogebank so Gerald could run an errand. "There's one advantage of having special needs," he said. "You get special service at the bank. Otherwise you wait two hours in the line, because banks are very crowded, especially now because many banks collapsed." The Sogebank building was notable for one of the very few handicapped ramps in Haiti. As Ben filmed Yovens wheeling him up it, Gerald looked into the camera and cried, "Here is what we're fighting for!"

✷

One morning Gerald dropped us at the office of Fonkoze, the microfinance organization I had worked for during my visits to Haiti in 2004. On a wall nearby was spray-painted:

BON RETOUR
J.C. DUVALIER

Welcome back, Jean-Claude Duvalier—Baby Doc. Gerald indicated a building: "This is the office of the political party of Duvalier." It was called Parti Unité National, the Party of National Unity.

"Does he want to come back, Gerald?" I asked.

"I think so. But there are some political and legal problems."

I remembered Fonkoze's director, Anne Hastings, fondly and was gratified that the feeling seemed mutual. In 2004 she had liked me enough to invite me to spend an evening with her in her apartment, watching the Edwards-Cheney vice-presidential debate. When Pete and Ben and I arrived at her office six years later, she hugged me. I was even happier to learn that the summit of microfinance practitioners that Fonkoze had hosted on the Central Plateau in 2004 seemed to have borne fruit, and that Anne felt my contribution to it had been useful. Knowing she was still at it, earthquake or no earthquake, as wiry and white-haired and tenacious and plain-spoken as ever, that the continuity of her leadership and the force of her personality were still at work on behalf of the Haitian poor, was comforting and encouraging. She was, of course, in the middle of urgent phone calls and an unforeseen crisis when we arrived, but she welcomed us warmly.

"There's been such a problem with psychological trauma with our clients, and our staff, and everyone, that it's kind of difficult to get people back to any sense of normalcy," she said. "We lost eleven buildings, we lost five employees. We found a building to rent where we could open up the Port-au-Prince branch, but it's a three-story concrete building, and it's right down across from Champ de Mars, and right down from that fire station. I looked at the building, and I said, 'Wow, this is fabulous.' Every other building around it is totally on the ground, and this is the only building that's still standing. And then when the employees saw it, they said, 'No way, we're not going in that building.'" She laughed heartily. "First we had a structural engineer come in and look at it. And he said, 'This is one of the best-built buildings I've ever seen. I'd really like to know the engineer's name on it.' So we started with that, to tell the employees that it was okay for them to come in. But then ultimately Father Joseph came in, and we went on the third floor, and we did a Mass to inaugurate the building and to remember the five people who had died. And that really had a major impact on people. And Father Joseph said at the time, 'We can't continue to live in fear. We have to move on with our lives.'"

Two women walked into Anne's office. "You want to meet these people?" she asked me. "I'd like you to. Ethan, this is Leigh Carter, the executive director of Fonkoze USA. And that's Ben, and Pete. Ethan is the one who helped me on the anti-poverty summit, so many years ago? He was the PR guy who was writing those little things coming out at the end of every day, and all that stuff?"

"A lot came out of that," said Leigh, and both women laughed warmly. "We got the letter," said Leigh to Anne.

"Oh, you did? Congratulations! I want to see it, and also I want a copy to put in the binder."

"It was quite an ordeal."

We chatted for a couple of minutes, Leigh invited me to visit her sometime at her office in Washington, and then Anne continued: "So that's kind of what it took, was to have a ceremony to somehow bring the Holy Spirit into this building, so the employees could come to work every day. And frankly, we haven't heard anything else bad since then. People have been seemingly pretty comfortable with the building. Now, if we could just do the same thing for the tent cities, but I don't think it's gonna happen. Anyway, getting people to overcome their fear has been one of the most difficult things. Leigh was here on the day of the earthquake, and we had our building down on Avenue Christophe, which is one of the buildings which is no good anymore. And right next door to it we had planned to rent another building, because we'd run out of space in that building. We were going to put a door in the wall between them, and the executive offices were gonna be in this new building. We had been over there that day, figuring out who's gonna sit where. We had the contract in the hands of the owner, but it hadn't yet been signed. And the earthquake hit, and she fell out of the second floor and broke her back."

"Leigh did?"

"Leigh did, yeah. She had the most awful external cast, with all this metal stuff. It was awful. But we walked out of the building and looked to our left, where the other building was, and it was totally on the ground. The whole building. I mean, we were just hours from moving into that building." She laughed again. "So we felt very, very fortunate, you know? That we had gotten out of there, and had not paid the rent yet. I think that was one of the things that was so hard to see: that there was no reason that we would have predicted that that building would have fallen, any more than the building that we were in, which did not fall, although one wall fell, and that's what she fell out of. So it was a complicated day, you know? And then just tryin' to get home was too much."

Leigh had left the office, and now she returned. "I just told them the story of you falling out—not falling out of, but falling *with* the wall," Anne told her. They both laughed again.

"It was a well-laid-out plan," said Leigh. "You wouldn't believe the conditions where the Archbishop is. It's unbelievable in there."

"Really? Are you kidding? Is it behind the Christ Roi church?"

"Christ Roi church," Leigh confirmed. "And that thing completely fell."

Anne explained to us: "You know, where she just went this morning is—" She named a Roman Catholic foundation. "They always require that the highest authority in your country sign off on the grant that they're gonna give you. And also somebody has to submit the proposal on your behalf in the United States. So you have to go to the nuns in the United States, and then you have to go to the Archbishop in Haiti, you know? Monsignor Miot had gotten to be a really good friend of ours over the years. He knew us well, he knew Father Joseph, he'd gone to Fondwa on a number of occasions and everything. We felt really comfortable asking him any time we needed to, to sign this paper. And he died in the earthquake. And there's a congregation of nuns called the Daughters of Mary, and they were having a meeting in that same building. *Twenty* of the top leadership of these nuns, wiped out. And they run a whole network of schools across Port-au-Prince. So now they have a new Archbishop, and this foundation said, 'Where's your letter from the Archbishop? We're willing to give this *tiny* grant.'"

"Well, they weren't willing to release it at first," said Leigh. "The administrator was like, 'We're not releasing this money without a letter from the new representative of the Church.' And I said, 'Well, you know, that might be a little hard right now.' She wrote back, she says, 'It should be simple. Just go over there and get it.' And I just went, 'There is *nothing* simple or easy in Haiti right now.' You know, the guy died, his staff died, the cathedral—y'know? And a few minutes later her boss e-mails me and says, 'The money's on its way. Just get the letter when you can.' His office is now in this kitchen, and there's cracks all on the walls, and he's sittin' at this kitchen table. You know, this is the monsignor, the head of the Church in Haiti. He's sittin' at a kitchen table, chain-smokin' cigarettes. He's as nice as he could be. He likes Fonkoze a lot, because they've given him good customer service, cashin' checks for him after the earthquake when nobody else would."

"Oh, great!" said Anne. "So he knew who we were already."

"Yeah, absolutely," said Leigh. "Customer service paid off once again! I had to type the letter myself. It was fun. Nice to meet y'all." She went out again.

"Anyway," continued Anne. "So the earthquake was, uh, quite something. But Fonkoze was totally dedicated to getting all of our branches up. For a day, you were kind of in shock. But then one of our branches, way up in the mountains, close to the Dominican border, called our chief financial officer to say, 'We're open, we're running out of cash, what are you gonna do?' And she said she just couldn't believe it, that twenty-four, thirty-six hours after the earthquake, more than half of our branches were operating. They didn't care that Port-au-Prince was completely down; they just kept operating. But we were running out of cash, so we all came in to work, and we set up the Port-au-Prince branch in the courtyard outside of the building. We had electricity, we had the computers. Our IT director had taken all of the networks, servers, and everything, taken 'em up to the mountain, hooked 'em up with all those—you know that place up there where all the satellites are comin' in and stuff like that. He had hooked the whole thing up. He was a real cowboy. And so we were up and running in just a couple of days. And the banks didn't open for weeks.

"But then we did run out of cash, so then we had the help of the U.S. military to bring the cash in for us. That was done on a Saturday—Friday night in the middle of the night, and Saturday morning. Then Monday morning, the central bank called us and said, 'Now that you've gotten all those dollars, would you like some *gourdes*?' They had refused to do anything for us in the weeks before. They've been very wonderful since then, really, really helping us to keep the cash flowing. Because the amount of money that is coming through our organization now is *unbelievable*. It's just *so* much more. We've probably quadrupled or quintupled since the earthquake. Not in terms of donations for us or something, just in terms of money that we're passing through."

"Remittances?" I asked.

"We have remittances. We do the payroll for all the cash-for-work programs. We take cash out into these neighborhoods where people are cleaning the rubble, and we hand out their pay envelopes with cash in them. We used to do about three thousand every two weeks, with one contract. Now we have twenty contracts; we're doing more than eighty thousand every two weeks."

"Eighty thousand dollars?"

"Eighty thousand envelopes. No, millions of dollars! Eighty thousand workers are getting paid. And then we have cash grants that we're distributing for the American Red Cross through Fonkoze. And remittances are way up, as you pointed out. I mean, we just have money flowing through the institution. There's tons of money, about eighteen million, that's going out in cash grants to schools. Private schools in the West Department, the Nippes, and the Southeast. There's more than four thousand, five thousand payments that we're making now, of two thousand five hundred U.S. a pop, to all these schools. And that's supposed to be a one-off payment, but they might come back and do it again. So when it comes to getting cash out, everybody's coming to Fonkoze, because we're so customer service-oriented, but we just don't bullshit around about procedure, we just feel like it's important to get the money out there! You know, and get it in the hands of people. Because we really feel strongly that the only way to make this thing happen is to get the economy going again. And then all the new loans that we've been putting out. So the total amount of money passing through the organization is much, much, much, much bigger than it ever has been in the past."

"Are you going to have an annual report for 2010?"

"Of course! But not soon." She laughed uproariously again. "We're barely getting 2009 out. It's not quite ready, but we're doing the final review this weekend."

"But that 2010 report is going to be quite a document, I think. Historic, really," I ventured.

"Yeah, you're right. We should start on it now."

"What about the tent cities, and economic life there?"

"It's my hot button," said Anne. "I cannot *stand* the fact that we have gotten no further than we have. The guy that I was talking to when you first came in, I was very surprised because he's an advisor in the UNDP, and he was just saying everything that I believe: that this debate that has gone on, and on, and on, and on, over 'Are we gonna put in temporary shelters or permanent homes?' is just a huge waste of time and energy. And as a result, *nothing* has happened. And we have said from the beginning: the solution is not temporary shelters. We've got to get permanent housing back for people. And the other thing is the issue of financing that construction. We're trying to say that our clients, there's just no way that we could ask them to take a mortgage on a one-room house that we're gonna build for them, that costs more than they've ever seen in their lives, even though it only costs three thousand dollars. They can't pay for that; there's just no way. So, talking about *loaning* them money to pay for those homes is just ridiculous. So this guy said he agreed. I mean, *he* told *me* that it has to be some combination of subsidy, sweat equity, and maybe a little credit. But he was saying that he thought the most that anybody could afford would be like ten percent of the cost of the structure. So he's tryin' to make some movement. I don't know if he'll be successful or not. But it just drives me nuts. It drives me nuts that people are just sittin' around six months, eight months later, and we're still not past the stage of debating whether we're going to temporary or permanent. And, as he said, it's *way* too late for temporary. If we were gonna do temporary, it should have been done back in February, March. But August is ridiculous. And temporary, everywhere in the world that they've tried it, it turns into *permanent* temporary. Ten years later, you have slums with people living in structures that are just gonna fall apart. So anyway, we've just gotten the money we could get to do home building, and we're just doin' it. We're working with two different partners, one in Cabaret, one in Fondwa, and we're just building homes."

"What you've been saying seems to underscore what I've been hearing about agencies not really cooperating, lots of competition among international agencies, lots of meetings ..."

"Well, fortunately, we're not an international agency. We've had some very, very good partnerships with a few international agencies, but we don't go participate in all the B.S. We've been trying to say that the government developed its plan, okay? And there was concern about whether the private sector was involved in the development of the plan. Well, they did have a plan for involving civil society and the private sector in the development of that plan, but did they really involve grassroots organizations like Fonkoze and many others out there? And, you know, I think the answer is, 'Not really.' There was some input. We were invited for input, but that's because we've gotten pretty big. And so we can also be viewed as part of the private sector, because we have a nonbank financial institution. So I didn't feel left out; I wasn't gonna argue about whether my institution had been left out of the planning. I just thought the whole thing was absurd, because I don't believe that you can do planning that way. You know, this comprehensive plan for the next ten years. Nobody can ever do that."

"Particularly not in Haiti."

"Particularly not in this kind of environment, in which every six to twelve months the whole world changes for Haiti. So, as usual, we're just about getting out there and making things work, which I think is also what Partners in Health does. Paul has a role where he's really trying to coordinate these international NGOs. I work with the ones we can work with. But I don't really get involved in their stuff. You know, they have all those, um, different—what do they call them? Those things where they meet interminably. Uh, clusters. They have the Shelter Cluster, the Health Cluster, this cluster, that cluster. And all it is, is a whole bunch of meetings and nobody's doing anything except debating."

Gerald had told us much the same thing: "You can spend a lifetime in seminars right now in Haiti. Because it seems all NGOs that come, they offer seminars, and they send you invitations. From time to time I send people to these seminars, but I don't attend myself. You can get some good information, but between talking and action, I prefer action."

"Does Paul get stuck in those?" I asked Anne.

"I don't know. I mean, Paul is in and out a lot. But I think he's in a position where he has to try to bring them together. We work with the Clinton Global Initiative Haiti Platform, and it's much better. And it's a combination of international and local. But it's smaller, and it's more about making real commitments and then showing the progress that you're making against those."

"Decentralization has been a buzzword," I said. "Various people have expressed disappointment to me that it hasn't happened or is not going to happen."

"Yeah, I think it's very complicated. Another one of my things that I found very, very frustrating was that for years and years and years, decades, we've been trying to stop or slow the migration of people from the rural areas into Port-au-Prince, and in thirty-five seconds we reversed the whole thing, and everybody started moving out. Six hundred thousand people, minimum, moved out into the provinces. And then all the cash for work was in Port-au-Prince! So there's no way for them to make a living out there, they're putting incredible stress on their families and people that they were trying to stay with, and so now they've all turned around and moved back. So we missed a tremendous opportunity to really make something of that. Had we gotten employment out there to those people, they might have stayed. And now they're all back in the city, living in the tents. Because in the tents you get medical care, and you get water, and you get whatever. I don't know. The thing I can't quite bring myself to reconcile is knowing how horrible it must be to be stuck in one of those tents, and yet seeing that your option to move out means you're moving away from whatever water, whatever health care, whatever schools—because they have schools in there now. You're living in less than human conditions, but you're receiving services that you never received before, and that you won't receive if you go out to the provinces. It's truly a dilemma. And so you sit there and let the rapes happen, and the theft, because you're afraid to do anything else. I think it's a horrible, horrible choice that we're asking people to make. You should go out there to Corail, where they moved people from Petionville. It's in the middle of nowhere! There's not a single tree anywhere. The first day that there was a storm coming across the mountains, and they had one of these model temporary shelters out there, the wind picked the shelter up and moved it a hundred meters from where it had been! There's no markets, there's no schools, there's nothing! And they talk about, 'Oh, we're gonna do that.' But when?"

"Well, who's in charge?" I asked.

"That's the problem. I think what has made this disaster so bad is that we started with a weak, fragile government, and then the government was just wiped out. Nothing was hurt as bad as the government. When you go down to the center of town, where all the government buildings are, every single government building is gone. And they lost so many employees and leaders. So it's very hard to figure out how you could expect any more from the government. They're all operational now, and that seems like a major step forward. But trying to coordinate this huge amount of money that's supposedly there, but it's not really there, it's not coming in – we're asking them to take on such a huge task, that it just seems incomprehensible to me that we would think that the government of Haiti could do any better than it is actually doing. They've got the problem of elections. They couldn't have a bigger set of problems right now."

"Are these elections going to be meaningful or useful in any sense?"

"You know, I've given up on predicting anything that's gonna happen in this country, and certainly on participating in Haitian politics. It's just hard for me to believe that people are going to get out there and vote. And yet, the other day I was driving up one of these streets, and there was one of the places where you can get your electoral card. You know, because everybody lost them. And there were *massive* numbers of people outside, standing around, sitting, waiting to get their electoral card. So, had Wyclef stayed in, I betcha we would have had the best participation we've had since Aristide's first election, you know? It's hard for me to imagine, but I don't predict. I have no idea. It would be surprising to me if a lot of people participated. But who knows what fireworks we could have before then?"

✳

"As a people, we need to take responsibility in our country," said Gerald later, back in his car. "We have to fight and work for Haiti. We have to love the country. We have no other country, and we have to cherish every bit of Haiti. We have to learn to love our compatriots, we have to learn to love our natural environment. We have to work and participate in volunteer activities as well. In that manner, we will work toward progress in Haiti."

"How do you go about bringing that sense of responsibility to the majority of people?" asked Ben.

"We need a stronger civil society. Local associations should be encouraged and developed. At the same time, we need more responsible leaders in public offices. We, as a society, need to take some tough decisions now. For instance, we've pretty much ignored the problems of *bidonvilles*. We've been acting like they didn't exist, and look what happened unfortunately during the earthquake."

"Hey Gerald," I called to him over the back of the front passenger seat where he sat. This was often how conversations went in the car, because he couldn't turn around to talk to us in the backseat. Sometimes I leaned around between the front seats and he would look at me sidelong; other times we made eye contact in the rear-view mirror.

"Uh-huh."

"Do you think that if I come to Haiti ten years from now, we might see piles of rubble that have just been overgrown, with trees growing out of them, and they never were cleared away?"

"Well, it's possible. It depends on the choices that we make as a society. But I'm hopeful, and I certainly do not look forward in ten years to having rubble around here. Let me tell you something, Ethan. The only people who are truly shocked right now are people like me. But for the poor, things were so hard for them already that it's just another challenge. Maybe it's even better for many poor now."

"The other difference is that many of them lost family and friends," I said.

"Yes, of course. I know a guy who lost his five children and his wife. But materially speaking, they are probably no worse off."

"I love the fact that privileged people in this country say that they're privileged," said Ben. "You try to tell people in the States that they're privileged, and they'll say, 'No, I worked for it!'"

"The political climate, although right now there is some stability, is very volatile," said Gerald. "Because if nothing is done, if there is no sense of hope, if there is no sense of direction that emerges after these elections, anything can happen. It's frustrating, it's certainly not acceptable the way things are evolving right now, and although I do live in a comfortable—but a comfortable what? Comfortable bubble. Once I step out of my house, once I step out of my car, I experience many of the same challenges and frustrations as the common people."

Gerald left his bubble every morning, by choice and with a sense of purpose. This day his purpose was to hold a *sensibilisation*, a public slide show and discussion on issues facing disabled people and the importance of including them in mainstream society and economic life, in Édrice's neighborhood. They had a stash of full-color posters showing Gerald's and Édrice's faces and the Fondation J'Aime Haïti and Direct Relief International logos, with blank lines where they could hand-write the date and time and location, and for days ahead they had pasted these on walls around the neighborhood. We arrived in Gerald's vehicle with a laptop, a screen, and a generator, and a couple of hundred local citizens sat on wooden benches and stood beneath a makeshift canopy to hear stirring orations—these were Édrice's specialty—and personal testimonials, followed by Q and A.

We try to highlight the capacities of disabled people and show the opportunities for Haiti if we integrate people with disabilities," Gerald had told us. "We do some PowerPoint presentations, in which we show images of people with disabilities, with no arms, no legs, but that are still able to paint, or people that are blind playing pianos. And we talk about these issues in Haiti, and how difficult the social environment is for people with disabilities. And how we, as a society, can make life easier for people with disabilities and allow them to play an active role in society, in which they are able to not only exercise their rights, but as well their duties." He used this word often, and he pronounced it the American way: *doodies*. "And this we've been doing for the past several years. Usually, we organize this activity in schools for the children, but recently we started doing it in communities as well."

"What kinds of responses do you get?" I asked him.

"Overall, the response has been very positive. But there is a tendency for people to think disabled people must be dependent on assistance, and should receive help from NGOs or the government, like regular coupons to go to the market, or free products, or maybe a stipend every month. I try to change this type of mentality. And I try to explain that a person with disability, certainly, in some cases, needs financial assistance, needs medical attention. But in most cases, a person with disability can participate actively in society and live a normal, autonomous life. Persons with disabilities can work, can provide for their family, and can be independent."

At today's *sensibilisation* he showed a video from a TV station in Minnesota showing teenage sisters, conjoined twins who essentially shared one body with two heads, going about their daily life with their very normal, suburban, middle-class parents and siblings. "Do you tell them what they're going to be watching?" Ben asked him afterward.

"No, I put it on mute and just show them the documentary. Did you guys take pictures?"

"I took a few," said Pete. "I got some negative responses when I first started."

"Will you send these pictures to me afterwards?"

"Oh, sure."

"Because I usually take pictures as well, but this time I didn't."

"What effect do you think the video has on people?" asked Ben. "Do you think it arouses their curiosity?"

"Yes, because sometimes people can be a bit timid to ask questions. But this really is something that is not common in Haiti. Not too many people know about it, and thus the video compels them to ask questions. Well, it's not common anywhere. But information flows much faster abroad, and obviously people know about Siamese. For instance, this video, I just downloaded it on YouTube."

"Ethan had stepped away, so he wasn't there to translate," Ben said. "What did that one guy ask you?"

"You know, they are not afraid to ask me personal questions," Gerald said. "He asked, 'How do you have sex?'" Gerald and his fiancée had a two-year-old daughter. "I said, 'I might be disabled, but my sexual organ has no disability!'"

We were stuck in traffic in the rain, on the way home. We had wanted to spend the evening with Philippe Allouard, Gerald's and my French mutual friend, who had introduced us to each other in 2004, but reluctantly we had decided it wasn't feasible because of the rain. Philippe now headed a nonprofit that worked on press freedom and media issues, which had been crucially helpful disseminating "news you can use" after the earthquake.

"Is traffic usually like this, this time of day?" I asked.

"When it's raining it's worse," said Gerald. "But also there might be something else, like an accident or a vehicle with a flat tire. For some reason many drivers in Haiti, whenever their car malfunctions, they try to fix it on the spot. They won't move it to the side. Oh, this is Miss Haiti, on the billboard. She's a lawyer. Her mother was also a lawyer. Her mother was a very outspoken lawyer during the embargo, and when Aristide came back, she got shot and killed. She was a very well-known lawyer."

"What was she outspoken about?"

"I don't remember well, but basically she was a political opponent of Aristide. I think Miss Haiti was five years old at the time her mother was killed, and she went to live in the Dominican Republic. And when she became Miss Haiti, a lot of people complained, saying that she was from the Dominican Republic, that she was not Haitian. Actually her father was a presidential candidate, but he was not allowed to run. Her father was one of the thirty-four original candidates. But he was eliminated for some technicality. Miss Haiti participated the other day in the Miss Universe contest. I thought she would make top fifteen, but unfortunately she got eliminated in the first round."

As we crawled through the evening rush hour, the windshield wipers flapped back and forth and the radio played music and then news headlines, read very elegantly in French by a female announcer.

"Did you hear that?" Gerald asked me.

"Yeah," I said. "Forty people killed in Pakistan."

"How?" asked Pete.

"Was it a suicide bomb, Gerald?" I asked.

"I don't know. I don't think she mentioned." After a pause, he added: "Oh, by the way, there was a candidate at our awareness campaign today."

"Oh really?"

"Yeah."

"A presidential candidate?"

"No, for Congress."

"Was he trying to get votes?"

"Yeah."

"He piggybacked on your thing."

"He tried. But I said no. Because that's not correct. Especially since the local committee that organized the event doesn't necessarily endorse his candidacy. He knows my number. He asked me for support already. But he didn't call. He just showed up. I only realized that he was there when he had the microphone in his hand."

"Yeah, that's not cool," said Ben.

"He's a nice guy," said Gerald. "But I think it was inappropriate. Don't you think so? But you know what? His visit also sparked some ideas. Maybe I should organize a local debate for the communities, with different candidates."

When we finally arrived back at Village Tecina, I went out through the rain and stood beside the passenger door talking to Gerald while his driver, Yovens, opened the house. "Well, another day full of adventures," I said.

"I like these types of activities," Gerald said happily.

"Like the presentation?"

"Yes. I like to interact with the population. It's work that needs to be done."

"And you're doing it," I said.

"*We* are doing it," he corrected me. "It's a whole team."

"It's a good team."

"Yes," he said with satisfaction.

※

"Do you mean Doog-lahs?" Père Noé said. "Doog-lahs is in prison in Florida, or somewhere in the U.S."

I had a queasy feeling. "For what?" I asked him.

"For misbehaving with some of the boys."

We had just arrived in Cap Haïtien from the Partners in Health compound at Cange on the Central Plateau, in Édrice's car with Ed-rice himself and Frantz, a driver he employed. Édrice had rescued five members of a better-off family from beneath the rubble of their house in Canot on the day of the earthquake, and to thank him they had sold the car to him at a steep discount. It brought him extra income when-ever he was able to hire it out. Édrice and Frantz had driven up from Port-au-Prince that morning to Cange, where we had spent a couple of days. Édrice couldn't drive himself because of his disability, but he came along to keep an eye on things and, I suspected, because he liked to meet people and check out whatever might be going on elsewhere around Haiti.

Frantz was a cheerful, husky fellow, but an alarming driver. From Cange to Cap Haïtien had taken us six and a half hours on National Route One, which was unimproved beyond Hinche, the first major town after Cange. It was a trip I had wanted to take in 2004 but had foregone in favor of Paul Farmer's invitation to ride with him down to the airport in Port-au-Prince, on a day he was due in Boston. If I had made this trip in 2004, I would have been taking my chances in a *publique* or a truck. Making it now, I could see the advantages of a private vehicle. Much of the northern part of the Central Plateau was a bleak and forlorn empty landscape punctuated by roadside villages and a few scruffy towns. We picked our way slowly around deep, muddy potholes, and at one point Frantz gunned the engine to cross a bridge at speed because some suspicious-looking characters looked as if they were moving in to head us off to stop and rob us.

It was a long, hot, dusty day on the road, an experience I had wanted to be sure to have before, so rumor had it, the EU-financed asphalting eventually extended from Hinche to Cap Haïtien. If and when the repaving was complete, it would transform travel from Port-au-Prince *au Cap* as well as, potentially, the economic geography of the Central Plateau. On a much smoother and faster road, mangos and other produce from around Hinche and points north would be able to reach market, and even export markets, via Port-au-Prince and—why not?— Cap Haïtien, rather than rotting on the ground or not being cultivated at all. Whether this would be done, and whether it would benefit the peasant farmers of the Central Plateau or contribute to the badly needed decentralization of Haiti as a whole, were open questions whose answers would depend on other factors, including the human factor. What was certain was that if the road was not improved, it would not happen. The potential was there.

Père Fritz Lafontant in Cange had given me Père Noé's phone number and had called him for us, to ask him to help us in Cap Haïtien. Père Noé Bernier was the pastor of the main Episcopal parish in Haiti's second-largest city. It was reassuring to have such a contact in hand, particularly since we might not have known—arriving *au Cap* for the first time since the earthquake, and overland without much reconnaissance—how to go about finding a place to stay, for starters. We had spent more than two hours with Père Lafontant in his apartment at the Zanmi Lasante campus in Cange, interviewing him about his life and work. There's a lot to tell about that, but for most purposes it's been told elsewhere very well by Tracy Kidder. My purpose, when offered the chance to sit with the 84-year-old mentor of Paul Farmer, onetime colleague of my own father, and patriarch of everything Partners in Health has accomplished, was simply to document as much of his life as I could in a couple of hours, in his own words, to give the raw video to Partners in Health for the enjoyment and edification of its own staff and whatever other uses it saw fit to make of it, and at some point to put a half-hour edit on the Web with English subtitles.

I wouldn't have presumed to ask Père Lafontant to introduce me to anyone. But as we stood at the top of the stairs outside his apartment saying our goodbyes, he had thought of Père Noé and urged his number on us. It was an unexpected grace note and felt like a good omen.

So Père Noé's house, in a compound belonging to the church behind a wall along the seaside boulevard, was our first stop *au Cap*, and here we were, sitting with him in his living room. His bearing expressed a confident sense of his own status as a well-situated and respected young professional and community leader. "We have our tent too, just in case," he was saying, meaning his own family.

"Did you see a large influx of people after the earthquake?" asked Pete.

"Oh yeah," said Père Noé. "In fact, the day after the earthquake."

I tried to pay attention and to take part in the conversation, but I was preoccupied with what Père Noé had just told us about Doog-lahs, Doug Perlitz. In 2004 I had been talking with Paul Farmer outside the guest house at Cange when Doug and Andy Schultheis had arrived. They had driven all the way from Cap Haïtien that morning to replenish AIDS medications for a teenager they worked with, and they were planning to drive all the way back the same day. I had jumped at their invitation to visit and stay with them. I had been impressed and moved by their work with street boys and had written about it. Now I had to figure out what to do with what I had just learned, and how it might change what I would publish. Was Doug still part of the story I needed to tell? My account of my time with him had been written years earlier, though not yet published. Should it be rewritten? Should it—could it—be edited out of my story? But wouldn't that amount to a lie of omission?

It was something I would rather not have had to think about or deal with. The account of Doug that I had written was admiring. Now, in an instant, new information had shaken the ground beneath me. What made it more jarring was that the information itself wasn't new; only my awareness of it was. But was it even information—was it true?[1] And if it was true, what did that change? Something Doug himself had said to me took on new overtones: "If you hold everyone at arm's length it's safe, it's neat, it's clean. But if you do this"—spreading his arms—"you get bloody."

Père Noé was offering to help us find a place to stay. There was a shortage of hotel rooms, especially these days, and rates were startlingly high. "All the hotels are full of UN, ONG," he said.

"Yeah, they're like pests," I agreed.

"Hopefully they're doin' some good," said Pete.

"Are they?" I asked Père Noé.

"Not a lot," he said.

In three words, Père Noé summed up the view of many people I spoke to in post-earthquake Haiti. "Just like in business, it's a competitive environment," was how Gerald put it. "They protect their turf. I was shocked to see that. A lot of money is being wasted. They tell you that they raised this much money, but we don't know where the money went. But I think that we complain too much about the NGOs. It's like we're spoiled children. I think that the NGOs, the international community, are here to provide some help. If you are wounded, they will give you a Band-Aid. But we as a people need to get organized. We need to determine what we really want and really need for the country. And we need to prepare our own development. We need to take action ourselves, to ensure that we are autonomous, we are able to fend for ourselves. Certainly I'm not satisfied. But I think that the primary responsibility lies within Haiti."

Édrice was more blunt. Sitting on the grass by the ruined Sans Souci palace in Milot, a day trip outside Cap Haïtien, I asked him: "*Ki sa ou pense sou solda Nasyonzini yo?*" What do you think of the UN soldiers?

"*Peyi kote Nasyonzini ale nan mond, gen pwoblem,*" he said. Countries the UN goes to in the world have problems. "It's not security that they provide. They look for the beautiful women, beautiful beaches, nice houses. If there's insecurity, they're happy. It's their job: per diem, salary, car. Wherever there's UN intervention, it creates problems. They

1 It was. See Michael P. Mayko, "Perlitz sentenced to nearly 20 years for sex abuse in Haiti," GreenwichTime.com, December 22, 2010.

give arms to twelve-year-old children. They trade arms with young boys for marijuana. They destabilize the economy. They make prices rise, because they have American money. That's why they encourage disorder: when there's disorder, they have jobs. That augments the NGOs in the country too. NGOs create jobs, but they don't create durable jobs, they create temporary jobs. Many young people abandon school to look for jobs with the NGOs. We should replace soldiers with agronomists, engineers, doctors, professors. In lieu of tacticians, we need technicians." (The last sentence was a characteristic *bon mot édricien*.)

As we talked, someone was broadcasting a speech over a loudspeaker in the market area below. I asked Édrice to help me understand what the person was saying.

"They're talking about the reconstruction of the country," he said.

"Is it political?"

"It's the UN who's talking."

"Is it good or bad?"

"Good words. *Bel pawol sans aksyon.* Beautiful words, with no action."

✳

On our last day in Cap Haïtien we sat down again with Père Noé, in his office. "Right after the earthquake, we had about 16,000 people that came to live in Cap Haïtien," he said. "We worked through the mayor. Sometimes we sent people to live with families, friends, or church people. For instance, in my church I said to people, 'Who wants to take care of this family?' And we had somebody raising their hand, saying, 'Okay, I'll take care of those people.' And they took care of them: they give them food, and they send them to school, they do everything for them. But the problem is after three months, you know, Haitian people want to do things, so they'd rather go back to Port-au-Prince instead of staying in Cap Haïtien. But sometimes you find the kids staying in Cap Haïtien, and the parents just went back to Port-au-Prince to look for jobs, cash-for-work, everything like that.

"In our school now, we have about two hundred students that stayed. We adopted them here, and they stayed. And they come to school for free. They don't pay anything. So we're still looking for funds from like USAID, CHF, OMI [International Organization for Migration]. In our school, right after the earthquake, we had about two hundred people living in this compound. We had to feed them twice a day, give them food, clothing, shelter, everything."

"How many days after the earthquake?"

"Within two and three days after the earthquake. By the 15th, really."

"And they just showed up and came into the compound?"

"Oh, no. The mayor and the church leaders sat down together and sent buses to Port-au-Prince to get those people. We call those buses Obama buses, because it's a gift that Obama gave to the Haitian people. They're brand new. There were about 120 buses. It's a lot of buses. It's same thing like 'Kennedy,' used clothes that President Kennedy asked people to share with people in Third World countries. Up to now, eight months since the earthquake, things are very difficult in Haiti. Especially places like Cabaret, Arcahaie, Petit Goave."

"Cabaret—that was Duvalierville, right?"

"Duvalierville, right. Things are really terrible there: people still living in tents, hundreds of people have no food, no shelter, nothing at all. The situation is very critical."

"You mentioned cash-for-work. I can't help but think if they had done cash-for-work in Cap Haïtien, then people wouldn't have gone back."

"Exactly. If we could have this program right here in Cap Haïtien, in terms of cleaning the canals, everything. At least the people would stay. Because Cap Haïtien was not really affected by the earthquake. But if they could stay, they have a better life here. And we have a lot of land. If you go to Limonade, to Milot, no houses. If they could build nice houses for those people, they could stay."

"Do you think it's too late for that?"

"It's not too late. It's just only the government needs to take a stand and say, 'This is what we're gonna do for the people.' Sometimes the problem in Haiti is that the government does not really think for the people, in terms of doing things for them. They just leave people by themselves. That's a big problem here. And everything is centered around Port-au-Prince."

"Do you have hope that after the election there could be some kind of new direction?"

"Um, personally, no. I don't think so. The problem in Haiti is that Haitian people don't realize that they can do things for themselves. They think somebody outside has to come and do things for them. But we have to say, 'This is where we want to go.' We need to realize this is high time to sit down together and have a talk. We have a lot of things that we can do. But we have to sit down and say, 'This is what we want for the country.' I was born in 1970. I never see any action from the government to help the people to go to school, to have clean water in the houses, to have like Medicare, Medicaid. They don't have things like that. Some people, when they're ill in Haiti, they just stay there and die. Or they pray, and a miracle happens. If you don't have money, you cannot go and see a doctor here."

"Unless you go to Cange," I suggested.

"Yeah. But a lot of people don't know about Cange. Because they don't have a radio, they don't have electricity. They will not know. But the good thing is that I'm an Episcopal priest, I can refer somebody to Cange, because I know there is a Cange there. And a priest in Cayes will do the same thing too. But we have a lot of people."

"Could there be similar hospitals like in Cange? Could there be a hospital like that here?"

"Yeah, we can have that. But you need to have the leadership. I mean, Père Lafontant has done a great job, but he's taken a long time. Thirty years."

"How did Père Lafontant get away with never getting transferred away from Cange?"

"Remember also, he's a retired priest. He was a very active parish priest in Mirebalais. So when he got the age of 65, he had to move somewhere. 'I'm retired now. The main parish is St. Pierre Mirebalais. So I have to resign from this parish and start a little something on my own.' But it is for the Church. I can do the same thing when I retire; I can take a very little village and say, 'This is where I'm going to work.'

Because if you retire and you don't work, you're gonna die, because that means you have nothing to do! Because he was very active. If you're very active and you retire and you don't do anything, you'll be in trouble. He's very smart. And also, he had an assistant priest that was there with him when he was not in Mirebalais. Somebody was there and taking on the service. He was able to go to Cange and do all these things that he was doing. I mean, Cange is like Heaven!"

"So Paul Farmer couldn't have done all the things he's done without Père Lafontant?"

"Oh, definitely. If you have the idea, the vision, you need somebody to help you with the vision, and sit down and put things together. He was there, looking for funds in the U.S. and everywhere, and Père Lafontant was the guy *in Haiti*, that could really implement the idea that he had. And you know also that here in Haiti, if you want to have something done quick, and in a very serious manner, you go to the Church. Because most of our priests, I would say like 99 percent, those guys are very serious. If you give them something for the people, the real people will get it. We say evangelism, education, and health care—those three all go together."

"What are relations like between the different churches? Do you get along?"

"Yeah. Everywhere I go, I get along very, very well with the Catholic, Episcopal, all the churches really. Like this school, this is the best school in the whole northern region. People from Gonaïves will come here to study. Hinche. Port de Paix. Everywhere. And the Catholic priests always ask me for favors for students to send here. So they know me. And they come here and sit down, as you sit down, and ask me for scholarships for the kids. Pastors, same thing too. So we have good relationship. And we work for CHF. They take young women and young men in the streets, and we give them some training here in, like, air condition, plumbing, electricity, like for six months, and send them away to work. USAID are funding some projects here. They send fifty or a hundred students every six months here, and they pay us to train them. We do this also for MINUSTAH, the UN guys. And even sometimes, the good thing is, in these projects you do this evangelism also, because they come to know Christ!"

"Mm-hmm," I said.

"I tell them to go to church on Sunday, talk to them, do some pastoral care of them, and then on Sunday sometimes they show up, they come to church, they keep coming, and their life just change! And some even testify, like they used to kill people, they were bad boys, now they've become good people."

"Well, that's great," I said. "Did the people who came after the earthquake put a lot of stress on the community that was already here?"

"Yeah," he said. "Even for myself, I didn't really understand what was going on. We Haitians, we're not really educated for that matter. I was sitting in my office when that happened, and my office was shaking. But I thought that was a big truck passing through the road. I didn't know anything about that. I went down and talked to my wife. And we had an American priest that was staying in my house for a week, and his wife sent him a text message saying, 'There was an earthquake in Haiti, the Palace collapsed and everything.' But we didn't know."

"You were here."

"I was right here, in my office." He slapped the top of his desk. "And after that we could not get any phone calls at all. For three days, no phone calls. And after that, when I called my mother, there was no house, nothing." His family came from Léogâne, near Port-au-Prince. "You know, Léogâne was the epicenter. We lost everything. And people crying, you know, people calling people, you see a lot of people crying in the streets, somebody who just lost their loved ones. And some people just died because they went to Port-au-Prince for an ID. Just an ID. They just went there just for one night, and that was the night. That was the 12th. For a passport, for an ID, or for some paper. Just for one night. Cap Haïtien people don't like to stay in Port-au-Prince. They have this prideness in them: *la fierté christophienne*. They're so proud of Cap Haïtien."

"So during those three days when you didn't have any phone calls, you didn't have Internet either?"

"Yeah, I could find Internet, but it was not really reliable."

"So how soon was it that you knew how serious the situation was?"

"Because we had an American priest that was staying in my house, and he kept sending messages, and we knew from that. And after three days we tried to call home in Léogâne, and then they keep telling my wife, 'Oh, So-and-so dead, So-and-so dead, So-and-so dead, So-and-so dead, So-and-so dead.' Cousins, friends, relatives, parents. You know? And my brother, he was in medical school, at Kiskeya. We found him after three days. Alive, after three days. Because there was some French students that was at Kiskeya. When the French Army came after 72 hours, they went straight there. He was alive, but very shaky. And they took him to the boat. There was a boat, the USS *Comfort*, that was there. And now he's safe, he's alive, he's okay."

"Was he hurt badly?"

"Yeah, he was hurt badly. His face, everything. He was in the middle of a classroom."

"And your parents both survived."

"Yeah, they both survived. My father, he told me that he was in his yard when that happened, and he fell three times on the ground. And my mother was sitting—she has a little booth in front of the house where she sells goodies, like cookies. She was there. And she heard a noise, and the house just collapsed. In one second." He snapped his fingers. "But she was outside at the little booth, and that saved her. Yeah, it was really tough."

"So what was it like for the community when all the people came here to Cap Haïtien?"

"You can't imagine. It was really a mess. Some buses when they come, they come with bodies, dead bodies. They trying to save some people, and they dead on the way. In all the houses you pass, somebody just crying. They lost their loved ones, brothers and sisters. It was really a shock."

"It's been eight months now. Psychologically, how is the society handling it? It was an enormous event, something really huge that the whole country had to come to terms with."

"I go to Port-au-Prince from time to time. What amazes me is that you see the houses being destroyed, but you see life is just normal. You see people just …" He laughed, helplessly. "There was a time when we buried bodies. Now it is time to move on, you know? But in the same time you see some people that are really distressful. Because some people just lost everything. Some people just can't take it. And then some people, life is normal, and they're going back in their old ways and walks."

"If you're one of the people who survived, you have to get on with your life," I suggested.

"Yeah. If you survived, you're lucky. Because three hundred thousand people died. That's a lot, you know?"

"And your parents, they're handling it okay?"

"Yeah, they're handling it okay. My father and mother, they have ten kids, so from time to time we went and talked to them. We're trying to build a house. I mean, there is hope. There is hope."

"And you and your brothers and sisters …"

"We're all alive. We all escaped from that."

"Your brothers and sisters are all in different places?"

"Yeah, we have some in France, some in Miami, some in Haiti."

"Any in Léogâne?"

"Only one. He's a teacher. We have three in France, we have two in Florida, we have one in Boston, we have two in Port-au-Prince. To rebuild the house we budget, and we then say, 'Okay, we can give this, that, that.' If I have a better job, I give more. If you have a less job, you give what you can. That's how we do it. We're trying to build a house right now. And things are okay."

Chapter 14

To Be Continued

The writing of this book has become more difficult as I've approached the end of it. Maybe I fear the end of the writing will be the end of the story. I don't want it to end. I hope that, just as the story of Haiti that I have to tell begins thirty years—almost to the day—before the publication of this book, it will continue another thirty years or more. "People's interest in Haiti has peaked," the myopic book agent informed me in 1995. Well, mine still hasn't. My life without Haiti would be like my world without Haiti: meaningless, out of context, a contradiction in terms.

There's so much more to tell. Events of the highest drama punctuate Haiti's history, but it takes more than punctuation to tell a story. Just before we met Père Noé in Cap Haïtien, Pete and Ben and I spent several days at the Zanmi Lasante/Partners in Health compound in Cange. I have a memory of visiting Cange from Mirebalais with my father and Father Fritz Lafontant, probably in 1983, when it was as bleak and bare as any other hilltop in Haiti. Twenty-one years later, in his little house shaded by trees and giant bamboo, Paul Farmer enthused to me about what he called his "hobby" of planting trees and gardening. Farmer never tells a story without having a point. Another six years after that, Cange was more than ever both a refuge and a living model of what's possible. When Joan Van Wassenhove of Partners in Health met us at Village Tecina in late August 2010 to take us up the mountain to Cange, we loaded her vehicle with fifty or so seedlings as a gift from Ti Gerald Oriol. On the way up, at a place called Corporant, we left them in the care of Ghislayne Warne, a rugged and cosmopolitan Australian woman who heads Zanmi Lasante's agriculture project, Zanmi Agrikol. "They'll be at La Colline," she assured us, "they'll be at Corporant, they'll be at Kay Polo" – Paul's house – "and we'll just keep spreading the goodness."

"Gerald will be very happy," said Pete.

Relaxing later on the balcony of the Maison d'Amitié at Cange, Pete asked me: "How do you say 'It's a beautiful day' in Creole?"

"*Se youn bel jou,*" I suggested.

"*Se youn bel jou,*" he repeated.

"That's pretty good," I said in encouragement.

"Well, it is," said Pete. "It's great just to see birds in the trees, and hear 'em singing."

Ghislayne belongs to the group of Episcopalians from the Diocese of Upper South Carolina who were already working with Father Lafontant when my father and the Diocese of Milwaukee were also working with him, in the 1980s. "People in Greenville cross the street when they see me, because they don't want to hear any more about Haiti," she told me. The Milwaukee group now works in Jeannette on the southern peninsula; my father co-founded the Colorado Haiti Project, which supports St. Paul's parish in Petit Trou de Nippes; the Diocese of Upper South Carolina has walked the walk all these years in and around Cange. Over three long, hard decades there have been many obstacles and setbacks in Haiti, and there still are, and the Episcopal Church in the United States has rent itself asunder with unseemly factionalism and ideological correctness. The institution to which my father devoted his life's work broke his heart, but its Diocese of Haiti is administratively equivalent to any other of its regions, which is to say that it's not foreign to us. And Haiti is in a position of moral leadership. *Bay kou blie, pote mak sonje,* goes the proverb: He who gives the blow forgets; he who bears the bruise remembers.

For my part, I don't believe the tale about Jesus redeeming the sins of mankind by dying on the cross. If you do, that's fine with me. I don't care what you believe, as long as you make yourself useful here and now, in this world. Any other world is hypothetical at best, and we are stewards of this one. The damage we've done as bad stewards is nowhere more evident than in Haiti.

✳

Ghislayne first went to Haiti after being recruited to translate from French for Father Lafontant during one of his visits to Greenville. Seemingly her proudest accomplishment is a nutritional supplement for children called Nourimamba, "made from peanuts, powdered milk, multivitamins and minerals, little bit of oil, little bit of sugar. And it is massively, massively high calorically, and it can turn around the life of a child in six to eight, nine weeks."

"I'm very interested and impressed that you went from showing up once to sticking around," I told her.

"It's been absolutely great for me," she said. "It's built and built and built. My family's starting to scream a bit, you know, saying, 'Mum, your grandchildren would like to know you too!'" She laughed happily.

"Do you spend most of your time here now?"

"I'm spending a lot of time here now, yeah. The next thing we're going into now is another very exciting part of Zanmi Agrikol. We're starting a vocational school, a trade and agricultural school. Everything will start with agriculture, but there are no trade schools up here, that are qualifying people that need to go out and rebuild Haiti."[1]

"So this is analogous to the teaching hospital," I suggested. Partners in Health and the Haitian Ministry of Health were about to break ground on a 300-bed teaching hospital outside Mirebalais.

"Absolutely," said Ghislayne. "Already we have classes here, we have students all through the summer that have come up from Port-au-Prince, and local kids we're teaching here. We have formations for the neighbors all around. We're doing bees the last two days, and they've just gone off to transfer the bees from the old hives into the new ones

---

1 In a telephone conversation on December 29, 2011, Ghislayne gushed to me about all the progress she and her colleagues had made and told me that the trade school at Corporant was scheduled to have a grand opening in March 2012 as the Centre de Formation Fritz Lafontant. "We're forming the rebuilders of Haiti," she said.

that we just built. That structure over there, when it gets a green roof, is our outdoor classroom, so that when we have teachings and gatherings we can all be outside. Agronomists and farmers don't need to be inside. And the other big thing we're doing is growing mangos. Mangos and fruits and supplying reforestation trees. These are our mangos. They start here, in little bags, and then they go into the nursery there for the first growing period. Then they're moved into larger bags, then they come out into the open, and then next year they all get planted out."

"What do you do with the plastic bags?" I asked her.

"They can't be reused," she said. "They have to be burned."

"They can't be reused?"

"They tear. If we had an alternative, I wouldn't be using plastic. But the alternative is peat or something like that, and it's so expensive. The other thing I found this summer, up in Nantucket, there was a great artisan who was taking strips of paper, rolling it around a piece of wood, and then there's a little cap that you bang on the bottom of it, which seals the underneath of it, and you take out your wood and you've got a paper cup. And they're planting in that with all kinds of herbs and small seeds and things. But the paper's not going to last here, in this rain and with all the watering that has to happen. It would just go 'Phhht.' I bought two, because I thought, 'This is going to be fantastic, and I can use all the paper down there.' You just plonk it right in the ground, you don't have to take it out of a bag or anything. But I don't think the paper's going to last."

"Maybe there's something," I said.

"Peanut shells," said Pete.

"Yeah, you're right," said Ghislayne. "If we milled them and molded them. You're right! You may have hit paydust there."

"Thanks for revolutionizing everything we do," said Joan cheerfully. "You can stay." She turned to me: "Pete's not going with you anymore."

"And not only that," said Ghislayne. "Maybe we could even use the same process as the charcoal, using the manioc as the binder. Everybody grows manioc. It's really, really easy to grow. And if we use manioc as the binder we may have something, and it goes right back in the dirt."

"I know peanut shells tend to hold up as far as the moisture, and they don't degrade as fast," said Pete.

"They would hold up for as long as you'd need them, probably to get into the ground," said Ghislayne.

Someone brought us a few ears of roasted corn, which we munched on happily while we talked. A young Haitian agronomist, Jean-Philippe Dorzin, was sitting with us, though Ghislayne was doing most of the talking.

"The corn remember me something," said Jean-Philippe now. "After the earthquake, we grow a lot of corn we deliver to the people coming from Port-au-Prince. They are very, very happy for the corn."

"We invited them to come down and harvest the corn themselves," Ghislayne elaborated. "The men went ahead across the fields and cut the cornstalks, and the women came and broke them all off, and they carried them all the way up to the top farm, and we put them in bags, so that everybody got some, and it was distributed all around the community. That was such a great day! *C'était une belle journée, n'est-ce pas?*"

"Oh yeah," said Jean-Philippe. "*Oui.*"

"*C'était formidable,*" said Ghislayne.

"*C'était quand?*" I asked. When was that?

"*Avril, mai,*" said Jean-Philippe. April or May.

"*Trois fois,*" said Ghislayne. "Three times."

That evening, Ghislayne escorted us to the small house that had been built, in the same concrete as everything else at Cange, for Jackie Williams, one of the community's revered elders. Jackie was a very Southern woman whose late husband had designed the compound's innovative running water system and who now, in her late seventies, was determined to remain active and useful. "To feel old and in the way is probably the worst way to finish up your life," she told me. "I want to go out with my boots on." She was in astonishingly good physical shape from walking up and down the Cange hillside every day. She was an independent soul and enjoyed describing herself as "a Republican in South Carolina, and a Communist in Haiti."

"I'm bringing three gatecrashers, but they're all very nice and good-looking," Ghislayne told Jackie by way of introduction, when she met us at her door.

"You have a very nice little house," I said.

"Well, it's just right for a little old lady, and I do enjoy it," she said.

Over drinks and hors d'oeuvres, Jackie regaled us with a well-polished yarn about how an ancestor of hers in Virginia hid in a barn or an attic (I can't remember which) from the approaching Yankees and later escaped and went to Florida. I was charmed and intrigued, and still am. At breakfast in the Maison d'Amitié a couple of mornings later, she got my attention by saying, "Ever' time I google 'Haiti Alerts,' I get something about Pakistan. You know, comparing."

"Wow, that's interesting," I said. "You know, I'm probably the only guy in the world who cares as much about those two particular countries as I do."

"Really?"

"Well, I've spent a lot of time in both countries. How many people like that can there be?"

"It is an odd combination. Do you know the Google Haiti Alerts?"

"I probably should," I said.

"Sometimes it's just a Boy Scout troop collecting shoes, you know, or Wyclef Jean is mad at somebody. But usually there's at least one good article every day."

After our days with Père Noé in Cap Haïtien, we returned to Mirebalais to attend the groundbreaking ceremony for the new teaching hospital. For a change of scenery and because the roads were better, we returned the roundabout way, over the hills to Gonaïves and then inland from there through the Artibonite. We approached Mirebalais in the dark and in the rain, and when we arrived at the river just outside town sometime after eight o'clock, we couldn't cross because the bridge was out. People were standing around waiting for the river to subside, but we were told that could be hours. We couldn't cross the river, so we were forced to negotiate with a rather hard-nosed local woman to pay an extortionate amount to spend the night in her house. The bridge was a temporary one that had been built just higher than the river's normal level, to allow the river when in flood to overflow the bridge without damaging it. The original bridge, we learned, had been destroyed when a UN shipping container had come loose upstream and smashed into it.

Late the next morning after the ceremony, as people were milling about and getting into vehicles to go to lunch or to the airport, I found Paul Farmer briefly alone and took the opportunity to approach him and say, "I'm not going to take your time, but I just wanted to say that I'm very happy to be here."

"Thanks, Ethan," he said. "I'm thinking about Pakistan a lot these days."

✳

A few months later, in February and March 2011, Pete and I went to Pakistan again. We visited three areas that had been severely flooded the previous summer: the Swat valley, the agricultural breadbasket of the central Punjab along the Indus River, and an area dominated by the Baloch ethnic minority in the far southwestern corner of Punjab province. The people of Swat had just begun rebuilding their lives after fighting between the Pakistan Army and the Taliban in 2009 forced nearly three million to flee, when the flooding washed it all away again. We saw the valley floor in Swat, where fields and orchards had been, completely stripped of topsoil and covered instead with huge boulders from upstream. In the Punjab we found brick-and-mud villages only just starting to be rebuilt, mostly by the devastated local people them-selves, and heard complaints of incomplete and feckless responses by the provincial and national governments and of international NGOs obtusely continuing to give food aid, when what people now needed urgently was paid employment helping rebuild the damaged dykes, to control the coming monsoon season's anticipated flooding. As in Haiti, there was a depressing sense that no one in particular was in charge and that there was no overall plan.

In the meantime cholera had broken out in Haiti for the first time in fifty years, probably caused by Nepalese UN soldiers dumping human waste in the Artibonite River. And then there was a revolution in Egypt and, just after Pete and I returned from Pakistan, a massive earthquake and tsunami that killed tens of thousands and caused a nuclear disaster in Japan. After little more than a year, the Haitian earthquake was old news. Haiti's election did happen in November 2010, and Michel Martelly, formerly known as the raunchy singer Sweet Mickey and a relative of Gerald's by marriage, became the new president. Both Jean-Claude Duvalier and Jean-Bertrand Aristide returned from exile. Aristide was keeping a low profile but was rumored to be very active behind the scenes, possibly laying the groundwork for another return to power.

I returned to Haiti again in August and September 2011, partly to give my wife, Jenny, a chance to see the country she had heard so much about from me. "Welcome home," said Gerald when he met us at the airport. We attended a graduation ceremony at a school for handicapped children and adults, and we made a long day trip to Les Cayes for a meeting of people receiving training and small-business grants through the regional office of the Secretary of State for the Integration of Handicapped People. Gerald told us that the office had an operating budget but very little program budget, so the funds for the grants came from Fondation Voilà and were managed by Gerald's Fondation J'Aime Haïti. It was important for the secretary of state's office to participate actively in the program, he said, to reinforce the state's capacity. "NGOs can help alleviate the problems, but they cannot really help develop a country," he said. On the office wall were posters:

Yon sel espas
Yon sel fanmi
Nou tout dwe viv!

Only one space
Only one family
We all must live!

Other posters read *Planifier pour tout le monde c'est aussi planifer pour personnes handicappées, planifier pour les personnes handicapées c'est aussi planifier pour tout le monde.* Planning for everyone is also planning for handicapped people; planning for handicapped people is also planning for everyone.

On the drive back to Port-au-Prince, Gerald reminisced fondly about Sister Kathy, an American nun I had introduced him to at Hospice St. Joseph, where I had stayed briefly in 2004. Sister Kathy was no-nonsense but kindly, and she wore a white tank top; it was hard to think of her as an honest-to-gosh nun. She and Gerald had debated Haitian politics. Hospice St. Joseph had a big balcony with a beautiful view of the city and the bay. It was destroyed in the earthquake.

"She was very left-wing, that nun," I remembered.

"Yes," agreed Gerald. "She was very nice, though."

I also took Jenny to Cange, where Jackie Williams hosted us. Ghislayne wasn't there, so we stayed in the room in the back of the Sant Art, the crafts center that Jackie oversaw, where Ghislayne had been staying before. I seized the opportunity to ask Jackie for her memories of the earthquake.

"We were sitting in English class at 4:53 on the 12th of January 2010 and felt this terrific jolt," she told me. "Everyone jumped up and rushed outdoors, and the schoolchildren were rushing outdoors too. And I noticed kind of crossly that a couple of nice pottery pieces had fallen. But we thought no more about it. This is my third earthquake, and I wonder if I'm doing something wrong. I was in a minor one in California, and then in the major one in '89 in San Francisco."

"I was in that one too!" I exclaimed.

"Where were you?"

"I was in Berkeley."

"Well, we were in the Holiday Inn on the Embarcadero. We were getting dressed to go out to dinner, and we really thought our time had come. It was a memorable experience. And what we felt at Cange was nothing like that. Somebody called Port-au-Prince, no answer, then a number of people began kind of frantically calling. Dead silence. And we didn't really know anything until the next day, when the vehicles started coming up with the victims. It was just horrifying. Sarah Marsh, who is a midwife and a trainer of midwives, took charge, did a superb job. She came into the artisans' center and said, 'Give me every piece of cloth you've got that can make a pallet.' So we emptied the shelves of anything thick and soft, and we lined the church with pallets for people to lie on. Somebody had given us a roll of very, very tough stuff that we used for making trash bags, and we made that into stretchers. The doctors who were here did what they could. It was mostly stopping shock, stopping bleeding, there was not much they could do. The piano in the church became the supply table, with alcohol and bandages and rubber gloves, and all that sort of stuff. The hospital was full immediately, and they started bringing a few supplies. And I rose to the very height of my medical ability; I emptied bedpans. A friend had given me some very fancy French soap, highly perfumed. So we washed patients with that. And, you know, took sips of water, and somebody wanted a Bible, I gave 'em my Bible, and that sort of thing. Just general coping. A few more doctors ambled up the next day, or were flown in, and that's when Ghislayne's husband and son came in through the Dominican Republic and said, 'We have got to put in some kind of waste system, or we'll have a really nasty epidemic.' Because along with the patients, the horrified family members were coming, and just camped out all over everywhere."

Our conversation rambled, and after a while she mentioned some international CNN reporters who had come to Cange. "They came to church, because they had heard that this was a church community. I don't know what their beliefs were, but anyway they came to church. And they said afterwards, 'Father, I can't tell if you're Catholic or charismatic.' Well, a little of both. You've been to a lot of churches here, I'm sure, and it's fun."

"Yeah, it's great fun," I said. "It's part of the Haitian experience. What are your beliefs?"

"My beliefs? Oh, let me see. I'm a sort of practicing Episcopalian, but definitely skeptical about some things. I think creation is wonderful, I've got great faith in that. My husband's spirit appears at the upstairs door for anything goin' on at church, and I sit over on this side, so I commune with him during church, as he's chuckling. I think they're like in a glass-bottomed boat, and they look down and see what's goin' on. I can't think that everything is gone."

"But you seem more concerned with what's actually going on day to day, and what needs to be done."

"Oh yes, yes, I come from very pragmatic, practical people. I got into a flap at the church back home. What was the issue? Church fights are like family fights, very ugly, very bloody. I don't know whether it was the issue about gays, or changing the Prayer Book, or ordaining women, one of the big issues. I guess you're very aware of what goes on in the Episcopal Church. And there were factions. And I belong to a Sunday school class that the clergy comes down to spy on us every now and then, to see if we're gettin' a little bit too far afield. It's called Faith Perspectives. We talk about all manner of things. I got kind of sick of this back-and-forth about, you know, 'Are we being scriptural about ordaining gays?' or something, and I said I really did not have an answer, I would leave it to the good Lord to decide what's the right or wrong of that. What I see in Haiti is that the sick are healed, and the hungry are fed, and the illiterate are educated. Well. One of my dear friends called me up and said she was really worried about my immortal soul. She says, 'You're just making the Church into a Rotary Club.' So be it."

*

And we were privileged to spend more than an hour touring the teaching hospital with Dr. David Walton, who was supervising the project. Dr. Walton was a young man of impressive, obvious competence and self-confidence and, considering how busy he was, very generous with his time and views. He had become involved with PIH after meeting Paul Farmer fourteen years earlier as a first-year student at Harvard Medical School. "We old folks been tryin' to get David married," Jackie told Jenny and me. "He needs a helpmeet."

What had been a vast gravel lot a year earlier was now a full-blown construction site, with the two-story shell of the hospital already in place. The women's health and outpatient wards were now scheduled to open in January 2012, and the rest of the hospital in June or July. "I like the idea that it can be an economic magnet," I told Walton, to get him started talking.

"Yeah," he said. "I mean, just around here, the price of real estate has increased rather significantly. And in fact, there are efforts underway to really transform the city of Mirebalais. I don't know all the details, because I'm a little busy with this project. However, I do know the Kellogg Foundation has chosen Mirebalais as one of their sites on which they're going to be focusing, so I think there is a global vision. But this really is the anchor, drawing more business, more professionals, decentralizing Port-au-Prince to the extent that we can draw many more people here, and really transform this particular city."

The repaving of Highway One "has already kind of transformed the economic corridor that is Port-au-Prince to the Central Plateau," he said. "From Port-au-Prince, even Croix des Bouquets, to Mirebalais used to take two and a half hours. It takes forty-five minutes now. It's a commute now, where before it was really a journey. Vis-à-vis this hospital, it has significant implications for the amount of patients we'll see. Because still, the health infrastructure in Haiti, particularly in Port-au-Prince, hasn't really recovered post-earthquake." Improving roads had been a pet project of President Préval's since well before the earthquake. "Préval has been criticized a great deal. I don't weigh in on any of that. But what I do know is what I can see, and I can see the transformation of the roads and the effect that it's had."

"So you're a medical doctor," I said.

"Correct."

"And you're also, like, the boss of this construction project?"

"Turns out I am, yeah," he laughed. "I've been interested in medical infrastructure for a long time. It started really in the early part of the last decade, when I was working in Las Cahobas. Las Cahobas evolved to La Colline, because we were overwhelmed with patients, we needed more space. And really La Colline has evolved to this. I am the head of this particular project, but I am working with some incredibly talented and incredibly good people, who make me look really good. Still, it's a herculean task to get this thing done. We're a very small team, and we have no shortage of adversity. But we're making progress, as you can see. The entire roof is going to be covered by photovoltaic panels. So, if we can get the funding, we'll probably be able to run the hospital on solar during the day."

"So it was originally not going to be this," I said. "Pre-earthquake, the plan was something different."

"It's a long, long story, but the short version is that the cell tower that you see is at the top of a hill. At the bottom of that hill is a hospital. That was the hospital for Mirebalais. It was run in a public-private partnership by another NGO. The NGO was providing suboptimal services, and the community was really, really upset, for a long time. We, Partners in Health, couldn't really set up another, competing hospital, for a variety of reasons, mainly political. But as you know, we traverse Mirebalais to get to almost all of our sites on the Central Plateau. So people would see our ZL cars going through, and it created difficulty, because people would say, 'Why doesn't Partners in Health, Zanmi Lasante, come here?' And we'd say, 'Well, we can't, there's already a hospital.' And they felt both disenfranchised and—because this was actually a fee-for-services hospital—incredibly upset that they had to leave their own city to go to La Colline or Belladere or Cange to get quality care.

"And so a variety of public uprisings crescendoed to a point that, on January 22, 2008, we inaugurated La Colline. We were anticipating a very slow transition to clinical services: moving the patients, moving the physicians, all the equipment. But the next day the mayor of Mirebalais, who is still the mayor, he was just here this morning, led a popular uprising, walked into the hospital, took everybody out, put 'em in tap-taps, drove 'em to the empty hospital that was La Colline, and then put a huge chain with a big lock on the door [of the original hospital], and said, 'We refuse to accept this anymore, you guys gotta get outta here.' Pretty dramatic, but Haitians are dramatic people. So we scrambled to deal with it, and that was really the turning point. That NGO pulled out months later. The Ministry of Health then asked us to fill the void. Originally just redoing that hospital."

The Ministry of Health offered Cuban doctors funded with Venezuelan petrodollars the defunct hospital to set up a CDI, or center of integrated diagnostics, to provide sub-specialty services. "But that ultimately proved to be too small," said Walton. "And then we were given this land here. A few months later, when we were still drawing up plans, the earthquake happened. The Minister said, 'We know you're building the hospital; we've signed off on it. But you need to go back to the drawing board. We need it bigger, you need to build it faster, and we need it to be a teaching facility, because the General Hospital in Port-au-Prince is in such bad shape.' An adjunct teaching facility, not to ever replace the General Hospital. But really, in the vein of decentralization, one of these should be present in every department of Haiti. Right? Decentralizing clinical services, but also training for doctors and nurses, particularly in the public sector. So we went back to the drawing board, and a hundred-bed lower Central Plateau referral center became a 320-bed national teaching hospital."

"The thing that struck me from the groundbreaking last year, and from Paul's speech, was 'biggest hospital in the Caribbean,'" I told him.

He laughed. "It won't be the biggest in the Caribbean. Paul, sometimes he exaggerates things. But it will be the biggest functional public hospital in Haiti, and certainly the most advanced public hospital. Probably the most advanced hospital, because the private hospitals were either destroyed or kind of floundering along. This will be transformative for Haiti and redefine the way the public sector can provide care."

"And that's enough," I suggested.

"Yeah."

Nothing had been done about the lack of an adequate bridge over the Artibonite River nearby in the year since Pete, Ben and I had been forced to spend the night on the other side.

"The temporary bridge is there because the MINUSTAH container took out the original bridge," I said to Walton.

"Correct," he said.

"You need a good bridge, don't you?"

"That temporary bridge, that was always designed to be temporary, hopefully will not be permanent. I still don't know what the government's plan is to rebuild the bridge. But that bridge floods, right? So if there's heavy rainfall, it floods. It's designed, in fact, for water to flow over it. I've been on the wrong side of that bridge during a storm. Could be two hours, could be eight hours. It's a real problem. We're having a tough time just doing all the things we need to do. We don't have the capacity to lobby the government to fast-track that. But that was 2008 when that happened, so it's been a long time. Three years."

"Shouldn't it be MINUSTAH's responsibility to replace the bridge?"

"Uh ..."

"And if that's something you'd rather not comment on, just say."

"No, I mean, you know, you break it, you buy it. That's kinda how I see things. Right? So I think MINUSTAH does have a responsibility. Although I don't actually know what their party line is on their culpability. For cholera they actually said, 'Uh, yeah, sort of, us, but not intentional.'"

"Eventually they said that, right? They didn't say that at first?"

"Oh no. They were like, 'What?!? Are you accusing us? This is outlandish! These rumors, we will not accept them!' But to their credit, they had a panel of independent, scientific cholera experts. I met these guys, I know these guys. They came, they did their work, it was really, really good work, they presented their report to the director-general, which implicated MINUSTAH in introducing this microbe to Haiti, and he said, 'Publish it.' So it was published on the Web two days later. So there was an impressive amount of transparency around it. However, containers destroying the bridge? I actually don't know if they even admitted guilt, even though everyone knows they were guilty. But ultimately it would be nice if they did something. Is it realistic for them to do something? No. Do I feel they should step up? Absolutely. But from a pragmatic point of view, should we waste time lobbying them, or find some other, probably easier way to do it? Probably the latter. But I don't know MINUSTAH enough to know whether they'd be willing to rebuild probably a multi-million-dollar bridge. I'm betting no."

As we talked, we were walking around the building site. At one place we stopped he said, "This is just doing the site work, preparing the land, for the men's ward that's going to be started probably next week."

"So the men's ward that we saw in the plan doesn't exist yet?"

"Nope. This is it, right here. We'll start digging the foundations next week."

"So, do you consider yourself to have professional skills as a general contractor?"

"No way. Absolutely not. I'm a trained physician. I have confidence in my clinical abilities, and that's as far as I go. But I have programmatic experience with medical infrastructure. I know enough to know that I couldn't direct the construction. I work very, very closely with a guy who's our director of construction. His name is Jim Ansara. Retired contractor out of Boston. Founded and grew a hugely successful company. He and his wife have been philanthropists for a long time. But he's a pragmatic philanthropist and, with his skill set, he's really making this a reality. We were able to do La Colline, but this is orders of magnitude more complicated."

✳

On our last day in Cange I had a jarring but salutary realization, after encountering Father Lafontant in the small parking lot in front of the Sant Art. When Jenny and I came out of the building to wait for our vehicle I saw him standing nearby, in conversation with another Haitian. After hesitating, I approached him and introduced myself and Jenny. He introduced himself by name, as if we hadn't met before. He didn't remember me, at least not in that moment. He had no reason to know that I was in Cange; he was distracted; he was 85 years old. It was sad and humbling, but it was helpful. As Joan Van Wassenhove had said, in reference to Americans who had imposed on Partners in Health staff time and other resources after the earthquake because they were desperate to help Haiti: "It's not about you." This book is the story of Haiti as I've known it, and of all that I've learned from it, but it's not about me.

The moment was like one I had experienced many years earlier in Srinagar. One morning in July 1995, at the end of what turned out to be my last trip to Indian-occupied Kashmir, I had struggled to say the right thing, make the right gesture, to an old man who had opened his home to me and gone well out of his way to help me know his country and its situation. I felt profoundly grateful, and I knew that anything I might write or say would be a pittance in recompense. In my book *Alive and Well in Pakistan*, I wrote: "He was polite as ever but distracted, perhaps thinking of his own worries."

I would move on, I realized that evening on the pier, and life and death would go on in Kashmir as before. This was their life; it was only a slice of my varied, attenuated experience. I had no right to claim Kashmir, to feel sure that it was mine. I was not suffering and dying; I was not losing my livelihood. On the contrary, as a journalist I was literally making money from other people's suffering. And in more important ways, I had been given more than I deserved or felt I could repay.

In the same book I compared that man to Père Lafontant's brother, Octave: "Haji reminded me a bit of a Haitian priest I had known who spoke in riddles and who, like Haji, radiated an indulgent patriarchal air and a seemingly ill-founded calm that was both alluring and slightly maddening. ... It had taken me time to see that the priest's enigmas were his surrogates for answers, carefully cultivated over a long lifetime of asking questions." I also wrote, about that same return visit to the Vale of Kashmir, of "the familiar, ineffably sad sensation I had felt too many times before, in Kathmandu, in Haiti, in Milwaukee, of coming home to a place I was only passing through." Sixteen years later here I was again, same sensation. What lesson there is in that I don't know, except that human experience everywhere in this vale of tears is essentially the same.

Jenny teaches English as a second language at the University of Washington for a living, and she had volunteered to spell Jackie that afternoon. Jenny held the lessons around a table on the second floor of the Sant Art, and Jackie sat in. Jenny had the two intermediate students, a dentist named Richmond and a lab tech named Sonel, read aloud and discuss an article I had written a year earlier, titled "What Does Pakistan Have to Do with Haiti?"[2] In it I had quoted Ti Gerald saying, "It's funny how an abnormal situation can be normal. The only people who are truly shocked right now are people like me. But for the

---

2   See http://www.ethancasey.com/2010/09/what-does-pakistan-have-to-do-with-haiti/. I later expanded the themes in that article into a speech I delivered at a TEDx event hosted by the Princeton Public Library in Princeton, New Jersey on June 1, 2011. The full text of that speech is online at http://www.ethancasey.com/speaking/tedx-princeton-library/.

poor, things were so hard for them already that it's just another way to organize themselves. Maybe it's even better for them now."

Jenny asked the students what they thought Gerald meant. "I agree with him," said Richmond. "Because like he says, materially, there is not much difference between how they lived before and how they live now."

"Because the friends and relatives are the things that are most expensive for people," said Sonel.

"That are dearest?" I suggested.

"Yes, dearest," he said.

When Jenny asked them what my purpose had been in writing the article, Richmond said: "He wants people who are not Haitians to see how some people who are Haitian see the earthquake."

Jackie asked me if the U.S. had done things to Pakistan that were similar to the way it had imposed the building of the Peligre dam—the dam that had displaced the people of Cange to this hilltop—on Haiti. I replied that there was a lot that could be said on that subject, but I decided to give the specific example of the Afghan war of the 1980s, and how the intended and eventually successful result of forcing the Soviet Union out of Afghanistan had wrought a string of unintended consequences, such as the proliferation of arms, heroin, and refugees. The war "was necessary and successful," I allowed, "but it had results that were bad. It's important to pay attention to the bad results that you didn't expect – or," I amended, "that you didn't want to believe might happen."

At the end of the lesson, Richmond asked me when I might return to Haiti. I liked Richmond; he was intelligent and had a gentle manner.

"Soon, I hope," I told him, because that was the truest answer I could give. His face registered disappointment, and a resignation that I had seen many times before on Haitian faces. I was returning to *l'autre bord de l'eau*, the other side of the water. When I would be back, I didn't know.

"I test people's blood and urine," said Sonel. "And speetle."

"Spittle," Jenny corrected him.

"Spittle," he repeated. Sonel had an aspiration to host a radio show about the Gospel. "Because I am a Christian," he said. "Are you a Christian?"

Wrapping things up, Jenny gave a little instruction on emphasis and pronunciation of verbs, articles, and some other words, especially *can* and *can't*. She asked each of them to name something they can do.

"I can pull teeth," said Richmond with an engaging laugh.

Sonel asked what it had been like for me when I returned to Wisconsin after my first trip to Haiti. I have pat answers to this and similar questions, but it was an unusual challenge to be asked to tell that story not to Americans but to Haitians. I explained that I had lived a *bourgeois* life in a town where all the people were *blancs*. I said that, after returning from Haiti, I could no longer live in my hometown in the same way as I had before. "I was grouchy and angry," I told them. Jenny explained the meaning of the word *grouchy*.

I had been "too young," Richmond said. "He was only sixteen when he first came to Haiti," he told Jenny. "And—" He paused, seeking words, but I knew what he was trying to say. "And—and a sixteen-year-old boy should be in school."

✳

On our last full day in Haiti, Gerald took Jenny and me and his friends Edrice, Fritz, and Marseille from Port-au-Prince to Saut d'Eau, the waterfall famous as a voodoo pilgrimage site, beyond Mirebalais. It was an outing that would not have been possible as a day trip before the highway was repaved. For the guys, it was a well-deserved day off from their work in the neighborhoods. "We have a rather strange relationship," Gerald told me. "It's both work and friendship. They were supportive as volunteers of Fondation J'Aime Haïti from the very beginning, before there was any formal work engagement."

Reconnecting with Gerald after the earthquake was a grace note that had swelled into a major theme of my experience. I had liked him when I first met him in 2004; now, I considered it a privilege to consider him a friend. So many things he has said remain in my mind. "The thing is, good news doesn't make headlines," he said. "There are a lot of small victories, but they go unnoticed." And he said funny, touching things that conveyed his love for his country and his compatriots: "We are very folkloric in Haiti. There used to be one guy in my dad's office who had a very big mouth due to a medical condition. So people called him Little Mouth. Another guy had large ears, so people called him Ears."

In downtown Mirebalais, as we waited in the truck for Edrice, Fritz, and Marseille to pick up some lunch, a local woman grilled Gerald through the passenger-side window. He explained to Jenny and me that she didn't believe he was really Haitian, because of his light skin. "So you see, in provincial towns I'm a *blanc*," he said. "Every time, I have to explain. In Saut d'Eau they were arguing, saying that my Creole is good but I'm really a *blanc*."

"We'll miss you," I told him as we drove out of Mirebalais.

"Me too," he said. "But I hope that this is only the first of many trips to come, for Jenny as well as for Ethan."

✳

On October 15, 2011, I gave the keynote speech at a fundraiser for the Colorado Haiti Project in Westminster, Colorado. It felt like a fitting return full circle. My parents were there, and so were my father's co-founder, Father Ed Morgan, and his wife.

"Our purpose tonight is to honor, support, and carry forward the long-term partnership between the Colorado Haiti Project and the parish of St. Paul's, Petit Trou de Nippes," I said.

I'm going to try to serve that purpose by articulating what I believe to be some of the important context, both geographical and historical, in which the Colorado Haiti Project works.

If there's one organization working in Haiti that most Americans have heard of, it's Partners in Health. As Dr. Louis Marcelin, a Haitian professor of anthropology at the University of Miami, put it drily when we were discussing just this point in his office in September, the thinking process of many Americans goes: Haiti, *Mountains Beyond Mountains*, Paul Farmer, Partners in Health, "end of story." But in fact Partners in Health is only the beginning of the story of Haiti and all that needs to be done there, as its staff, to their great credit, are the first to acknowledge.

PIH works only on the Central Plateau, and it doesn't have the intention or, really, the capacity to expand its operations to other parts of the country. PIH staff I've talked to believe that if they did expand geographically, it would compromise their primary and overriding mission, which is to address the health care and other needs of the extremely poor people specifically of the Central Plateau.

This puts PIH in a paradoxical position because, as I'm told, with 5000 employees it's already the third-largest employer in Haiti, behind the government and the cell-phone company Digicel. The very impressive 300-bed teaching hospital under construction just outside Mirebalais represents an ambitious stretching of PIH's capacity. After the hospital is operational next year, PIH will employ another thousand Haitians, as well as training young Haitian physicians who will eventually work all around Haiti. But PIH is very mindful to deploy its considerable clout carefully and thoughtfully, and explicitly in partnership with the Ministry of Health. I want to emphasize here why it's important, especially after the earthquake, that we be mindful of the message that's conveyed by that stance and, even more, by the overall situation of Haiti itself.

I spoke of the importance of decentralization, and I told an anecdote about how my father, as a teenager, had played in a baseball game "somewhere in Dallas when there were only two, maybe three of us who were white," and how he remembered thinking that was "a mildly radical thing to do."

"If more of us did mildly radical things more often, the world would be a better place," I asserted. And I offered an idea that had come to me in September when Elizabeth van der Weide, director of the Haiti Project in Milwaukee, told me that some Episcopalians in Wisconsin had objected to being asked to contribute toward the $10 million that it was estimated would be needed to rebuild Holy Trinity Cathedral in Port-au-Prince, which had been the site of religious murals considered great masterpieces of Haitian painting, when they understandably felt there were more urgent human needs in Haiti. To honor the memory and carry forward the legacy of the cathedral murals, I suggested that we commission new religious paintings from some of the leading Haitian painters of our day: not for a rebuilt cathedral, but for

Episcopal parishes in provincial towns around Haiti. Such paintings could become landmarks and even tourist attractions, I suggested, as well as symbols of decentralization.

"In the twenty-two years since Father Casey, Father Morgan, and Father Lafontant sat down outside the cathedral gift shop, the Colorado Haiti Project has accomplished a great deal," I said.

> When I last visited Petit Trou, in 1993, we slept in tents and only the foundation of the church building had been laid. Now I understand that St. Paul's is a local landmark and that 700 children are enrolled at the school. With active and steadfast support from many people in this room over many years, and others not here – or no longer with us, notably Dr. Ted Lewis – the Colorado Haiti Project has drilled wells to bring clean water to Petit Trou and has projects in community health, nutrition, and women's entrepreneurship in partnership with Fonkoze.

> All of that adds up to a good start. Now, since the earthquake, what the Colorado Haiti Project has been doing all along in Petit Trou is more relevant than ever. It's time to build on our excellent beginning.[3]

✱

A month after that, I was in the Bay Area staying with my friend Kathy Sheetz, whom I met at Wall House in 2000, and whose encouragement and concrete help have been crucial to much of all that I've experienced and witnessed in Haiti since then. Kathy and her husband took me to a meeting of the local Haiti Action Committee in Richmond, the hardscrabble town at the northern end of the East Bay where they live. One of the speakers was Pierre Labossiere, a Haitian active for decades in labor and protest movements in the Bay Area as well as Haitian causes. "The struggle is one," he told the meeting. "It's the same struggle. It's that same one percent that operates internationally." Labossiere told us that, when Oakland police attacked Occupy Oakland protesters on October 25 and fractured the skull of young Iraq War veteran Scott

---

3   The full text of the speech is online at http://www.ethancasey.com/speaking/haiti-on-doing-something-mildly-radical/.

Olsen with a tear gas canister, "I said, 'That looks like Haiti!' A lot of times, we don't see the global connection. They don't want us to see that."

Richmond mayor Gayle McLaughlin also spoke at the meeting. "America is awakening to the fact that we need to take the power back, just like the people of Haiti are taking the power back and trying to build a better society," she said. McLaughlin had taken heat nationally the previous week, when Fox News made hay from her decision to visit the Occupy Richmond encampment instead of a Veterans Day event. She got an appreciative ovation for her unapologetic explanation: "Chevron sponsored the Veterans Day event, and the people of Richmond sponsored the Occupy Richmond event."

If there's anything we can say we learned during the first decade of the twenty-first century, it's that life goes on, even in the aftermath of the previously unthinkable. When the earthquake hit Haiti on January 12, 2010, Cange, and the string of Zanmi Lasante clinics across central Haiti from Las Cahobas near the border to St. Marc on the coast, and the relationships and credibility and track record of Partners in Health in the United States, all husbanded mindfully over a quarter-century, were lifesaving assets. Afterwards there was plenty more work still to do, in a changed context. Ghislayne pointed out to me some of what had changed locally, in Cange itself, such as the much greater number of market stalls on the road outside the Zanmi Lasante compound. "People come here from all the scattered communities around, to sell to the people who have relatives in the hospital," she said. "And, as you can imagine, it tripled in size after January 12. And people thought they had it pretty good, so they stayed." With the pending construction of the teaching hospital, and the trade school at Corporant, and the repaved highway, the Central Plateau was poised to become a hub of the most promising trends in post-earthquake Haiti, and an example of the potential that could be realized if decentralization were to be pursued with active intention.

Even so, not all the results would be positive. Ghislayne fretted about how motorcycles and trucks now roared past Zanmi Lasante, with no real speed limit or other traffic controls. "See what it's going to be like, with bikes like this?" she said. "I mean, how many people are going to have accidents? I wrote a whole list of things they should have, like speed bumps, mirrors coming out of the gate here ..." On our way back down to Port-au-Prince, Pete and Ben and I passed an accident scene that graphically proved Ghislayne's point: a woman had just been killed by a speeding truck.

My mother-in-law, who proofread this book, told me the one thing in it that bothered her was the suggestion that the millions of Americans who donated to earthquake relief after January 12 were somehow behaving selfishly or self-indulgently. They wanted to help, she insisted, and shouldn't be faulted for not knowing how best to do that. Elaine is very representative of the kind of middle-class American I hope this book will move and influence, and I readily grant her point: the outpouring of American generosity that followed the earthquake was extraordinary and encouraging.

But in itself, without understanding, even well-meaning action is inadequate or irrelevant at best, dangerous and damaging at worst.[4] "The first emergency food shipment we got—and we're up in the country, in the *Plateau Central*, normally without any electricity, certainly no ovens, no microwaves, no fridges, no nothing—we got shipped individual portions of frozen microwave lasagne," Ghislayne told me. "They'd never seen anything like this. People think they're doing really, really, really kind, good, wonderful things, without reflecting on how they actually can help." If people who meant well in early 2010 expect credit for that, without also doing the harder work of educating themselves, then it will be difficult to avoid the rueful conclusion that Haiti has been used again, albeit in a novel context, then promptly enough forgotten again. Over the thirty years that I've known Haiti, the country has been the subject of a series of American fads, iterations of the hula hoop or the Rubik's Cube. The Aristide craze was followed by the Paul Farmer craze, then the earthquake relief craze. Then ... what? Has people's interest in Haiti peaked?

---

4 A very useful, though flawed and incomplete, starting point for assessing the international community's response to the earthquake is "Beyond Relief: How the World Failed Haiti" by Janet Reitman, *Rolling Stone*, August 4, 2011. See http://www.rollingstone.com/politics/news/how-the-world-failed-haiti-20110804.

If so, that would be an enormous loss, not only for Haiti's own sake but because its story is more universally relevant now than ever. The same big questions apply everywhere, such as this one: How is it that the social class that, by definition, has most of the money and power in the first place, and whose wealth and power always constrain and often brutalize everyone else, is the one that presumes to accuse the poor of class warfare? The rich have any moral standing at all to hold their position at the top of society only if they use at least some of their disproportionate resources and influence to maintain a decent life for everyone. Otherwise, they're little better than parasites. That's as true in the United States as it is in Haiti. Perhaps now that the middle class of the most successfully broad-based middle-class society in history is suffering and fearful, we'll see more clearly what has been happening in other societies all along. "The feudals should give half their land to the people that have been living on it all these years," Todd Shea told me about Pakistan. "Isn't it time? Give them hope, for God's sake." And Betsy Wall said to me at Wall House in Port-au-Prince in 2000: "People come here, and they think Haiti is so corrupt. Well, you know what? It's that way everywhere in the world. Haiti is what we all are."

One striking thing about many representatives of the Haitian elite that I've met is their self-awareness about the fact of their privilege. "Guys like me, we live in an oasis," said a friend of Gerald's, a businessman named Philippe Armand. "My first oasis is right here, this office. My second oasis is the beach, where I go for weekends. The rest of it, I don't see. I don't even listen to the radio; I play CDs. That's how we survive. And I tell myself that in my business I employ a thousand people, and that that's a contribution."

"It is a contribution," I assured him, for whatever that might be worth.

"It's pretty micro."

"But it's important for those thousand people."

"And their families," said Pete.

"Haiti has been a great education for me for twenty-eight years," I said.

"But have you seen any progress?" asked Armand.

"I haven't seen much progress," I admitted. "But I've learned a lot."

We all need compassion, even the elite. I live modestly by American standards and am not financially secure, but the fact I can't avoid is that I am one of the world's haves. As such I need for myself, from the have-nots, a compassion that I've done little to deserve and can claim only by appealing to shared humanity. I wouldn't want to be *déchouké* or occupied. This is the significance to me of the subtitle I've chosen for this book. Not only has Haiti been a repeating grace note in the symphony of adventures that has been my life, but it has graced me with gifts I could never claim to deserve or begin to repay. But of course the point of a gift is that you don't have to repay it. Anyway, you don't have to be a Christian to rely on grace; it's the only thing that makes life in this bruised world liveable.

So this is one place where the progressive version of history breaks down: to demonize the elite, and/or lionize the poor, doesn't suffice. For one thing, human nature crosses class lines. For another, the world, from Wisconsin to Haiti to Germany to Detroit to Burma to Nepal to Pakistan to California, is a borderless whole. If we want a revolution for Haiti, we should have the courage to insist on a revolution everywhere, and be willing to pay the price. Haiti has already had one revolution, has already led the vanguard of world history, more than two centuries ago, and it's been paying the price for it ever since. We can't wall off Haiti, either for its own sake or in order to avert our eyes. Hiding the truth is like trying to bury water; it seeps out everywhere. And the truth is that both Haiti's history and its current situation have everything to do with each and all of us, wherever and whoever we are.

Acknowledgements
and Further Reading

Bearing the Bruise itself is a book-length acknowledgement of the influence of some of the most important people in my life, above all my father, Dayle Casey, without whom I would never have gone to Haiti in the first place. My mother, Judith Casey, has also been staunchly supportive of my unconventional life and career choices and has "modeled behavior," as they say in her line of work, of diligence, thoroughness, cultivation of mutually respectful and productive professional relationships, and seriousness of purpose.

My entire family has been unstintingly supportive, and Paul and Cindy Haralson in particular gave me not just a home base, but a home, in Miami throughout the action-packed second half of 2004. My wife Jennifer Haywood, and Cleo, Princess of Pookistan, have made my own home a warm and welcoming one for most of the years since then, and it means everything to me that Jenny's belief in my work as a whole, and especially in this project, goes beyond spousal understanding to loving and very active partnership.

Kathy Sheetz has egged me on since 2000 and has always been actively available to me with moral and, on a couple of crucial occasions, material support. Kathy gave me a copy of *Mountains Beyond Mountains* soon after it was published in hardcover and urged me to make a point of meeting Paul Farmer; needless to say, I'm glad I did. Kathy also introduced me to the extraordinary Anne Hastings and her colleagues at Fonkoze. Anne herself gave me paying work in late 2004, at a time when I needed it both to make ends meet and as an excuse to spend more time in Haiti. Sarah Cardey introduced me to Philippe

Allouard, and Philippe introduced me to Gerald Oriol Jr., and anyone who has read this book knows how important those friendships have been.

It's a great honor to acknowledge having been graced by the hospitality, generosity of spirit, and help of Father Fritz Lafontant, Dr. Paul Farmer, and others at or associated with Partners in Health: Mary Block, Kate Greene, Tracy Kidder, Todd McCormack, Katharine Mathews, Cate Oswald, Joan Van Wassenhove, Jon Weigel. I feel especially fond of and grateful to Ghislayne Warne and Jackie Williams. Past and current staff, board members, and supporters of the Colorado Haiti Project have also been encouraging and supportive: Paul Casey, Sharon Caulfield, Sally Hubbell, Patricia Laudisio, Marti O'Dell, Bill Oliver, Anne Skamarock, Don Snyder. I also want to thank Mark Pasternak and Myriam Kaplan-Pasternak of the Bay Area Haiti Network.

Many Pakistani and Pakistani-American physicians, toilers on the coal face of the dysfunctional American health-care system, dropped everything to volunteer in Haiti in early 2010. Many others did too, of course, but these are the ones I know personally and through my work networks. Some of them I'm honored to call personal friends: Dr. Shahnaz Khan, Dr. Farzana Naqvi, Dr. Salman Naqvi. Salman, Farzana, Laila Karamally, and others at the Southern California-based nonprofit SHINE Humanity either went to Haiti to work at the emergency clinic Todd Shea set up and maintained at Bojeux Parc in the first weeks after the earthquake, or did the online and California-based networking and fundraising that were needed to sustain the clinic, or both. Todd Shea is a big man in every sense, and a dear friend.

Pete Sabo and Ben Owen shared my journey for three fascinating weeks in Haiti in August and September 2010, and Jenny shared it for ten days a year later. Sharon Green, who edited my previous book *Overtaken By Events: A Pakistan Road Trip*, was there for me again as a tactful and helpful editor and hand-holder through the publishing process. Kate Myers once again proofread the text, for her standard fee: one signed copy of the book. Elaine Haywood also proofread it and offered thoughtful, incisive feedback just when I needed it. Jennifer Haywood did a beautiful job on the page design.

Jason Kopec deserves special mention for designing the book's cover. Jason is my former neighbor and an admired Seattle-based graphic artist and musician. Working with him during 2009 and early 2010 on the cover design for *Overtaken By Events* was a great pleasure both personal and intellectual, and one of the delights of promoting that book at public events around the United States has been to be told by appreciative Pakistanis that the cover looks "just like a Pakistani truck." I always make a point of responding by telling them it was designed by a white guy who has never been to Pakistan. Jason has never been to Haiti either, and it's a testament to his talent and sensitivity that, in the cover of *Bearing the Bruise*, working with the life-affirming dominant green color and mango and mango-leaf images that his client urged on him, he has similarly captured something of the vibe of a Haitian painting.

A few friends and associates in my home and refuge, Seattle, have been notably helpful and supportive: Wier Harman of Town Hall Seattle, Paul Rogat Loeb, Ray and Sandra van der Pol, Jeb Wyman. Eric Amrine, Jeff Mandell, and Dennis Rea have stuck with me through it all, meeting almost daily around the virtual water cooler and too infrequently at the actual baseball stadium or bar. I'm also grateful for the professional and personal friendship of John Singleton, James English, and Lizbeth Branch of the International Student Services office at Texas Christian University.

Some of the people I have known in Haiti over the years are no longer with us: Mme. Lisette Lafontant; Père Octave Lafontant, who mercifully passed away (in Cange, cared for by his brother) the year before the earthquake; Mme. Yolande Lafontant; Sister Joan Margaret of St. Vincent's School for the Handicapped; Père Gerard Jean-Juste; Marc Bazin; Dr. Ted Lewis, a longtime pillar of the Colorado Haiti Project; Ti Jean Gabriel; Pierre-Richard Sam.

There are many books one could recommend to anyone who wants to continue learning about Haiti; I'll mention only a few here. Tracy Kidder's bestseller about Paul Farmer, Cange, and Partners in Health, *Mountains Beyond Mountains*, is excellent but is a starting point, not the last word. Farmer's own books *The Uses of Haiti* and *Haiti After the*

Earthquake are important. C.L.R. James's classic account of the Haitian Revolution, *The Black Jacobins*, is a masterpiece, a tour de force of both scholarship and historical narration. *Papa Doc and the Tontons Macoutes* by Bernard Diederich and Al Burt is the standard history of the regime of François Duvalier. Graham Greene's 1966 novel *The Comedians* is classic too, though no longer contemporary in terms of the Haiti it depicts; Brian Moore's neglected 1993 novel *No Other Life* is fascinating as an attempt to understand the personality and the phenomenon of Aristide. But I've saved the best for last: *Brother, I'm Dying,* by the Haitian-American novelist Edwidge Danticat, is a wrenching, beautifully written nonfiction memoir of her 81-year-old uncle's 2004 death in U.S. Immigration custody, and of her family's immigrant experience. I think it's one of the finest American literary accomplishments of the past decade.

If you would like to support organizations working in Haiti, please consider Gerald Oriol Jr.'s Fondation J'Aime Haïti (www.jaimehaiti.org), the Colorado Haiti Project (www.coloradohaitiproject.org), the Haiti Project of the Episcopal Diocese of Milwaukee (www.haitiproject.org), and Fonkoze (www.fonkoze.org), Haiti's leading microfinance institution. SHINE Humanity (www.shinehumanity.org), whose board I now serve on, also works in Haiti. You also can't go wrong by donating to Partners in Health (www.pih.org).

Ethan Casey
January 1, 2012
Port Orchard, Washington

Ethan Casey visited Haiti for the first time in 1982 and most recently in September 2011. He worked as a foreign correspondent in the 1990s, covering Asia for *The Globe and Mail*, the *Boston Globe*, the Observer News Service, and other publications. He wrote about the Zimbabwe farm crisis for *Geographical* magazine and the November 2000 Haitian election for the *Financial Times*.

He edited, in collaboration with Jay Rosen and the New York University Department of Journalism, *09/11 8:48 a.m.: Documenting America's Greatest Tragedy*, the first book-length collection of writings about the September 11, 2001 terrorist attacks. His book *Alive and Well in Pakistan* (2004) has been described as "magnificent" by Ahmed Rashid, "intelligent and compelling" by Mohsin Hamid, and "wonderful ... a model of travel writing" by Edwidge Danticat. He has also written *Overtaken By Events: A Pakistan Road Trip* (2010).

He speaks frequently to university students, civic and religious groups, and other audiences around North America. To contact him, or purchase his books, visit www.ethancasey.com or www.facebook.com/ethancaseyfans.